Studies in Moral Philosophy

John Kekes
General Editor

Vol. 3

PETER LANG
New York • Bern • Frankfurt am Main • Paris

Hume's Place in Moral Philosophy

Nicholas Capaldi

Hume's Place in Moral Philosophy

PETER LANG
New York • Bern • Frankfurt am Main • Paris

Library of Congress Cataloging-in-Publication
Data

Capaldi, Nicholas
   Hume's place in moral philosophy / Nicholas
Capaldi.
      p. cm — (Studies in moral philosophy ; vol.
3)
   Bibliography: p.
   1. Hume, David, 1711-1776—Contributions in
ethics.   2. Ethics, Modern—18th century.   I. Title.
II. Series.
   B1499.E8C36   1989   170'.92—dc20   89-8258
   ISBN 0-8204-0858-1   CIP
   ISSN 0899-4897   74905

CIP-Titelaufnahme der Deutschen Bibliothek

Capaldi, Nicholas:
Hume's place in moral philosophy / Nicholas Capaldi. –
New York; Bern; Frankfurt am Main; Paris: Lang, 1989
(Studies in moral philosophy; Vol. 3)
   ISBN 0-8204-0858-1
NE: GT

Printed by Weihert-Druck GmbH, Darmstadt, West Germany

for

Richard H. Popkin

and

Paul Oskar Kristeller

TABLE OF CONTENTS

Table of Contents

ix

PREFACE

This book reflects a professional lifetime of preoccupation with the fertile mind of David Hume. Having written and spoken on a wide variety of issues in Hume's philosophy in general and his moral philosophy in particular, I have decided to attempt to construct a coherent account of Hume's moral philosophy both with an eye to those issues which have persistently vexed his readers and commentators and with the intent of underscoring those novel and challenging aspects of his moral philosophy which, in my judgment, remain unnoticed or unappreciated. It is because Hume still represents a significant alternative to much of what has passed in moral philosophy in the last two centuries and because his approach to philosophy and morals is so fundamentally different from most contemporary work that he can still address us as a contemporary voice.

Let me take this opportunity to thank four people, all of whom read the entire manuscript and offered me the inestimable benefit of their constructive criticism: John Kekes, who is the editor of the series in which this book appears and whose scrupulous attention to detail and whose good judgment has earned my deepest admiration; James King and Donald Livingston, with both of whom I have shared a personal as well as a professional dedication to understanding Hume and from both of whom I have learned more than I can recount; and Stuart Warner, who since the time he was my student has pressed me to think more deeply about the text of Hume's writings. All of these readers raised important issues that I was not able to pursue within the constraints of this book. Of course, final responsibility for what is said in this book rests with me. Other Hume scholars to whose work I am indebted and who continue to give life to the renaissance in Hume scholarship include Annette

Baier, David F. Norton, Tom Beauchamp, Sandy Stewart, John Biro, Peter Jones, J.P. Montiero, Stanley Tweyman, Robert Anderson, Pall Ardal, Terence Penelhum, Ronald Glossop, Craig Walton, Eugene Miller, John Danford, Knud Haakonsen, and Kenneth Merrill. I would also like to acknowledge the assistance of Jaganathan Muraleenathan, my student at the National University of Singapore, and Lynn McIntosh, both of whom helped with the copy editing of the manuscript.

Special thanks must go to my wife Pamela and my daughter Meredith for their patience with and encouragement of the writing of this book.

Finally, in dedicating this book to Richard Popkin and Paul Oskar Kristeller I wish to acknowledge the profound debt we all owe to them for establishing such high standards of scholarship in the history of philosophy.

CHAPTER ONE

HUME AND HIS PREDECESSORS: THE INTELLECTUAL FOUNDATIONS OF HUME'S MORAL PHILOSOPHY

Modern Moral Philosophy

David Hume's moral philosophy is part of the remarkable renaissance in moral philosophizing that took place in the seventeenth and eighteenth centuries iñ Great Britain. This renaissance in moral philosophizing is distinctly modern in the questions it raised, the way in which it raised them, and the kinds of answers it was willing to consider. One of the most salient trends of modern philosophy in general is its turning inward in the search for standards. Some brief and broad indications of this shift to the modern perspective in which standards are thought of as internal can be seen in (1) the Cartesian orientation of modern philosophy; (2) the discovery of perspective in Renaissance painting; (3) the awareness of perspective in Copernicus' claim that the earth moves and not the sun; (4) the turning inward of the Protestant Reformation and the finding of the voice of God in one's own interior conscience; (5) the decline of the scholastic Aristotelian view that nature is suffused with purpose or teleology and the substitution of the view in sixteenth and seventeenth century science that nature is a machine operating according to mechanical and deterministic laws, with the consequence that mankind must now look inward in order to discover purpose or moral order.

What significance does this shift have for modern moral philosophy? The shift in perspective raises four distinct issues: *(a) Is there a specific internal (i.e. inwardly discoverable) moral domain? (b) How, if there is such a domain, do we have access to it? (c) How is moral motivation related to moral apprehension? and (d) How is moral motivation related to non-moral motivation?* We shall be discussing all four of these questions.

The *first issue* faced by modern moral philosophers is to determine whether there is an *inwardly discoverable moral domain.* One response to this issue, the response of Hobbes and Mandeville, was to deny the existence of a specific moral domain. That is, one of the ways in which some modern philosophers handled this problem was to eliminate ethics altogether in favor of social philosophy. Critics of Thomas Hobbes and Bernard Mandeville are partly correct in their charge that both of these thinkers deny the existence of morality, but often the critics missed the extent to which both Hobbes and Mandeville try to compensate for this by developing a social theory with external constraints on our non-moral passions. At the same time, the relation among ethics, social philosophy, and political philosophy becomes problematic for these modern philosophers. All of the other modern moral philosophers are indeed reacting against Hobbes and Mandeville by proclaiming that there is a specific moral domain. Yet the anti-Hobbes consensus immediately breaks down because the protagonists will disagree amongst themselves on how we apprehend that domain.

The *second issue* concerns the *source of moral apprehension or insight*. The great debate among those who assert the existence of a moral domain is whether the source of moral insight is *reason or sentiment*. Three different answers were given to the question regarding the source of moral apprehension. The first answer, reflected primarily in the works of Samuel Clarke and John Locke, alleged that *reason* is somehow the source of moral insight. Clarke likened moral apprehension or insight to *a priori*

2

reasoning as found in mathematics, whereas others such as Locke and Reid likened it to empirical reasoning concerning matters of fact. The second answer, represented mainly by Shaftesbury, asserted that the source of moral insight was *sentiment*. The third answer, asserted primarily by Joseph Butler, Francis Hutcheson, and David Hume, opted for some combination but one in which sentiment was the dominant element.

Amongst those who advocated that sentiment is the source of moral apprehension a special problem emerges, namely, how can we guarantee or account for the uniformity of apprehension or an intersubjective consensus on moral apprehension? The response of Butler and Hutcheson was to invoke some sort of pre-established harmony, often in the form of a theological guarantee about the uniformity of the moral sense. What is different and unique about Hume's response to the problem of guaranteeing some sort of intersubjective consensus was the claim that moral apprehension involved in an integral way conventional social standards which human beings were able to incorporate both because of their sociability and the workings of sympathy, a process about which we shall have more to say later.

The next set of issues in the debate among modern British moralists had to do with the *springs of moral action*. Here the protagonists in the debate lined up differently, which is precisely why we must keep in mind which issue is being debated. The *third issue* concerned the *relationship of moral apprehension to moral motivation*. Those who argued that reason was the source of moral insight, e.g. Clarke, had a special difficulty in accounting for moral action. They revived the traditional doctrine of the conflict of reason against passion, as well as the traditional Christian notion of the divine origin of reason and the sinful nature of basic human impulses. This position remained problematic and unpersuasive within the modern context. In an increasingly secular world the notion of human depravity was on the defensive. Such thinkers as Shaftesbury, Hutcheson, and Hume challenged the assumption of human depravity, espe-

3

cially in its Calvinistic form. Moreover, there was a new tendency amongst modernist thinkers to conceptualize the issue of motivation in technological terms. That is, whereas classical thinkers tended to think in their practical decision making primarily in terms of discovering an external structure and then trying to conform to it, modern thinkers began to think in terms of changing and controlling the external world in order to make it conform to our internal vision. This is seen not only in the growth of physical science's ties to technology as proclaimed by Bacon and Descartes but in the growth of the belief in a social technology aligned with social knowledge in much the same way.

In denying the very existence of a combat between passion and reason, Hume was saying nothing novel but rather aligning himself with the more thoroughgoing modernists. He was thus making an important conceptual point about the terms of the debate among modern British moralists and not advocating some kind of human irrationalism.

A second response to the issue of moral motivation came from Hobbes and Mandeville who had declined in the first place to make a distinction between the moral and the non-moral realms. This group now found itself aligned with the sentimentalists (or, hereafter, those who argued for sentiment as the source of moral insight) against the rationalists on the issue of the springs of moral action. Of course, there will be differences. Hobbes, Mandeville and their followers, claimed a great advantage when dealing with the springs of all action. If there is no intrinsic difference between moral motivation and non-moral motivation, which follows from collapsing the moral into the non-moral, then there is no special problem of moral motivation as such. These protagonists will not have to consider the internal integration of motives. Instead, when faced with the practical problem of how to get people to behave, they can treat this as a legalistic or social issue of what *external sanctions* will most effectively achieve this objective. Solving the social philosophical problem is all there is, and this particular problem is solved by using ex-

4

ternal sanctions to get people to maximize their collective long term self-interest. This is recognizable as the eventual position and solution of Bentham, and it is this propensity which creates the misperception of all British moral philosophy as reducing morality to self-interest.

The third response to the issue of moral motivation comes from those sentimentalists who had recognized the existence of a moral domain, who had claimed that sentiment was the source of moral insight, and who believed that there are specifically moral motives to serve as the springs of human moral action. This group, which includes Hutcheson and Hume, had to discuss both the third issue, the relationship of insight to motivation, and *the fourth issue, the relationship of moral motivation to nonmoral motivation.* As opposed to the rationalists, Hutcheson and Hume denied the combat of reason against passion. Since moral apprehension is a sentiment it connects with passion and therefore motivation directly. This is how both Hutcheson and Hume handled the third issue. As opposed to Hobbes and Mandeville, Hutcheson and Hume recognized the existence of *internal sanctions,* or a sense of duty which is capable of causing people to act morally. That was how both Hutcheson and Hume handled the fourth issue. External sanctions are recognized, but the external sanctions remain parasitic upon the presence of internal sanctions.

Since Hutcheson and Hume both reject the rationalist claim of a reason-imposed obligation independent of passion or sentiment, they are both taken mistakenly to fail to provide for a sense of obligation. That is, the answer given by Hutcheson and Hume to the third issue is confused with the answer they gave to the fourth issue. On the contrary, a sense of obligation is an integral part of their theories but understood as derived from sentiment or a moral sense.

There is a special problem that theorists like Hutcheson and Hume face, and that is that if there are specifically moral motives as well as non-moral motives there must be some way of reconciling potential conflict.[1] To argue that moral motives are re-

5

ducible to non-moral motives of self-interest would in effect eliminate the distinction between Hutcheson and Hume on the one hand and Hobbes and Mandeville on the other. Hume understood this and resisted it, which is one reason Hume could not accept Hobbes and why in the end Hume is not a utilitarian.[2] There is a persistent rejection of the move to reduce morality to self-interest. Nor does Hume believe in a purely natural and ahistorical harmony of self-interest and the social good, a form of the natural law theory. Nor does Hume accept the view that self-interest is ultimately and totally transcended by identification with some social whole, i.e. some sort of Hegelian synthesis. Rather, Hume argued that moral motivation is a developmental process that is both natural and artificial. It is artificial in the sense that moral standards are partly conventional, being social products over time. It is natural because of our capacity for sympathetic identification which can reconcile conflicts among self-interest, moral motives, and the social good. In short, as we shall see, Hume sought to transcend the conflict over moral motivation in a novel way by appealing to the notion of the historical development of a moral sense. This will also help to explain Hume's uniquely conservative political outlook.

Hume's Predecessors (Cudworth, Clarke, Hobbes, Locke, Mandeville, Shaftesbury, Butler, and Hutcheson)

In his major philosophical works, Hume specifically mentions all of the predecessors whom we have cited. In the Introduction to the *Treatise* as well as in the *Abstract* Hume mentions John Locke, Joseph Butler, Francis Hutcheson, Bernard Mandeville, and Lord Shaftesbury as "some late philosophers in *England*, who have begun to put the science of man on a new footing."(*Treatise*, p. xxi).[3]

In the early editions of *An Enquiry Concerning Human Understanding* Hume discussed within the introduction "those who, with so much success, delineate the parts of the mind, in which we are so intimately concerned,"[4] and he added a note naming both Hutcheson and Butler. In that note, Hume claims that Hutcheson "taught us, by the most convincing Arguments, that Morality is nothing in the abstract Nature of Things, but is entirely relative to the Sentiment or mental Taste of each particular being; in the same Manner as the Distinctions of sweet and bitter, hot and cold, arise from the particular Feeling of each Sense or Organ. Moral Perceptions, therefore, ought not to be class'd with the Operations of the Understanding, but with the Tastes or Sentiments."[5] In the following paragraph of the same footnote, Hume praises Butler for criticizing the division of the passions "into two Classes, the selfish and the benevolent." Further, Hume praises Butler for pointing out that "even the Passions, commonly esteem'd selfish, carry the Mind beyond Self, directly to the Object; that tho' the Satisfaction of these Passions gives us Enjoyment, yet the Prospect of this Enjoyment is not the Cause of the Passions..."[6]

In Hume's *A Letter from a Gentlemen to his Friend in Edinburgh* (1745)[7] he specifically refers to the moral controversy we have mentioned earlier and takes sides with Hutcheson in direct opposition to Clarke and Wollaston.

> He [here Hume refers to himself] hath indeed denied the eternal Difference of Right and Wrong in the Sense in which *Clark*[sic] and *Woolaston*[sic] maintained them, *viz*. That the Propositions of Morality were of the same Nature with the truths of Mathematicks and the abstract Sciences, the Objects *merely* of Reason, not the *Feelings* of our internal *Tastes* and *Sentiments*. In this Opinion he concurs with all the antient Moralists, as well as with Mr. *Hutchison*[sic] Professor of Moral Philosophy in the University of *Glasgow*, who, with others, has revived the antient Philosophy in this particular.[8]

In *An Enquiry Concerning the Principles of Morals*, Hobbes is first mentioned in a specifically moral context and linked with Locke as the two thinkers "who maintained the selfish system of morals."(*EPM*, p. 296).[9] Also in the same work Hume mentions Cudworth and links him with Clarke. "Father Malebranche, as far as I can learn, was the first that started this abstract theory of morals [supposes all right to be founded on certain *rapports* or relations], which was afterwards adopted by Cudworth, Clarke, and others..."(*EPM*, p. 197n1).

It should be clear from this brief survey that Hume was well aware of and explicitly mentions in his works all of the major proponents of the different positions held by the British moralists.

Let us briefly examine each of Hume's predecessors and focus only upon those features which will help us to clarify both by way of contrast and similarity the moral philosophy of David Hume. Thomas Hobbes is of interest for several reasons. First, Hobbes denied a specifically moral domain. That is why his writings such as *The Elements of Law* (1640), *De Cive* (1642), and *Leviathan* (1651) are rightly read as part of social and political philosophy. Hobbes aimed to be the "first civil philosopher" and thereby give us the first scientific account of the social world. He sought also to derive from that science a practical social technology for bringing peace and order to the civil world. Second, following the modernist lead of Machiavelli and Bacon, Hobbes consciously seeks to dissociate his account of human nature from the ancient doctrine of the perfection of man.[10] He deduced the natural laws of human nature not from reason but from the powerful forces of the passions. In a passage that Hume will later restate, Hobbes insists that "the Thoughts are to the Desires, as Scouts, and Spies, to range abroad, and find the way to the Things Desired."[11] All social and political obligations are derived from the right of nature, the individual's right to self-preservation, to do or refrain from doing whatever one can to preserve one's life.[12] Laws of nature, as opposed to rights of nature, are the conclusions of prudential reason which inform us on how to avoid the obstacles to self-preservation.

Although the sentimentalists, such as Shaftesbury, Hutcheson and Hume, agreed in principle with Hobbes' rejection of the reason versus passion conceptualization of motivation in favor of the preeminence of passion, these same sentimentalists went to great lengths to distance themselves from Hobbes' "selfish system". Shaftesbury characterized Hobbes as trying to explain "all the social passions and natural affections as ... of the selfish kind. Thus, civility, hospitality, humanity towards strangers or people in distress, is only a more deliberate selfishness."[13] Even Adam Smith chastised those "who are fond of deducing all our sentiments from certain refinements of self-love."[14]

It is important for our understanding of Hume that we note first and foremost that Hume sides with those who reject Hobbes' denial of a specific moral domain. As we shall see in our discussion of Hume's *Enquiry Concerning the Principles of Morals*, Hume does single out Hobbes as the originator of the selfish system and distances himself from Hobbes. Second, Hume's contention that reason is the slave of the passions is the cause of much notoriety among Hume's critics, but the subordination of reason to passion had already been asserted by Hobbes and was a view held by most major British moralists, except for the rationalists so called. It was also the considered view of Machiavelli and Spinoza[15], both of whom had grasped the practical importance of this subordination for modern moral, social, and political philosophy. Within this historical framework, Hume's general position on the subordination of reason to passion is neither novel nor any indication of a particular theory of moral judgment. It is important, therefore, to be clear on what Hume accepts and what he rejects in Hobbes and why.[16]

Now, let us turn our attention to John Locke. The difficulty in interpreting Locke is trying to piece together a consistent view from scattered remarks in several different works written over a long period of time.[17] Yet, the importance of Locke cannot be overstated. The significance of Locke's discussion of moral relations for Clarke, Hume and others was best expressed by T.H. Green: "The place held by the 'Essay Concerning Human Understanding,' as a sort of philosopher's Bible in the last century [eighteenth century], is strikingly illustrated by the effect of doctrines that only appear in it incidentally. It does not profess to be an ethical treatise at all, yet the moral psychology contained in the chapter 'of Power' (II, 21), and the account of moral good and evil contained in the chapter 'of other Relations' (II, 28), furnished the text for most of the ethical speculation that prevailed in England, France, and Scotland for a century later."[18]

Locke, in opposition to Hobbes, did believe in a specifically moral domain even within the state of nature. Locke is also famous for having said that morality is "amongst the sciences capable of demonstration". The first principles of moral science are rationally abstracted from experience.[19] The resulting moral product Locke called a *relation*. Moral relations in one sense seem to be totally objective natural laws. On the other hand, Locke admitted that such moral relations were binding only on rational animals, i.e. man, and not other forms of animal life. Hume, in his discussion of alleged moral relations, is going to exploit this admission in order to indicate the dilemma it creates for Locke's theory. If the relations are truly objective then they hold for everyone and everything including animals. If the relations only exist for those who possess the capacity to perceive them, then there is an uneliminable subjective element which makes the alleged moral relations totally unlike other kinds of relations perceived by reason.

The other sense in which moral philosophy is supposed to be demonstrable is that Locke believed we could demonstrate the existence of a God who establishes both natural law and who punishes wrongdoers. Even if one accepted Locke's proof for the existence of God, Locke failed to demonstrate the moral attributes of God and our moral relation to him.[20] Recent scholars have argued that the main thrust of Hume's critique of theism and design was to separate the issue of God's existence from the issue of God's moral relationship to man.[21] It is the presumed demonstration of both God's existence and moral relation to man that, if successful, would have guaranteed both the cognitive nature and absolute objectivity of Locke's moral relations.

Despite Locke's belief in an objective moral domain, Locke did not believe in a specifically moral motive. In this respect, Locke acknowledged the gap between moral apprehension and moral motivation, or what we have identified as the third issue in British Moral Philosophy in the seventeenth and eighteenth centuries. There is no internal sanction or specifically moral motive for Locke as there is for Shaftesbury, Butler, Hutcheson, and Hume. On the contrary, it is only the fear of God's eternal damnation that serves as the external sanction restraining human beings. It is the denial of specifically moral motivation and the recognition of only external sanctions which account for why the other British moralists classify Locke together with Hobbes as partisans of the selfish system. Further, a careful comparison of Locke's theory of the social contract with that of Hobbes shows that despite all of the important political and social differences there are important similarities from the point of view of the moral and social theorist. Locke, like Hobbes, recognized that we must extricate ourselves from the state of nature which is the only place where a state of war can exist; Locke, like Hobbes, claimed that the fundamental law of nature is self-preservation and that reason is the servant of the passions; Locke, like Hobbes, urged the importance of the external sanction of civil government which is "the proper remedy of the inconveniences of the state of nature". All of this reinforces why from the point of view of Shaftesbury, Hutcheson, Hume and Smith we can classify Locke together with Hobbes in moral philosophy.

Another writer for whom Hume had the highest regard and from whom he borrowed many ideas was Anthony Ashley Cooper, the third Earl of Shaftesbury (1671-1713). His most influential work was *Characteristics of Men, Manners, Opinions, Times,* published in 1711 and revised for republication in 1714. Although Shaftesbury was a friend of Locke's and his pupil in analyzing the psychology of moral experience by emphasizing the origin of our ideas and sentiments, Shaftesbury rejected the rationalistic element as found in Locke. Instead, Shaftesbury introduced the notion of a specifically *moral sense* as a peculiar faculty that we possess for apprehending a right and a wrong which are objects of that faculty.[22] According to Shaftesbury, this moral sense does not directly intuit virtue or vice, rather it is an internal reflection on outward objects. Shaftesbury's brief description of the moral sense stressed both an independent moral object and at the same time the internal feeling we have about it. Hume will reinterpret Shaftesbury's moral psychology as the apprehension of something like a secondary quality, thereby denying the existence both of a special faculty and of a completely independent external moral object.

Shaftesbury argued that moral judgments were like those of aesthetics, not mathematics. When we attribute moral virtue to someone we are asserting that a harmony of the affections in the agent produces in the disinterested spectator a kind of approbation. Our apprehension of that harmony or quality is a matter of feeling. Hume adopted this view but with the crucial qualification that we do not simply feel the virtue, rather the feeling is part of what constitutes the virtue. That is, Hume made the response of the observer a constituent part of the virtue.[23]

Shaftesbury was critical of Hobbes' doctrine of a contract because contracts can have no legitimacy or legitimating force unless there are prior standards of right and wrong. Shaftesbury was also highly critical of Locke for ignoring the classical notion of the social dimension of human nature, for reducing moral motivation to self-love and for making morality dependent upon religion by postulating an external sanction of future rewards and punishments. Instead, Shaftesbury argued that fear of divine retribution is not a moral motive at all.[24] Moreover, the presence of a moral sense eliminates the necessity of an external authority, such as God, for making moral determinations.[25] Shaftesbury exercised an enormous influence on later thinkers such as Butler, Hutcheson, Hume and Smith by emphasizing such notions as the need for social sympathy, the rejection of naive egoism, and the natural affections which lead to the good of the public.

Bernard Mandeville (1670-1733) was born in Holland but moved to London in 1692 where he practiced medicine. His most famous or notorious work was *The Fable of the Bees: or, Private Vices, Public Benefits* (1714). It was specifically intended as a critique of Shaftesbury, against whom Mandeville argued that there was in fact no moral realm, that benevolence was a sophisticated form of self-interest, and that the pursuit of self-interest (or vice) was socially beneficial. Like Hobbes, Mandeville denied a specifically moral realm and moral motivation, and like Hobbes he argued for an external sanction as the only way of maintaining social order. As Mandeville put it, "no species of animal is, without the curb of government, less capable of agreeing long together in multitudes than that of man."[26] Efficient political leadership involves the use of praise and blame to encourage the pursuit of a self-interest that is publicly beneficial.

What is original, interesting, and important about Mandeville, especially in relation to Hume, is that Mandeville makes the case that the desire for luxury is a spur to the growth of civilization. Hume will make precisely the same point in his economic and historical writings. The difference between Hume and Mandeville is that Hume will accommodate this point in his social philosophy and in a way that makes it compatible with his moral philosophy. Moreover, in Hume's moral philosophy there is both a distinctively moral realm and moral motivation apart from narrow self-interest. As we shall see, this will require both a distinction between moral philosophy and social philosophy and an argument to the effect that without a certain kind of moral philosophy the social philosophical defense of the pursuit of luxury is not viable.[27]

Joseph Butler (1692-1752) was a pivotal figure in the development of eighteenth century British moral philosophy. In 1726 he published a work entitled *Fifteen Sermons*. Butler, a Bishop, maintained that human nature and the teachings of religion are perfectly compatible. Hence, although morality is consistent with religion, it is not derived from religion. This is the thoroughly modern element in Butler.

In 1729 Butler published a second edition of his work and included a preface in which he clearly stated the present state of

moral philosophy after Shaftesbury and his own role as a com-
promiser among the factions:

> There are two ways in which the subject of morals may be treated. One
> begins from inquiring into the abstract *relations* of things: the other from
> a *matter of fact*, namely what the particular nature of man is, its several
> parts, their economy or constitution; from whence it proceeds to deter-
> mine what course of life it is, which is correspondent to this whole na-
> ture. In the former method the conclusion is expressed thus, that vice is
> contrary to the nature and reason of things: in the latter, that it is a viola-
> tion or breaking in upon our own nature.[28] [*italics mine*]

Butler rejected Clarke's attempt to establish morality on the basis
of abstract relations and argued instead for locating the source
of moral insight within human nature. The specifically human
capacity relevant to moral insight Butler identified as conscience,
the capacity to reflect upon our affections. Butler proposed to include both the affections and the reflective capacity of conscience as elements in his treatment and thereby criticized
Shaftesbury for not recognizing the authority of the principle of
reflection.

This dichotomy between those who locate morality in relations and those who locate it in matters of fact will reappear in
Hume's *Treatise* in a critical passage. There, Hume will argue
against both views narrowly construed by insisting that morality is concerned with facts but facts of a very peculiar sort having to do with human feeling. Thus, there is an important sense
in which Hume followed Butler's lead by making morality dependent upon human nature. Hume was so impressed with
Butler's views as expressed in both the *Sermons* and the *Analogy
of Religion, Natural and Revealed, to the Constitution and Course of
Nature* (1736), especially the appendix "of the Nature of Virtue",
that he wrote a letter in 1737 to Henry Home, the future Lord
Kames, in which Hume agreed to withdraw the essay on
"Miracles" from inclusion in the *Treatise* in the hopes of obtain-
ing a more favorable response from Butler.

Butler was the first moral philosopher to distinguish clearly between self-love and selfishness. Among the points enumerated by Butler was the important clarification of the relationship between benevolence and self-love, as well as an appeal to follow nature in which there is no conflict between a "perception of the heart" and "a sentiment of the understanding". These two elements, as we shall see, were taken more seriously when Hume wrote *An Enquiry Concerning the Principles of Morals*, but without Butler's notion of theological guarantees.

Among Hume's predecessors, Francis Hutcheson (1694-1746) influenced him the most. Hutcheson was the theorist who brought together the views of Shaftesbury on the moral sense and the views of Butler on the springs of moral action. In 1725 he published the *Inquiry into the Original of our Ideas of Beauty and Virtue*, consisting of two treatises, the second being one *Concerning Moral Good and Evil*, and in 1728 he published an *Essay on the Nature and Conduct of the Passions and Affections, with Illustrations on the Moral Sense*. The subtitle of the *Inquiry* makes clear where Hutcheson stands: "In Which the Principles of the late Earl of Shaftesbury are Explain'd and Defended, against the Author of the Fable of the Bees: And the Ideas of *Moral Good* and *Evil* are establish'd, according to the Sentiments of the Antient [sic] Moralists."

With regard to the moral sense, Hutcheson made clear in the second edition (1726) of the *Inquiry* that the moral sense "has no relation to innate ideas". The moral sense is a feeling of approbation for actions and dispositions that tend to the public good, and it is a benevolent passion to act in accordance with that tendency. As Hutcheson was at great pains always to make clear, the moral sense was not purely subjective. He consistently argued that differences of opinion were ultimately due to false opinions, and in this respect moral sense judgments were like judgments with regard to secondary qualities which depend upon accompanying circumstances. Hume would later follow the same path in asserting that moral judgments were not subjective but intersubjective, that they depended upon specific kinds of prior information or beliefs which were subject to revision, and that moral judgments were similar to judgments about secondary qualities.[29]

Secondary qualities like color are subjective in the sense of being "in the subject" or in depending upon the presence of a perceiver. They are not objective in that such qualities are not "in the object" independent of the perceiver. The only sense in which secondary qualities are objective is in the important sense of being intersubjective. To a modern or contemporary theorist who understands objectivity in the sense of intersubjectivity there is no problem or difficulty. To a traditional or classical realist such a view makes morality dependent upon man and not objectively independent of man. Recently, David F. Norton has defended the objectivity of moral judgments in Hutcheson and Hume by claiming that they are moral realists.[30] What Norton shows, in fact, is that Hutcheson and Hume are intersubjectivists and not realists in the classical sense of that term, that is Hutcheson and Hume would deny that moral qualities are exclusively "in the object".

Hutcheson, like Hume afterwards, was quite self-conscious in challenging his rationalist predecessors. Hutcheson argued that reason was neither the source of moral insight nor the spring of moral action. In a crucial paragraph of the *Illustrations*, he takes Clarke to task:

> We come next to examine some other explications of morality which have been much insisted on of late (see Dr. *Samuel Clarke's* Boyle's Lectures and many late authors). We are told, 'that there are eternal and immutable differences of things, absolutely and antecedently; that there are also eternal and unalterable *relations* in the natures of the things themselves from which arise agreements and disagreements, congruities and incongruities, fitness and unfitness of the application of circumstances to the qualifications of persons; that actions agreeable to these *relations* are morally good, and that the contrary actions are morally evil.' These expressions are sometimes made of the same import with those more common ones, 'acting agreeably to the eternal reason and truth of things.' It is asserted that God who knows 'all these *relations*, etc., does guide his ac-

16

tions by them, since he has no wrong affection (the word 'wrong' should have been first explained) and that in like manner these *relations*, etc., *ought* (another unlucky word in morals) to determine the choice of all rationals abstracting from any views of interest. If they do not, these creatures are insolently counteracting their Creator and, as far as they can, making things to be what they are not which is the greatest impiety.'[31] [*italics mine*]

Hume will repeat precisely this argument, and he will incorporate this attack on *"ought"* in his famous is-ought paragraph. According to Hutcheson, Locke was the source of the doctrine of moral relations.[32]

Hutcheson's attack on "ought" is not an isolated point. At the end of the first section of the *Illustrations*, Hutcheson raised the issue of how we are to relate approbation to the question of action. He concluded by saying that "Some farther perplex this Subject, by asserting, that 'the same Reasons determining Approbation, ought also to excite to Election". But Hutcheson expressly opposed this move and concluded with the statement, "As to that confused word (ought) it is needless to apply to it again all that was said about Obligation."[33]

The word "ought" is confused. An explanation of the confusion surrounding it is to be found in the explanation of obligation. Obligation, as Hutcheson argued, has nothing to do with the rationalist moral "ought". Rather it refers either to prudence and questions of means (hypothetical) or it refers to particular feelings on the part of the spectator.

When we say one is obliged to an Action, we either mean: 1. That the action is necessary to obtain Happiness to the Agent, or to avoid Misery; 2. That every Spectator, or he himself upon Reflection, must approve his Action and disapprove his omitting it, if he considers fully all its Circumstances. The former meaning of the word Obligation presupposes selfish Affections, and the Senses of private Happiness; the latter Meaning includes the moral Sense.[34]

Hutcheson recognized that others will use the word 'obligation' differently, but he contended that such usage is confused. His opponents argued that he failed to capture the full meaning of the term. Likewise, against Hume it will be urged that he failed to provide a theory of obligation. What this means is that neither Hutcheson nor Hume accounted for the *ought* which is supposed to hold between what reason discovers on the one hand and human action on the other. Of course they failed to provide such an account because they denied the necessity or the need for it. Such an account is only necessary if one is committed to the view that reason is the source of moral insight and/or the spring of moral action. That is precisely what Hutcheson and Hume rejected. Their rejection is part and parcel of a rejection of rationalistic preconceptions about morality. Hume's account of obligation is, as we shall see, almost identical to that of Hutcheson.

Hutcheson continued the attack on reason by arguing that reason is always about means and never about ends. This is precisely the claim made by Hume. In addition, Hutcheson was the first to offer an explanation of the origin of the confusion in the minds of his opponents by claiming that they confused reason with calm desires. Hume will offer the same explanation. As opposed to the confusion created by those who asserted that reason was both the source of moral insight and the spring of moral action, Hutcheson introduced a distinction: "The qualities moving to Election, or exciting to Action, are different from those moving to Approbation".[35] Hume will also argue that some moral judgments simply express approval and some incline us to action. The difference will be crucial. Moreover, in the case of action it is not reason but passion which is the spring or motive. "There can therefore be no exciting Reason previous to Affection".[36] This view is one of the hallmarks of Hume's moral philosophy.

One final point of similarity between Hutcheson and Hume is the former's assertion, following Butler, that benevolence is a desire for the happiness of others and not for the pleasure that happiness will give us. In the *Treatise*, Hume considered benevolence to be one of the direct passions that are original and do not spring from pleasure or pain but produce pleasure or pain.

In the light of the foregoing summary it is little wonder that A.N. Prior could say that "there is little or nothing in Hume's moral philosophy that cannot be traced to Hutcheson, but in Hume it is all more clear and pointed."[37] This point is found as well in Kemp Smith: "Book III of the *Treatise* is a masterly restatement with a clarity and self-consistency beyond anything possible to Hutcheson, of Hutcheson's own main theses, and leads by its rigor and consistency, as also by the very different context which Hume supplies, to conclusions quite other than any Hutcheson would himself have been willing to draw."[38]

A clearer statement of the differences between Hume and Hutcheson is suggested by Duncan Forbes. Hutcheson subscribed to the typical eighteenth century program of trying to construct a science of morality based on human nature and the nature of the physical world as we discover both in our experience. The science is intended to be a form of natural law with a hierarchical ranking of goods (what Hume described and rejected as final causes and what we commonly refer to as a teleology). Most important, this Hutchesonian moral science is grounded in natural theology: "just opinions concerning God are taught in natural theology and metaphysics....We take these principles as granted in treating of morals."[39] Furthermore, in connecting the source of moral insight with the springs of moral action, Hutcheson appealed to the guarantees of God's providence.

Hume, Forbes stresses, went further than anyone else in detaching moral philosophy from natural theology. As we shall see, Hume's discussion of the process of sympathy in his moral psychology provides a totally naturalistic as opposed to supernaturalistic explanation of the connection between the source of moral apprehension and the springs of moral action. As Forbes puts it: "what was really and radically new, apart from the attempt to apply the principle of association consistently, was what set Hume apart from the [other] Newtonians: the discovery that a genuine experimental philosophy ruled out final causes and involved a conscious separation or bracketing off of the natural from the supernatural."[40] Forbes also reminds us that Hume's rejection of the social contract theory was, in part, a rejection of the common assumption that the social contract presupposed a natural theology.

Hume's Newtonian Program[41]

So far, we have discussed Hume's conception of moral philosophy with specific regard to his predecessors. It is now time to raise the question of how Hume's moral philosophy relates to his philosophy in general. Following a hint given at the close of the *Opticks*, Hume proposed to take seriously the program of a Newtonian explanation of human nature, i.e. a Newtonian explanation of the human thinking process, the passions, and morality. Hume self-consciously adopted the four rules of reasoning given by Newton in *Philosophiae Naturalis Principia Mathematica*, Bk. III (1686). In the introduction to the *Treatise*, Hume summarizes the four rules:

> We must endeavour to render all our principles as universal as possible, by tracing up our experiments to the utmost, and explaining all effects from the simplest and fewest causes, 'tis still certain we cannot go beyond experience; and any hypothesis, that pretends to discover the ultimate original qualities of human nature, ought at first to be rejected as presumptuous and chimerical. (*Treatise*, p. xxi)

Specifically, the Newtonian program involves:

a) isolating the objects of analysis,
b) conducting experiments for the sake of arriving at
c) some general principle which explains the relationships among the isolated units, and then
d) extending the general principle to other phenomena.

The isolable units in Hume's philosophy are ideas and impressions; the general principle is the principle of association, and the most general principle corresponding to Newton's principle of gravitation is, in Hume, the communication of vivacity. The communication of vivacity explains belief in Book I, it explains the passions and sympathy in Book II, and in Book III sympathy as the communication of vivacity explains moral judgments.

It is clear from the subtitle of the *Treatise*, "An Attempt to introduce the experimental Method of Reasoning into Moral Subjects," that Hume is moving from the assumed truth of Newtonian mechanics and methodology to creating a science of man. It is the glory of the *Treatise* and its author's claim to originality, as put in the *Abstract*, that it elucidates the principles of association. Finally, it is the extension of this method to morals that, following Newton's rule about testing a generalization by extending it to other contexts, accounts for Book III of the *Treatise*. As Hume put it in the very first paragraph of Book III, "the present system of philosophy will acquire new force as it advances; and that our reasonings concerning *morals* will corroborate whatever has been said concerning the *understanding* and the *passions*." (*Treatise*, p. 455). It would appear from this that Hume's genius lay, in part, in incorporating Hutcheson's moral philosophy and teachings into a more fundamental framework which can only be described as Newtonian.[42]

Hume's Copernican Revolution in Philosophy[43]

Side by side with the Newtonian program is a much more novel and original aspect of Hume's general philosophy. Part of Hume's originality was that he was thinking in pragmatic or action-oriented terms and that he tested his theoretical conclusions against the standard set by practical requirements. In order to emphasize the revolutionary character of Hume's philosophy, I shall introduce the following distinctions among philosophical perspectives:[44]

The classical perspective, carried over into modern philosophy by Descartes, is the *I Think* perspective, i.e. the perspective of the egocentric, outside, disengaged observer. From the point of view of this perspective, human beings are conceived of as isolated thinking subjects in contrast with a world of objects. The task of this human being is conceived of as a theoretical one, namely to discover how the world of objects really is. Even when the transition to modernity locates the standards internally the major task is conceived of as ratifying that the internal standards are a legitimate indication of external objective structures. What modernist philosophers, starting with Descartes, add to this theoretical task is the practical task of gaining technical mastery over nature. As Descartes once put it, by knowing the force and action of fire, water, air, the stars, the heavens, and all other bodies that surround us we should be able to utilize them for all the uses to which they are suited and thus render ourselves *masters and possessors of nature*. Whereas classical thinkers for the most part conceived only of conforming to external order, modern thinkers for the most part strive to rearrange the physical universe in order to suit and to conform to the axiological order we discover internally.

There are many well known and serious philosophical problems which confront the *I Think* perspective. All of these problems are compounded and magnified in the modern philosophical enterprises. In dualist versions such as Descartes', and rationalism in general, the separation and distinction between an immaterial mind and a material world containing our own body in a special causal nexus, leads to the inability to explain the relation between thought and action, between mind and body. The alleged conflict between reason and passion within rationalistic British moral philosophies is a reflection of this problem. In monistic materialistic versions of the *I Think* perspective, such as Hobbes, we seemingly avoid the problems of dualism, but only to be confronted with (a) the inability to explain how a material being whose activities are caused by external events can be said even to have a practical task and (b) how the tasks of atomic individuals can be conceptualized in a socially coherent and responsible way. Briefly stated, these are the familiar problems of modern philosophy, and they are problems aggravated by the *I Think* perspective.

What Hume is proposing is to circumvent these problems by adopting the *We Do* perspective. Hume viewed human beings fundamentally as agents, as doers, immersed in both a physical world and a social world along with other agents. Hume saw mankind's primary task as practical, not theoretical. This is not only a radical shift in perspective, but it is an intrinsically social view of man. Instead of attempting to scrutinize our thought process in the hope of uncovering principles of rationality which could be applied to directing our action, Hume reversed the procedure. He began with our practice, our action, and sought to extract from it the inherent social norms. Efficient practice precedes the theory of it.[45]

Hume announced this revolutionary change in perspective at the beginning of the *Treatise*:

> Tis evident, that all the sciences have a relation, greater or less, to human nature ...Even *Mathematics, Natural philosophy, and Natural Religion*, are in some measure dependent on the science of man....we ourselves are not only the beings, that reason, but also one of the objects, concerning which we reason....Here then is the only expedient, from which we can hope for success in our philosophical researches,...to march up directly to the capital or center of these sciences to human nature itself....In pretending therefore to explain the principles of human nature, we in effect propose a complete system of the sciences, built on a foundation almost

entirely new, and the only one upon which they can stand with any security....We must therefore glean up our experiments in this science from
a cautious observation of human life, and take them as they appear in the
common course of the world, by men's behaviour in company, in affairs,
and in their pleasures. Where experiments of this kind are judiciously
collected and compared, we may hope to establish on them a science,
which will not be inferior in certainty, and will be much superior in utility to any other of human comprehension. (*Treatise*, pp. xix-xxiii)

The *We Do* perspective is specifically advocated at the
beginning of *An Enquiry Concerning Human Understanding*:

Man is a reasonable being...But so narrow are the bounds of human understanding, that little satisfaction can be hoped for in this particular...Man is a sociable being, no less than a reasonable being...Man is also
an active being...It seems, then, that nature has pointed out a mixed kind
of life as most suitable to the human race...Indulge your passion for science, says she, but *let your science be human, and such as may have a direct reference to action and society.* Abstruse thought and profound researches I
prohibit, and will severely punish, by the pensive melancholy which
they introduce, by the endless uncertainty in which they involve you,
and by the cold reception which your pretended discoveries shall meet
with, when communicated. Be a philosopher; but, amidst all your philosophy, be still a man. (*EHU*, pp. 8-9) [*italics mine*]

The relevance of the *We Do* perspective for moral philosophy
is noted by Hume at the very beginning of *An Enquiry Concerning the Principles of Morals*:

The end of all moral speculations is to teach us our duty; and, by proper
representations of the deformity of vice and beauty of virtue, beget correspondent habits, and engage us to avoid the one, and embrace the other.
But is this ever to be expected from inferences and conclusions of the understanding, which of themselves have no hold of the affections nor set
in motion the active powers of men?...Extinguish all the warm feelings
and prepossessions in favor of virtue, and all disgust or aversion to vice:
render men totally indifferent towards these distinctions; and morality is
no longer a practical study, nor has any tendency to regulate our lives
and actions. (*EPM*, p. 172)

This novel Humean starting point has been previously identified by Capaldi as Hume's common sense philosophy[46] and by Livingston as Hume's appeal to common life.[47] Hume repeatedly argued for the validity of common sense beliefs as a touchstone of philosophical positions. Hume never challenged these common sense beliefs, rather what he questioned were the philosophical accounts of these beliefs. When Hume criticized the alternative philosophical accounts of common sense beliefs, he specifically had in mind the *I Think* perspective of both modern rationalism and modern empiricism.

Hume's unrelenting attack on rationalism is an attack on the *I Think* perspective, not an attack on reason. What Hume persistently tried to bring to the reader's attention is the inability of reason alone to make sense of itself when viewed from the *I Think* perspective. Let us remind ourselves how skillfully Hume exploited the blind alleys into which we are led by taking reason in this purely theoretical way. Hume led us into the desert of scepticism but only to reemerge by way of the path of the *We Do* perspective, as exemplified in the discussion of the passions in Book II of the *Treatise*. Recall Hume's refutation of extreme scepticism:[48]

1. If reason operated solely in terms of the rationalist model (i.e. demonstration from unassailable foundations), and

2. If men were guided solely by reason, then

3. Men would not act!

4. This is equivalent to the truth of extreme scepticism.

   BUT

5. Men do act!

6. Therefore, extreme scepticism is false.

7. Either, reason does not operate solely in terms of the rationalist model,

   OR

   Men are not guided solely by reason.

With regard to (7), Hume argued both that reason did not operate solely in terms of the rationalist model, so we need a much
broader conception of reason, and mankind are not guided
solely or even fundamentally by reason but by passion.

   The difficulty many readers face is in trying to conceptualize
Hume's position by adopting the language of the *I Think* perspective. To do so is to concede the debate in advance. What
Hume is suggesting is that we reconceptualize the very notion
of reason itself. Reason cannot be understood from an independent theoretical perspective, rather it must be understood relative to action. Within our own action we can discern principles
which it is the function of the philosopher to explicate.[49]
Having explicated the norms behind the practice, we are in a position to guide future practice. Of course, this Humean refutation of extreme scepticism will not satisfy those who cling to the
I Think perspective by demanding that we be given independent
rational assurance or foundations for the principles embedded in
our action. Hume's only recourse at this point is to remind them
that reason left to itself subverts itself and that the demand for
self-justifying foundations is illegitimate.

> When we see, that we have arrived at the utmost extent of human rea-
> son, we sit down contented; tho' we be perfectly satisfied in the main of
> our ignorance, and perceive that we can give no reason for our most gen-
> eral and refined principles, beside our experience of their reality; which is
> the reason of the mere vulgar...And as this impossibility of making any
> farther progress is enough to satisfy the reader, so the writer may derive a
> more delicate satisfaction from the free confession of his ignorance, and
> from his prudence in avoiding that error, into which so many have fallen,
> of imposing their conjectures and hypotheses on the world for the most

certain principles. When this mutual contentment and satisfaction can be obtained betwixt the master and scholar, I know not what more we can require of our philosophy. (*Treatise*, p. xxii)

Terminological disputes aside, other than calling attention to Hume's rejection of the *I Think* perspective and the limitations of reason when taken on its own, it is difficult to see what advantage there is in calling Hume a sceptic. *Scepticism*, since Descartes, connotes a negative position. Hume offers us a positive alternative. It is important that we do not miss all of the positive things Hume had to say about reason when reason is conceptualized as subordinate to action. One does not have to agree with Hume's alternative, but it should be recognized and understood for what it is. Whatever Hume did or did not share with traditional forms of scepticism, what is unique, original, and revolutionary about Hume is the *We Do* perspective.[50]

The standard objection to what we are here calling Hume's *We Do* perspective is that it confuses psychology with logic or replaces logic with psychology. It is clearly not a confusion, for it is done self-consciously and deliberately introduced as an innovation. It is a replacement, but a replacement argued for by Hume on the grounds that a strictly rationalistic account based on an *I Think* perspective is both inadequate and creates artificial and intractable philosophical difficulties.[51]

Noting Hume's Copernican revolution in philosophy and the perspective from which he operates will, we claim, overcome the difficulties usually attributed to Hume, and it will show him to be a consistent and powerful moral philosopher. This does not mean that there are no problems in Hume's philosophy in general and in his moral philosophy in particular, but I think we can show that those particular problems can be more fully understood and appreciated in terms of the Copernican Revolution.[52]

Summary

In this chapter we have provided two things: a thesis about Hume's conception of philosophy in general and his conception of moral philosophy in particular. It is our contention that when these conceptions are noticed we may achieve a concise view of what Hume was doing, a view which shows Hume's moral philosophy to be consistent, revolutionary, and provocative. Much of the controversy which continues to surround Hume's theory is due to the failure of Hume's readers to understand both his general orientation and his conception of moral philosophy. Once we grant Hume his general orientation, it becomes impossible to argue against his consistent development of that orientation in moral matters. Moreover, if we are correct then we shall be able to understand the recurrent patterns into which the criticisms of Hume's moral theory usually fall.

Our second aim in this chapter has been to provide a brief sketch of the intellectual milieu in which Hume was writing. This intellectual background is of more than merely historical interest, for it is our further contention that the misunderstandings, as opposed to the criticisms, of Hume's moral philosophy are largely the result of failing to see the specific issues and opponents Hume had in mind. A writer writes for his contemporaries and against his predecessors. Yet such an obvious point is frequently ignored by some of Hume's readers who either read into him current debates in a slipshod manner or who are so devoted to textual criticism that they see nothing but the text. In short, the former ignore the text in both the broad and the narrow sense, and the latter ignore everything but the text in the narrow sense. There is, of course, no substitute for an accurate reading of the text, but the text cannot be fully understood without understanding the intellectual climate in which it was conceived.

We hasten to add that we do believe that Hume is relevant to present day debates in moral and social philosophy, so that we do not reject attempts to apply Hume's thought to contemporary debates. In fact, we shall make just such an attempt ourselves. Nevertheless, it is our contention that the process of intellectual translation cannot be satisfactorily achieved unless we first see Hume within his own context. Part of that context consists of Hume's conception of what constitutes moral philosophy and his role as a moral philosopher. This brings us back to the first aim. It is precisely because Hume was a revolutionary figure in moral philosophy, one who challenged previous models of what philosophers were doing and who offered a provocative new vision, and it is because Hume's vision has still not been fully seen and absorbed that his views are both relevant and crucial for contemporary moral philosophy.

CHAPTER TWO

OUTLINE OF THE MAIN ARGUMENT IN HUME'S MORAL THEORY AS PRESENTED IN THE TREATISE, BOOK III, PART I

Introduction[1]

Book III, Part I, of the *Treatise* is entitled "Of Virtue and Vice in General". It is divided into two sections, the first of which is entitled, "Moral Distinctions not derived from Reason," and the second of which is entitled "Moral Distinctions derived from a moral sense". The overall organization is thus self-explanatory. Hume is focused on the first major issue that concerned all British moralists of this period, namely, the source of moral insight or moral apprehension. He also touches upon, as we shall see, the second issue, the springs of moral action, and as is usually the case with Hume's subtle analyses the relationship between moral apprehension and moral motivation. But the primary focus here is on the issue of moral apprehension and its source.

As is obvious from the section titles, the first section is designed to provide a refutation of those moralists who had argued that reason is the source of moral insight. Therefore, the very next section of our chapter will provide a summary of Hume's arguments against the moral rationalists. In the second section of our chapter we shall concern ourselves with Hume's positive and peculiar account of the moral sense. The only omission from our discussion will be Hume's so-called "is-ought" paragraph, to which we have devoted the whole of Chapter Three.

Moral Distinctions Not Derived From Reason

Hume begins this section of the *Treatise* by stating in both the first and the fifth paragraphs his conception of morality, his conception of a theory of morals, and the relationship between the two. He begins by noting that there is a distinction within philosophy between "*speculative* and *practical*; and as morality is always comprehended under the latter division, 'tis supposed to influence our passions and actions, and to go beyond the calm and indolent judgments of the understanding" (*Treatise*, p. 457). In other words, morality is a practical subject having reference to human behavior, and it is not merely a theoretical pursuit. Hence, any attempt to understand morality, and any attempt to provide a philosophical analysis of morality, and Hume does believe that "the question lies within human comprehension" (*Treatise*, p. 456), must make reference to the relationship between morality and human behavior. It is thus clear at the very beginning that Hume would disagree with any attempt to distinguish between ethics and meta-ethics as many contemporary moral theorists have done.[2] Failure to note this crucial presupposition on Hume's part will lead to misunderstandings of his theory of morals. The major point in Hume's critique of alternative moral philosophies is that they fail to provide an analysis that squares with the facts, and among those facts unaccounted for Hume cites one about "common experience, which informs us, that men are often governed by their duties, and are deterred from some actions by the opinion of injustice, and impelled to others by that of obligation" (*Treatise*, p. 457). Hume never fails to remind us that "Morality is a subject that interests us above all others: We fancy the peace of society to be at stake in every decision concerning it" (*Treatise*, p. 455).

The relationship of theory to practice is of crucial importance in this context. We have already remarked on an important difference between the modern approach as opposed to the classical and medieval approach. In the classical approach, practice is subordinate to theory in the sense that one first discovers a theoretical structure and then seeks to conform practice to that structure. In the modern approach, theory is supposed to make clear what is already implicit within practice. That knowledge should have a direct relationship with practice instead of an adversarial one and that science should be viewed in terms of its technological applications are modern attitudes.

We have also stressed the extent to which Hume is responsible for the Copernican Revolution in philosophy. Within the Copernican framework there can be no ultimate bifurcation of theory and practice. Hume is a perfect instance of this Copernican point of view. In Book II of the *Treatise*, Hume concluded his discussion of the passions by noting that curiosity or the love of truth is itself one of the human passions. He went on to assert that there is no such thing merely as love of the truth itself. "The satisfaction, which we sometimes receive from the discovery of truth, proceeds not from it, merely as such, but only as endowed with certain qualities." (*Treatise*, p. 449). For, as Hume maintained, "the truth we discover must also be of some importance" (*Ibid.*). At the beginning of Book III he is content to talk about the relationship of theory to practice only to chide those who fail to account for practice. His own positive views of the strong tie are stated unequivocally at the end of Book III:

> The most abstract speculations concerning human nature however cold and unentertaining, become subservient to *practical morality*; and may render this latter science more correct in its precepts, and more persuasive in its exhortations. (*Treatise*, p. 621)

The first section of *An Enquiry Concerning Human Under-standing* is devoted to a discussion of the different species of philosophy, wherein Hume sought to encompass both the theoretical and practical dimensions of the human intellect. Hume's final view on the relationship is to make practical knowledge primary: "let your science be human, such as may have a direct reference to action and society" (*EHU*, p. 9). The first section of *An Enquiry Concerning the Principles of Morals* raises the same dichotomy and arrives at the same conclusion: "The end of all moral speculations is to teach us our duty" (*EPM*, p. 172).

Having stated the perspective from which Hume approached issues in moral philosophy, we may now state the particular question which he raised in Part I of Book III. "The question with which we shall open up our present enquiry concerning morals, is *Whether 'tis by means of our* ideas *or* impressions *we distinguish betwixt vice and virtue...*" (*Treatise*, p. 456). What does this question mean, and why does Hume raise it in this particular manner? The meaning of this question is clear given the historical context in which Hume wrote. The major issue that concerned British moralists was the source of moral insight, and Hume is asking if moral insights or moral distinctions arise as either ideas or impressions. The reason for raising this issue in the terminology of ideas and impressions is explained in both the previous two paragraphs and in the following one. In short, the question is raised in paragraph three and the explanation of the question is given in paragraphs one, two, and four.

In the first paragraph of Part I, Book III of the *Treatise*, Hume stated that his "reasonings concerning *morals* will corroborate whatever has been said concerning the *understanding* and the *passions*" (*Treatise*, p. 455). The moral philosophy, in good Newtonian fashion, is to confirm the previous accounts of the understanding and the passions. In the second paragraph, Hume reminded us that his analysis always begins with a classification of all mental acts or objects under the generic category of "*perception*" (*Treatise*, p. 456). In the third paragraph, he reminded us that perceptions are subdivided "into two kinds, viz. *impressions* and *ideas*" (*Treatise*, p. 456). Given Hume's terminology, it follows that moral distinctions must be either impressions or ideas.

In paragraph four, Hume noted the existence of philosophical opponents who claimed that "virtue is nothing but a conformity to reason" and that "morality, like truth, is discerned merely by ideas, and by their juxta-position and comparison" (*Treatise*, pp. 456-57). In Hume's terminology, ideas are always the object of reason. If someone claimed that moral distinctions are discerned by reason, then within Hume's system this must mean that moral distinctions are discerned as ideas. So now it is clear that Hume raised the question in terms of ideas and impressions because he wished to consider the view that moral distinctions are discovered by our reasoning faculty.

It is equally clear from the title of this section of the *Treatise*, "Moral Distinctions not deriv'd from Reason", that Hume did not believe that moral distinctions were discovered by reason. The explanation for Hume's opposition follows from Hume's presupposition of what moral philosophy must ultimately explain, namely, the relation of morality to human behavior, or the relation of moral insight to moral motivation. At the beginning of the next paragraph, paragraph five, he reminded us that "If morality had naturally no influence on human passions and actions, 'twere in vain to take such pains to inculcate it" (*Treatise*, p. 457). "Since morals, therefore, have an influence on the actions and affections" and "because reason alone, as we have already proved [in Book II of the *Treatise*, "Of the Passions"], can never have any such influence" then "it follows, that they [i.e. morals, by which he means moral distinctions] cannot be derived from reason" (*Ibid.*). Hume's argument is invincible unless, as he said, someone denied "that principle, on which it is founded" (*Ibid.*). That principle is that passion, not reason, accounts for all of human action. Hume noted at the beginning of paragraph eight that this principle has been argued in an earlier discussion of the passions. Instead of repeating his whole position, Hume selected just one argument in order to render it "more applicable to the present subject" (*Treatise*, p. 458).

As the following context in Book III, Part I, section 1 of the *Treatise* makes clear, the argument Hume recalled is from pp. 415-16 of the *Treatise*. There Hume had argued that something can be contrary to or contradictory to reason or truth only if it is an entity of which truth is predicable. Only "judgments of our understanding" (*Treatise*, p. 415), and for Hume we must recall that judgments are ideas (*Treatise*, pp. 96-97), are capable of being true or false. This follows from the premise that ideas are true or false, consistent with or contradictory to reason, only when such ideas are "considered as copies, with those objects, which they represent" (*Treatise*, p. 415). It is the referential quality which is crucial, and only ideas or judgments "have this reference" (*Treatise*, p. 416). In the earlier context, Hume went on to argue that passions, not being ideas but impressions, do not have this referential quality and hence can never be considered as either true or false, or as reasonable or unreasonable. "A passion must be accompanied with some false judgment, in order to its being unreasonable; and even then 'tis not the passion, properly speaking, which is unreasonable, but the judgment" (*Ibid.*).

How exactly is the foregoing argument relevant to Hume's contention that moral distinctions are not discerned as ideas? The objects of our moral approval or disapproval are "passions, volitions, and actions," (*Treatise*, p. 458) for as Hume said "actions may be laudable or blameable" (*Ibid.*). Now if it can be shown that actions are somehow like judgments (ideas in Hume's terminology, or alternatively propositional entities in modern logical terminology), then judging an action or passion would be like judging a proposition or idea. Just as some ideas are false or contrary to reason so actions would be immoral in an analogous way. As opposed to this possibility, Hume argued that:

Truth or falsehood consists in an agreement or disagreement either to the *real* relations of ideas, or to *real* existence and matter of fact. Whatever, therefore, is not susceptible of this agreement or disagreement, is incapable of being true or false, and can never be an object of our reason. Now 'tis evident our passions, volitions, and actions, are not susceptible of any such agreement or disagreement; being original facts and realities, complete in themselves, and implying no reference to other passions, volitions, and actions. 'Tis impossible, therefore, they can be pronounced either true or false, and be either contrary or conformable to reason. (*Treatise*, p. 458)

It is clear from the foregoing that Hume's discussion presupposes a tight connection between morality and human behavior, a connection which cannot be made intelligible if moral distinctions are discerned by an inert faculty. In fact, throughout this first section Hume consistently distinguished between and then related two key issues: the question of the source of moral insight and the question of the springs of moral action. That is why he could say that the foregoing argument "is of double advantage":

For it proves *directly*, that actions do not derive their merit from a conformity to reason, nor their blame from a contrariety to it; and it proves the same truth more *indirectly*, by showing us, that as reason can never immediately prevent or produce any action by contradicting or approving it, it cannot be the source of moral good and evil, which are found to have that influence. (*Ibid.*)

Only a theory that made behavior a kind of propositional entity could escape this objection, at least initially. Interestingly, Hume was not merely manufacturing the possibility of such a moral theory which equated actions with propositions as a straw man destined for demolition. Hume continued to discuss this alternative theory in paragraphs ten through fifteen, and then in a concluding footnote identified Wollaston as the formulator of such a theory. (*Treatise*, p. 461)

The reference to Wollaston is interesting and important because it is a reference found as well in Hutcheson's *Illustrations*. Hutcheson had attacked Wollaston on precisely the same grounds.[3] Hutcheson's manner of putting the case is worth quoting: "This is a Truth, 'Rhubarb strengthens the stomach', but tis not a proposition which strengthens the Stomach, but the Quality in that Medicine. The Effect is not produced by Propositions shewing the Cause, but by the Cause itself."[4] Truth is a property of propositions and not of actions. Therefore, in judging the morality of an action we are not doing something analogous to judging its truth.

It is always open for the opponents of Hutcheson and Hume to reply to this refutation of Wollaston that it follows merely from the definitions and preconceptions which those two moral philosophers have about reason. Rather than quibble about terminology, Hume granted for the sake of argument Wollaston's position and then went on to offer an even more telling objection.

Wollaston had affirmed that the origin of immorality was in the tendency to produce false judgments in spectators when we performed certain actions. So, for example, when I steal my neighbor's purse this creates the false judgment that the purse is really mine. Hume's rebuttal of this position takes the form of pointing out that such a view would apply to animals and inanimate objects. Animals, for example, commit incest thereby creating the false impression or judgment that they are having sexual relations with a spouse as opposed to some other family member. Since animals and inanimate objects are not morally judged (at least in Hume's culture), it follows as a *reductio* that such actions are not the origin of immorality. Throughout his moral theory Hume will appeal to the applicability to animals as a *reductio* of all alternative moral theories that make moral distinctions totally independent of man. If it is replied on Wollaston's behalf that animals lack liberty of choice, Hume would respond that liberty of choice is irrelevant because moral distinctions are on the Wollaston theory, and in those of all the rationalists, objectively independent of such considerations. Wollaston's propositional view can only be defended by surrendering the claim to objectivity. Finally, Hume contended that if the agent caused no false judgments in others by taking the precaution of not being caught (assuming we exclude an allseeing God who would in any case not be fooled), then none of the agent's acts could be immoral.

> If I had used the precaution of shutting the windows, while I indulged myself in those liberties with my neighbor's wife, I should have been guilty of no immorality; and that because my action, being perfectly concealed, would have no tendency to produce any false conclusions. (*Treatise*, p. 461n)[5]

The foregoing argument as a *reductio* does not depend upon Hume's definition of what constitutes reason. The close connection of action and proposition which Wollaston assumed was not typical of the period, yet Hume did consider it and separately because it is a special case of a more general position. If actions were propositional in nature then Hume's argument about the inadequacy of alternative moral theories to account for action would not hold. That is why he eliminates it first and prior to his presenting the main argument of this section of the *Treatise*.

After summarizing the case against Wollaston in paragraph sixteen, Hume returns in paragraph seventeen to the main argument against reason as the source of moral distinctions. The structure of his argument for the remainder of the section is worth noting:[6]

1. *Theoretical reason*[7] operates in two ways only:
   a. forming *relations* of ideas, and
   b. *inferring* matters of fact (idea).

2. Moral distinctions are not relations
   a. because such relations apply to animals and inanimate objects not judged morally, and
   b. because such relations cannot directly influence human action.

3. Moral distinctions are not apprehended as inferred ideas or inferred matters of fact.

4. Moral distinctions are apprehended immediately as impressions.

The first step is presented in paragraph seventeen. The second step in paragraphs seventeen through twenty-four: part (a) appears in paragraphs eighteen through twenty; part (b) in paragraph twenty-one; paragraph twenty-two summarizes the second step. Paragraphs twenty-three and twenty-four are illustrations or examples of (2a) and (2b) respectively. Step three is given in paragraph twenty-five; and step four is given in paragraph twenty-five as well.

Hume begins by stating the kinds of operations that he recognizes as operations of theoretical reason in the strict sense of the term, namely, forming relations of ideas and inferring matter of fact.

> If the thought and understanding were alone capable of fixing the boundaries of right and wrong, the character of virtuous and vicious either must lie in some relations of objects, or must be a matter of fact, which is discovered by our reasoning. (*Treatise*, p. 463)

The word 'relation', given Hume's rather specific and technical discussion of relations,[8] calls for some clarification. Consequently, Hume makes his argument more specific. The first version of a view against which Hume is arguing is the view that moral distinctions are demonstrative relations apprehended by something akin to *a priori* reason. According to Hume there are only four demonstrative relations: resemblance, contrariety, degrees in quality, and proportions in quantity and number. Hume then denies that any of these are moral relations, and he further denies outright that moral distinctions are any other kind of relation of ideas. (*Treatise*, pp. 463-64).

Whom might Hume have in mind as protagonists of the view that moral distinctions are apprehended as *a priori* demonstrative relations? I believe that he has Cudworth and Clarke in mind. In *A Letter from a Gentleman to his friend in Edinburgh* (originally published in 1745 to defend the *Treatise*), we find Hume making reference to Descartes, Huet, Malebranche, Berkeley, Clarke, Cudworth, Hutcheson, Locke, Newton, Tillotson and Wollaston. Moreover, in *An Enquiry Concerning the Principles of Morals*, Hume specifically mentions Cudworth and Clarke as proponents of the view that morality is founded on abstract relations and goes on to trace the original source of that view to Father Malebranche.[9]

There is a second version of the view that moral apprehension involves 'relations'. According to the second view, morality is demonstrable from first principles, but unlike the Clarke view these first principles are discovered in or abstracted from experience. John Locke is the proponent of this second view. Immediately after criticizing the Clarke version of the view that morality is demonstrable in the form of relations, Hume brings up the Lockean view. In a footnote to paragraph eighteen, Hume notes a highly confused view which can only be attributed to Locke:

> As a proof, how confused our way of thinking on this subject commonly is, we may observe, that those who assert, that morality is demonstrable, do not say, that morality lies in relations, and that the relations are distinguishable by reason. They only say, that reason can discover such an action, in such relations, to be virtuous, and such another vicious. It seems they thought it sufficient, if they could bring the word, Relation, into the proposition, without troubling themselves whether it was to the purpose or not. But here, I think, is plain argument. Demonstrative reason discovers only relations. But that reason, according to this hypothesis, discovers also vice and virtue. These moral qualities, therefore, must be relations. When we blame any action, in any situation, the whole complicated object, of action and situation, must form certain relations, wherein the essence of vice consists. This hypothesis is not otherwise intelligible. For what does reason discover, when it pronounces any action vicious? Does it discover, a relation or a matter of fact? These questions are decisive, and must not be eluded. (*Treatise*, p. 464n)

Why are these questions decisive? The answer lies in Hume's previous assertion that " 'tis allowed on all hands, that no matter of fact is capable of being demonstrated" (*Treatise*, p. 463). One may place a set of empirical matters of fact into a demonstrative or deductive framework, for example in a syllogism or in a formal system or an axiomatic presentation (think of Newton's *Principia* being written in geometric form), but it still remains the case that the initial empirical facts however general or certain they might be are discoverable either as impressions or as inferred ideas. If they are discovered as inferred ideas then they are still ultimately dependent upon experience in some way or ways. If they depend upon experience as they must on the Lockean view, then they are not scientific relations (*a priori*) capable of being discovered by demonstrative reason. The demonstrative (theoretical) reason that discovers the invariable relations (*a priori*) of resemblance, degree of quality, contrariety, and quantity or number, must be distinguished from the (theoretical) reason that discovers inferred ideas as matters of fact. It is, therefore, highly misleading to call this 'demonstration' or to trade upon the ambiguity of the term relation. According to Hume, this is precisely what Locke had done, not unlike Locke's indiscriminate use of the term 'idea' for which Hume also criticized Locke. Before taking on Locke, we note only that Hume has so far refuted the Clarke version which argued literally for demonstratively discovered moral relations, and shortly Hume will specifically refute the assertion that moral distinctions are discovered or apprehended as inferred matters of fact (ideas).

The most influential discussion of morals in Hume's day was not to be found in a moral treatise but in Locke's *Essay*, especially in Book II, chapter 28, entitled "Of Ideas of other Relations," with specific reference to moral good and evil. It had been Locke who acknowledged "the *eternal* and *unalterable* nature of right and wrong," who had also argued that "morality is capable of demonstration" (III,xi,16), and in the famous section in question had asserted that "there is another sort of relation, which is the conformity or disagreement....that men's *voluntary actions* have to a *rule* to which they are referred, and by which they are judged of; which, I think, may be called moral relation" (II, xxviii,4). The rules to which Locke alluded are referred to three sources, "1.the *divine* law. 2. The *civil* law. 3. The law of *opinion* or *reputation*" (*Ibid.*,7). The relation is abstracted from a particular situation, "so that whencesoever we take the rule of moral actions; or by what standard soever we frame in our minds the ideas of Virtues or vices, they consist only, and are made up of collections of simple ideas, which were originally received from sense or reflection; and their rectitude or obliquity consists in the agreement or disagreement with those patterns prescribed by some law" (*Ibid.*,14). To make clear what he meant, Locke compared moral relations to such relations as "equal, or more or less" (*Ibid.*, 19) and "measuring" (*Ibid.*,20).

In a later discussion of morality, Locke declared that "morality is capable of demonstration, as well as mathematics" (III,xi,16), a view which he repeated when he said we could "place *morality* amongst sciences capable of demonstration: wherein I doubt not but from self-evident propositions, by necessary consequences, as incontestable as those in mathematics, the measures of right and wrong might be made out....The *relation* of other modes may certainly be perceived, as well as those of number and extension" (IV,iii,18). See also IV,iv,7-8, and xii,8. Locke went on to speculate that if an animal had the capacity to reason, it too would be subject to moral law. "For, were there a monkey, or any other creature, to be found that had the use of reason to such a degree, as to be able to understand general signs, and to deduce consequences about general ideas, he would no doubt be subject to law, and in that sense be a *man*, how much soever he differed in shape from others of that name" (III,xi,16).

From Hume's point of view, Locke is trading on the ambiguity involved in the term 'relation'. When pressed and despite his language in some contexts, Locke is arguing that moral distinctions are abstracted from experience, an experience involving a set of related elements. That is clearly different from demonstrative relations apprehended *a priori*. Hume also repeats as a criticism of the notion that morality is demonstrable an argument found in Berkeley's *Philosophical Commentaries*. Berkeley had pointed out that "to demonstrate morality it seems one need only make a dictionary of words, and we see which included which. At least, this is the greatest part and bulk of the work. Locke's instances of demonstration in morality are, according to his own rule, trifling propositions."[10] Hume repeats this criticism when he notes that "no one has ever been able to advance a single step in those demonstrations; yet 'tis taken for granted, that this science may be brought to an equal certainty with geometry or algebra" (*Treatise*, p. 463).

Let us return now to the main thread of Hume's argument. The reason why moral distinctions cannot be relations of ideas in either the strict *a priori* sense or the extended Lockean empirical sense is that such alleged relations would hold for animals and inanimate objects.

> If you assert, that vice and virtue consist in relations susceptible of certainty and demonstration, you must confine yourself to those *four* relations, which alone admit of that degree of evidence; and in that case you run into absurdities from which you will never be able to extricate yourself. For as to make the very essence of morality to lie in the relations, and as there is no one of these relations but what is applicable, not only to an irrational, but also to an inanimate object; it follows, that even such objects must be susceptible of merit or demerit....'Tis unquestionable, therefore, that morality lies not in any of these relations, nor the sense of it in their discovery. (*Treatise*, pp. 463-64).

There are two possible replies to Hume's rebuttal. First, one may argue that Hume has failed to note specifically moral demonstrable relations. On the contrary, Hume denied that there are such relations. There is no "new relation" (*Treatise*, p. 464). He also recommended by way of challenge to his opponents that until there is some evidence that such relations exist, we best avoid thinking that morals depends on them. The second reply to Hume might be that animals do not possess the reason or mental capacity to discover the alleged moral relation.

Recall that Locke's monkey needed reason to become a moral creature. This reply to Hume will not due for it constitutes a circular argument. As Hume answered, "before reason can perceive the turpitude, the turpitude must exist; and consequently is independent of the decisions of our reason, and is their object more properly than their effect" (*Treatise*, p. 467). Applicability to animals and inanimate objects is a *decisive argument* against the existence of moral relations for "reason must find them, and can never produce them" (*Treatise*, p. 468).[11] Hume's argument or rebuttal is decisive because his opponents have opted for a totally objective account of morality, not an intersubjective one, an account which seemingly placed moral distinctions in the object beyond human tampering. The price of such objectivity is now apparent, and the advantage of a Copernican orientation more obvious.

The second objection to the existence of moral relations, and one which Hume considers to be equally decisive, takes us back to the presupposition that morality is directly relevant to human conduct. Even if the alleged moral relations existed, and Hume denied their existence but considered them here in a polemical sense, we could not show the relationship between such alleged moral relations and human conduct. As he stated it in the summary paragraph, twenty-two:

> Thus it will be impossible to fulfill the *first* condition required to the system of eternal rational measures of right and wrong; because it is impossible to shew those relations, upon which such a distinction may be founded: And 'tis as impossible to fulfill the *second* condition; because we cannot prove *a priori*, that these relations, if they really existed and were perceived, would be universally forcible and obligatory. (*Treatise*, p. 466)

The reader may well ask why if one objection is decisive is it necessary to give two decisive objections. The answer to this question lies in a further distinction which Hume took from Hutcheson: a distinction between the apprehension of a moral distinction and the relation between moral distinctions and human conduct. As Hutcheson had put it: "The qualities moving to Election, or exciting to Action, are different from these moving to approbation".[12] As Hume put it: "These two particulars are evidently distinct. 'Tis one thing to know virtue, and another to conform the will to it." (*Treatise*, p. 465). This distinction reinforces a fundamental assumption in Hume's moral theory, namely, that a moral theory must account for the relationship between morality and human conduct. No theory is adequate that fails to accomplish this.[13]

Given Hume's rebuttal of the notion of totally objective moral relations, objective in the sense of being totally independent of human beings, one can understand Hume's argument against the notion that moral distinctions refer to matters of fact totally independent of human beings and which are discovered by matter of fact inference or reasoning. It is exactly the same argument: "nor does this reasoning only prove, that morality consists not in any relations, that are the objects of science; but if examined, will prove with equal certainty, that it consists not in any *matter of fact*, which can be discovered by the understanding" (*Treatise*, p. 468). The relationship between the two arguments is obvious. The major argument against treating moral distinctions as relations of ideas is that such relations "must antecedently exist in order to their being perceived" (*Ibid.*). If they existed independently of human perception such relations would be ascribable to animals and inanimate objects. Animals and inanimate objects are not subject to morality. Hence, moral distinctions cannot be relations which exist unperceived. Analogously, if moral distinctions were matters of fact "in the object" (*Treatise*, p. 469), [i.e. primary qualities], then they would exist independently of perception and would thus also be applicable to animals and inanimate objects. The same objection applies to both cases.

For Hume, theoretical reason in the strict sense of the term operates in one of two ways: discovering relations of ideas and inferring matters of fact. In neither sense can moral distinctions be the object of reason. Hence, reason cannot be the source of moral insight. Nevertheless, we do perceive or apprehend moral distinctions. If moral distinctions are not apprehended by reason, then moral distinctions are not apprehended as ideas, which are always the object of reason. If moral distinctions are not apprehended as ideas, then by the process of elimination moral distinctions are apprehended as impressions. This is precisely what Hume says. Moreover, these impressions must not be impressions of qualities which are totally independent of human nature for then such qualities would apply as well to animals and to inanimate objects. There is at least one kind of quality which exists only when perceived, that is, it exists only as an interaction of objects or events with human nature, namely, a secondary quality. Moral distinctions would therefore be analogous to the traditional secondary qualities like color. The analogy with secondary qualities was precisely what Hutcheson had stressed in the *Illustrations*.[14] In one argument Hume has combined the position of Hutcheson with a rebuttal of their common rationalist opponents. As a crowning achievement to this position, Hume noted that this conception of moral distinctions as a kind of secondary quality reinforces his Newtonian program by showing to what degree human nature can be illuminated by applying to it the categories of Newtonian physics. Finally, by stressing the dependence of morality on human nature, Hume has reasserted the basic insight of the Copernican philosophical perspective that man is central to any philosophical analysis.

> Here is a matter of fact; but 'tis the object of feeling, not of reason. It lies in yourself, not in the object....Vice and virtue, therefore, may be compared to sounds, colours, heat and cold, which according to modern philosophy, are not qualities in objects, but perceptions in the mind: And this discovery in morals, like that other in physics, is to be regarded as a considerable advancement of the speculative sciences... (*Treatise*, p. 469).

Once more we see how Hutcheson's moral theory has been incorporated into Hume's Newtonian and Copernican frameworks.

Hume's Place in Moral Philosophy

Moral Distinctions Derived From a Moral Sense

In the second section of Part I of Book III of the *Treatise*, Hume tells us what a moral distinction is. Just as the title of the first section was negative, "Moral distinctions not derived from reason," so the title of the second section is positive, "Moral distinctions derived from a moral sense." Moral distinctions are not apprehended by reason, so reason is not the source of moral insight. Therefore, moral distinctions are not perceived as ideas. By elimination, Hume concludes that moral distinctions are perceived as impressions. From this point on, following Hume, we shall speak of *moral sentiments*, since it has been established that moral distinctions are impressions or feelings or sentiments.

Hume has arrived at the conclusion that moral distinctions or sentiments are impressions.

> Since vice and virtue are not discoverable merely by reason, or the comparison of ideas, it must be by means of some impression or sentiment they occasion, that we are able to mark the difference betwixt them. Our decisions concerning moral rectitude and depravity are evidently perceptions; and as all perceptions are either impressions or ideas, the exclusion of the one is a convincing argument for the other. (*Treatise*, p. 470)

In denying that moral distinctions were relations of ideas or qualities totally independent of human perception, Hume made two objections: moral relations cannot be specified; and moral relations even if they existed could not influence conduct. In asserting that moral distinctions or sentiments are impressions, Hume must answer two corresponding questions: "Of what nature are these impressions, and after what manner do they operate on us?" (*Treatise*, p. 470)

Moral impressions are "particular pains or pleasures" (*Treatise*, p. 471). "The impression arising from virtue" is "agreeable, and that proceeding from vice" is "uneasy" (*Ibid.*). In order to avoid the decisive error in the theory that moral distinctions are perceived as relations or ideas referring to qualities totally independent of human perception, namely, that moral distinctions would then be applicable to animals and inanimate objects, Hume must explain why it is not the case that "any object, whether animate or inanimate, rational or irrational, might become morally good or evil, provided it can excite a satisfaction or uneasiness" (*Treatise*, p. 471). Hume replied as follows. Not every impression or sensation of pleasure and pain is a moral impression. "'Tis only when a character is considered in general, without reference to our particular interest, that it causes such a feeling or sentiment, as denominates it morally good or evil" (*Treatise*, p. 472). Moral sentiments are thus pleasures and pains felt under a certain set of specific circumstances.[15] In addition, moral impressions give rise to the indirect passions of love and hatred, pride and humility (*Treatise*, p. 473).[16] These indirect passions can only arise within us when there is an object which "must necessarily be placed either in ourselves or others, and excite[s] pleasure or uneasiness" (*Ibid.*). Since only other human beings or ourselves are capable of arousing the indirect passions, animals and inanimate objects alone cannot cause us to have either the indirect passions or a moral sentiment. Finally, it should be noted that in causing us to have the indirect passions of love and hatred the moral impressions can influence human conduct. That is why Hume can say that the arousal of the indirect passions is "the most considerable effect that virtue and vice have upon the human mind" (*Ibid.*).[17]

By identifying the source of moral apprehension as sentiment or feeling, Hume has placed himself within the camp of the moral sense theorists. To what degree is Hume a moral sense theorist? The moral sentiment is an impression which is "felt by an internal sense" (*Treatise*, p. 466). Morality is felt, not judged (*Treatise*, p. 470). Because moral sentiments are impressions, we may speak of a moral sense or a sense of virtue. "To have the sense of virtue, is nothing but to *feel* a satisfaction of a particular kind from the contemplation of a character" (*Treatise*, p. 471). "We do not infer a character to be virtuous, because it pleases: But in feeling that it pleases after such a particular manner, we in effect feel that it is virtuous" (*Ibid.*). Following Hutcheson's lead, Hume has himself compared the perception of a moral impression to secondary qualities in particular and to "all kinds of beauty, and tastes, and sensations" (*Ibid.*) in general.

Let us paraphrase Hume's argument by analogy with the color red or the perception of redness. To have the sense of redness is nothing but to feel (have) sensations of color of a particular kind. The very sensation constitutes our sense of redness. We go no further; nor do we inquire into the cause of the sensation of color. We do not, for example, infer a tomato to be red because we feel a sensation of color. In having the sensation of color after a certain manner we in effect sense that the tomato is red. The sense of redness is implied in the immediate sensation of color. In short, our immediate perception of the redness of a tomato is not an inferential process but a direct apprehension.

We do not infer virtue from pleasure. The sense of virtue *is* the feeling of a particular pleasure. Moreover, the sense of virtue is an instance of pleasure because while all sentiments of virtue are pleasurable not all pleasurable feelings are impressions of virtue. Analogously, we do not infer redness from the sense of color because the sensation of redness *is* the sense of a particular color. Redness is an instance of color although not all sensations of color are sensations of redness. Finally, just as the sense of virtue is not a quality over and above the feeling of pleasure and it is not a matter of fact inferred from pleasure, so the sensation of redness is not a quality over and above the sensation of color and not a matter of fact inferred from the sensation of color. Both virtue and redness are facts perceived as immediate impressions, and that is what it means to make them objects of feeling.

So far Hume's views are not appreciably different from those of Hutcheson. But there is an important set of differences between Hume's version of the moral sense and Hutcheson's. To begin with, Hume does not accept the view that the moral sense is an additional faculty in human nature. The moral sense is a set of feelings not the faculty that perceives the feelings. "To have the sense of virtue, is nothing but to feel..." (*Treatise*, p. 471).

Hume specifically contrasted in a later context his own theory with one that treated the moral sense as an "original instinct of the human mind" (*Treatise*, p. 619). Hume rejected the whole notion of unknown senses. "It is absurd to imagine, that in every particular instance, these sentiments are produced by an original quality and primary constitution" (*Treatise*, p. 473). Hutcheson, on the contrary, had viewed the moral sense as a special kind of original instinct.

Part of the reason for Hutcheson's insistence on a separate faculty was his desire to have that faculty, in a manner of speaking, pass judgment on our feelings. Hume specifically denied that there was an approbation over and above the feeling itself. "Our approbation is implied in the immediate pleasure" (*Treatise*, p. 471). In a letter written to Hutcheson (January 10, 1743) Hume contrasted himself on this point with both Butler and Hutcheson: "You seem here to embrace Dr. Butler's Opinion in his sermons on human Nature; that our moral sense has an authority distinct from its Force and Durableness, and that because we always think it *ought* to prevail. But this is nothing but an Instinct or Principle, which approves of itself upon reflection; and that is common to all of them." Hutcheson, like Butler, was concerned not to draw the full and apparently "subjective" implications of the moral sense position, the total reliance upon human nature. That is why, again following Butler, Hutcheson tied his version of moral sense to some theological basis. Hutcheson had in fact gone so far as to speculate on the moral sense in God Himself. Hume, on the contrary, pointedly distinguished between morality and theology.[18] In another, earlier, letter to Hutcheson (March 16, 1740), Hume had stressed this difference: "I wish from my heart, I could avoid concluding, that since Morality, according to your Opinion as well as mine, is determined merely by Sentiment, it regards only human Nature and human life. This has been often urged against you, and the Consequences are very momentous. If you make any Alterations on your Performances, I can assure you, there are many who desire you would more fully consider this Point; if you think that the Truth lyes on the popular Side. Otherwise common Prudence, your Character, and Situation forbid you touch upon it. If Morality were determined by Reason, that is the same to all rational Beings: But nothing but Experience can assure us, that the Sentiments are the same. What Experience have we with regard to superior Beings? How can we ascribe to them any Sentiments at all? They have implanted those Sentiments in us for the Conduct of Life like our bodily Sensations, which they possess not themselves."

Once freed of the notion that the moral sense is literally a special sense with a special authority of its own, Hume can pursue his project of incorporating a nonsupernaturalistic version of Hutcheson's theory of morals into Hume's own Newtonian and Copernican frameworks. Hume's critique of the notion that the moral sense is a separate instinct fits in well with his project to explain the moral sentiments by the principles of association.[19] Hume plans to explain the operation of the moral sentiments in terms of his own theory of sympathy. This also explains Hume's disagreement with Hutcheson about the naturalness or artificiality of certain virtues. Hume insisted upon the artificiality of justice in his own sense of the term. "If anyone, therefore, would assert, that justice is a natural virtue....he must assert....a certain conduct and train of actions, in certain external relations of objects, has naturally a moral beauty or deformity, and causes an original pleasure or uneasiness" and "it seems sufficiently evident....that nature has annexed no pleasure or sentiment of approbation to such a conduct" (*Treatise*, pp. 527-28). The objection to such a moral instinct is made even clearer in *An Enquiry Concerning the Principles of Morals*: "though it seems a very simple proposition to say, that nature, by an instinctive sentiment, distinguishes property, yet in reality we shall find, that there are required for that purpose ten thousand different instincts" and "Can we think that nature, by an original instinct, instructs us in all these methods of acquisition?" (*EPM*, pp. 201-02). No one who took Newton's rules of philosophizing as seriously as did Hume, could possibly accept such a conclusion.

Having distinguished the moral sentiment as an impression, and having distinguished his own view from that of Hutcheson, Hume is now prepared to ask the really fundamental philosophical question about moral theory. The philosophical question concerns the general principle of morals. "It may now be asked *in general,* concerning this pain or pleasure, that distinguishes moral good and evil, From what principles it is derived, and whence does it arise in the human mind?" (*Treatise*, p. 473). Following the Newtonian rules of simplicity and universality, Hume insisted that there be "some more general principles, upon which all our notions of morals are founded" (*Ibid.*). This way of stating the question recalls Hume's previous statement of the moral question at the end of Book I of the *Treatise*, when he claimed that he had a curiosity "to be acquainted with the principles of moral good and evil" (*Treatise*, pp. 270-71). The question of the general principle of morals is then restated by Hume along with his rejection of alleged moral relations and occult moral qualities:

> Thus we are brought back to our first position, that virtue is distinguished by the pleasure, and vice by the pain, that any action, sentiment, or character gives us by the mere view and contemplation. This decision is very commodious; because it reduces us to this simple question, Why any action or sentiment upon the general view or survey, gives a certain satisfaction or uneasiness, in order to show the origin of its moral rectitude or depravity, without looking for any incomprehensible relations and qualities, which never did exist in nature, nor even in our imagination, by any clear and distinct conception. I flatter myself I have executed a great part of my present design by a state of the question, which appears to me so free from ambiguity and obscurity. (*Treatise*, p. 476)

The kind of problem that is central to Hume's moral philosophy should now be clear as well as his reasons for having raised it in his particular manner. Having seen what he takes to be his problem, we may anticipate his answer. Hume will divide the virtues and vices into two classes, the artificial and the natural. In the *Treatise*, Book III, Part II, he will examine the artificial virtues and vices. In Part III, he will examine the natural ones. In the conclusion to Book III, Hume will offer as his conclusion the view that "sympathy is the chief source of moral distinctions" (*Treatise*, p. 618). Sympathy is thus the general principle of morals. A fuller understanding of Hume's theory of morals would require an extended analysis of his theory of sympathy.

CHAPTER THREE

HUME'S REJECTION OF THE TRADITIONAL MORAL "OUGHT"

Introduction

For the past half century, Anglo-American moral theorists have been vitally concerned with an issue referred to as the *"is-ought problem"*. The so-called is-ought problem is a starting point for textbooks in moral theory. As one theorist has expressed it:

> The central problem in moral philosophy is that commonly known as the *is-ought* problem. How is what is the case related to what *ought* to be the case – statements of fact to moral judgments.[1]

Hume has been credited with being the first moral philosopher to call attention to this problem. R.M. Hare has even gone so far as to call this "Hume's Law".[2] The text in which Hume is alleged to have called attention to this problem is the now notorious is-ought paragraph, the last paragraph of Book III, Part I, section 1 of the *Treatise* (pp. 469-70). Because of the crucial importance of this paragraph for contemporary moral theory, I have reserved a special chapter for it.

Although almost all contemporary Anglo-American moral philosophers agree that there is an issue, the so-called is-ought problem, they neither all agree on what exactly the problem is nor how the problem is to be resolved. These differences are reflections of more fundamental disagreements about moral philosophy and philosophy in general. The alleged is-ought problem provides a convenient focus for discussion precisely because there is a host of other issues entwined with it. Given different and conflicting perspectives there will be different interpretations of Hume's is-ought paragraph depending upon the more fundamental outlook of the moral theorist involved. Yet while there are differences amongst those theorists who look at Hume's is-ought paragraph, almost all agree on one point: it is alleged that Hume is introducing some kind of distinction between what *is* and what *ought* to be in a moral context, and that he is discussing the relationship between "is" and "ought".

In this chapter, I shall provide an interpretation of the is-ought paragraph which is consistent with what I have said so far about Hume's moral philosophy, especially in the context of section 1, where the paragraph appears, and with what I shall say in the remainder of this book. Because my interpretation is so different from what is universally said about that paragraph even taking slight variations into account, a word of warning is in order. Not only is my interpretation different from the received opinion, but in an important sense it is the exact opposite of what is said. Rather than crediting Hume with making a distinction, I shall argue that Hume denies the intelligibility of one of the items so distinguished.

Since I am concerned in this chapter with explaining Hume's position, I shall concentrate on explicating the is-ought paragraph in the context of Hume's moral philosophy. I shall only make reference to recent discussion of other moral issues in so far as they are needed to clarify Hume's position in a narrow sense.

I know from previous experience that the title of this chapter is likely to cause some misunderstanding. On my own behalf I can only plead that it expresses exactly what I want to say, and that, in large part, the misunderstandings are a reflection of readers viewing the title from an alternative philosophical perspective. Recalling the earlier quotations from Clarke and Hutcheson, the problem of "ought", however it be conceptualized, was not first articulated by contemporary moral philosophers, nor by Kant, nor even Hume. The existence of a specific moral category, signified by "ought", had been discussed by Hume's predecessors. What I shall show is that Hume rejects the existence of and the intelligibility of this category.

This is not to say that Hume found all uses of the word 'ought' to be meaningless. It is the alleged moral "ought" he rejected, and hereafter I shall use double quotation marks to so signify that alleged category. Not only is Hume willing to use the word 'ought' but it is possible in some contexts to have the word 'ought' be synonymous with 'moral obligation'. But, as we shall see, for Hume, 'moral obligation' is not a special or unique category but a factual state of affairs. The whole thrust of Hume's moral philosophy is not to cut off moral philosophy from the rest of human experience but to show how much it is a part of ordinary human experience. What Hume tried to explicate was our moral experience and our moral practice. Other philosophers had conceptualized our moral experience and practice by means of the alleged moral "ought". What Hume rejected was that conceptualization because he found that it failed to capture our experience and practice. We as readers should not confuse the rejection of a particular conceptualization with the rejection of the practice the conceptualization was meant to capture.

The Paragraph

Let us begin by quoting the is-ought paragraph in full:

I cannot forbear adding to these reasonings an observation, which may, perhaps, be found of some importance. In every system of morality, which I have hitherto met with, I have always remark'd, that the author proceeds for some time in the ordinary way of reasoning, and establishes the being of a God, or makes observations concerning human affairs; when of a sudden I am surpriz'd to find, that instead of the usual copulations of propositions, *is*, and *is not*, I meet with no proposition that is not connected with an *ought*, or an *ought not*. This change is imperceptible;

but is, however, of the last consequence. For as this *ought*, or *ought not*, expresses some new relation or affirmation, 'tis necessary that it shou'd be observ'd and explain'd; and at the same time that a reason should be given, for what seems altogether inconceivable, how this new relation can be a deduction from others, which are entirely different from it. But as authors do not commonly use this precaution, I shall presume to recommend it to the readers; and am persuaded, that this small attention wou'd subvert all the vulgar systems of morality, and let us see, that the distinction of vice and virtue is not founded merely on the relations of objects, nor is perceiv'd by reason. (*Treatise*, pp. 469-70)

The Schema

The major elements in the is-ought paragraph are as follows:

A. The examination of previous moral systems reveals that they reason in the "ordinary way", that is, as follows:

   a_1. Establish the being of a God, or make observations concerning human affairs;

   a_2. (a_1) is expressed in propositions with the copulations "is" or "is not".

B. Previous moral systems also contain propositions connected by "ought" and "ought not".

   b_1. This connection or copulation surprises Hume.

   b_2. These propositions appear unheralded or *imperceptibly*, but Hume considers the *change* to be significant.

   b_3. "Ought" and "ought not" express a "new relation".

   b_4. Hume offers the following challenges: the *new relation* must be "observed" and "explained", presumably by those who have introduced it.

b_5. The new relation is a "deduction from others", presumably other relations, which are "different".

b_6. Hume finds the deduction "altogether inconceivable".

C. Paying attention to this *change* from (A) to (B) does three things:

c_1. It subverts all the "vulgar" systems of morality;

c_2. Shows that moral distinctions, specifically vice and virtue, are *not relations*;

c_3. Shows that moral distinctions are not "perceived by reason".

Let us examine each part of the schema in some detail. Hume begins in (A) by speaking of "every system of morality, which I have hitherto met with". Which moral systems might Hume have in mind? I believe that among others he is referring specifically to Samuel Clarke.[3] The reader will recall from Chapter One that Clarke had argued from the existence of alleged moral relations to something which ought to be done by us as subordinate rational beings. As Clarke put it:

> The same consequent Fitness or Unfitness of the Application of different things or different Relations one to another with regard to which the Will of God always and necessarily does determine itself, to chose to act only what is agreeable to Justice, Equity, Goodness, and Truth, in order to the Welfare of the whole Universe, *ought* likewise constantly to determine the Wills of all subordinate rational Beings...[*italics mine*][4]

There is another reason for believing that Hume has Clarke in mind. In (a_1) Hume noted that these previous moral systems do two things prior to making statements with the copulation "ought": first, they establish the being of a God, and second they make observations concerning human affairs. If we examine the three alleged self-evident moral principles or axioms that embody for Clarke the eternal rules of rightness or fitness, we find that the first one concerns God and the next two contain observations concerning human affairs. Axiom one is as follows: "First, in respect of God, that we keep up constantly in our Minds, the highest possible Honor, Esteem, and Veneration for him."[5] "Secondly, in respect to our Fellow-Creatures..."[6] "Thirdly, with respect to ourselves..."[7] Even the order in which Clarke presents his axioms conforms to Hume's description.

The important element in Clarke which epitomizes the position against which Hume is arguing is the concession made about moral axioms:

> The only difference is, that Assent to a plain speculative Truth (twice two is equal to four) is not in a man's Power to withhold, but to Act according to the plain right and reason of things, this he may, by the natural Liberty of his will, forbear. But the One he *ought* to do....as the other he cannot but do....[8] [*italics mine*]

Here we see clearly the shift from what is the case to what "ought" to be the case. There are other reasons for believing that in (A) Hume had Clarke specifically in mind, but they are best considered in a later context below.

Let us now examine (B). It will be easier to understand (B) once we have related it to both (A) and (C). Hume considers (B) to be some kind of extraneous element as shown in (b_1), (b_2), and (b_3). Hume objects to (B), specifically in (b_4), (b_5), and (b_6). Hume never states or implies that (B) is deduced, derived, or inferred in any way from (A). His description of the movement from (A) to (B) is in terms such as "change", "surprise", and "imperceptible", and these are certainly not the sorts of descriptions we would expect of an inference from one group of propositions to another.

In section (C), Hume claims that if we pay attention to the change – notice that Hume does not say deduction or inference – from (A) to (B), we shall see three things: (1) the subversion of vulgar moral theories; (2) that vice and virtue are not relations;

60

and (3) that vice and virtue are not perceived by reason. Hume believes that (b_3), (b_4), (b_5), and (b_6) are reasons for proving the three points of (C). In this context the word "For" has a strategic location. After mentioning the change, Hume claims that it has great consequence, proceeds to introduce reasons or premises by means of the word "For", and arrives at the statement of the three conclusions of (C). The question with which we are left is why does Hume believe that paying attention to the change from (A) to (B) proves the three conclusions of (C)?

Since Hume believes that (b_3) through (b_6) are reasons for proving the conclusions of (C), and since (b_3) through (b_6) deal with the nature of "ought", our problem becomes the explanation of the expressions "ought" and "ought not".

What role did "ought" play in previous discussions of moral philosophy? The reader will recall from Chapter One that Hutcheson in his *Illustrations* had argued that the word "ought" as used by previous moral theorists was "confused".[9] Specifically, Hutcheson had argued against the view that "Reasons determining Approbation, ought also to excite to Election." It is not possible, for reason alone cannot determine action. It is not possible, for obligation, according to Hutcheson, refers either (a) to prudential considerations or (b) to our feelings about our action or lack thereof. If "ought" in the sense of obligation does not mean one of these two things, then it is used in a meaningless way. Whom, may we ask, does Hutcheson believe to argue in a manner which makes "ought" meaningless? The answer is Clarke. Hutcheson specifically refers to Clarke as one who argues that "these relations, etc., *ought (another unlucky word in morals)* [*italics mine*] to determine the choice of all rationals abstracting from any view of interest."[10] In short, Hutcheson was among the first if not the first to attack the "normative ought", that is, to attack the notion that moral distinctions can refer to something other than our sentiments or interests.

It is my contention that Hume is presenting the same argument. That is, like Hutcheson, Hume is attacking the "normative ought", especially in Clarke, and he is questioning the meaningfulness of such a concept. This, of course, reinforces the point made above that Hume had Clarke specifically in mind.

That this is Hume's design can be seen from another crucial paragraph in the *Treatise*, this time taken from Hume's discussion of the passions. In it, Hume states the major purpose of his moral theorizing:

> Nothing is more usual in Philosophy, and even in common life, than to talk of the combat of passion and reason, to give the preference to reason, and to assert that men are only so far virtuous as they conform themselves to its dictates. Every rational creature, 'tis said, is obliged to regulate his actions by reason; and if any other motive or principle challenge the direction of his conduct, he *ought* to oppose it, 'till it be entirely subdued, or at least brought to a conformity with that superior principle. On this method of thinking *the greatest part of moral philosophy, ancient and modern*, seems to be founded....this supposed preeminence of reason above passion. The eternity, invariableness, and divine origin of the former have been displayed to the best advantage: The blindness, unconstancy, and deceitfulness of the latter have been as strongly insisted upon. *In order to shew the fallacy of all this philosophy*, I shall endeavour to prove *first*, that reason alone can never be a motive to any action of the will; and *secondly*, that it can never oppose passion in the direction of the will. (*Treatise*, p. 413)[*italics mine*]

Following Hutcheson, it is clear that it was Hume's intention to introduce a revolution into moral philosophy by challenging the meaningfulness of the "normative ought". It was not Hume's intention to show that the "normative ought" is different from what "is" the case, and it was not his intention to show that there was or was not a special way of getting from "is" to the "normative ought"; rather, it was his intention to challenge the very meaningfulness of the "normative ought". Finally, we should remind ourselves of the close connection between Hume's discussion of the passions and his discussion of morals. In Book III, Part I, section 1, Hume stated that his "reasonings concerning *morals* will corroborate whatever has been said concerning...the *passions*" (*Treatise*, p. 455), and again that "it would be tedious to repeat all the arguments, by which I have proved

(Book II, Part III, sect. 3) that reason is perfectly inert, and can never either prevent or produce any action or affection" (*Treatise*, p. 458).

Let us return now to the schema. What does Hume say about "ought" in (B)? First, "ought" is called a 'relation'; second, it is called a 'new' relation; third, Hume asks that this relation be observed and explained; finally, Hume requests an explanation for the deduction of this new relation from 'others', presumably meaning other relations. The other relations, claims Hume, are entirely different from "ought". In short, the nature of *other relations* is crucial for explaining "ought".

Hume's Theory of Relations

In order to determine the meaning of "ought" in the is-ought paragraph we must find in the *Treatise* Hume's theory of relations.

A relation is a complex idea produced by association or comparison.

> The word Relation is commonly used in two senses considerably different from each other. Either for that quality, by which two ideas are connected together in the imagination, and the one naturally introduces the other, after the manner above-explained; or for that particular circumstance, in which, even upon the arbitrary union of two ideas in the fancy, we may think proper to compare them. In common language the former is always the sense, in which we use the word, relation; and 'tis only in philosophy, that we extend it to mean any particular subject of comparison, without a connecting principle. (*Treatise*, pp. 13-14)

Hume distinguishes between natural relations and philosophical relations (*Treatise*, pp. 13-25; 69-74). The former include resemblance, contiguity in time and space, and cause and effect. They are connected through the natural force of association, a psychologically based feeling. Philosophical relations include the foregoing three relations and, in addition, the relations of degrees of quality, contrariety, quantity or number, and identity.

They are connected by comparison, a logical operation implying no binding or connecting principle of association. The ideas in philosophical relations may be compared quite arbitrarily.

Philosophical relations are further subdivided into the variable and invariable relations. The latter include resemblance, degree of quality, contrariety, and quantity or number. These relations are invariable in the sense that they depend upon the ideas under comparison and vary directly with the idea itself. When Hume speaks in his epistemology of "relations of ideas" he means the invariable relations. These *invariable relations* are also referred to as scientific relations because they involve demonstrative reasoning. These *are the relations of scientific knowledge* (narrowly construed as demonstrative) *to which Hume will refer several times when he argues against the notion that moral distinctions are the objects of reason.*

The variable relations include identity, time and place, and cause and effect. They are established by experience and observation and may vary without a variation in the objects. For example, two objects may vary in distance from each other without undergoing a change in themselves.

In the *causal relation* the mind moves from an object given in present experience to another object, either a cause or an effect, not immediately given. This inference does not involve an invariable relation, for the relation it finds among its objects is not given intuitively with the objects or terms of the relation. The causal relation can be either philosophical or natural. Any two ideas may be compared in terms of cause and effect conceived of as a philosophical relation and ultimately depending upon resemblance. The philosophical relation of cause and effect does not permit an inference to be believed about a real connection among objects outside of the imagination. We can imagine any one of these relations, but this implies nothing about the actual connection in experience. It is only as a natural relation that causal connections within experience can be made. This difference gives rise to the distinction between demonstrative reasoning, where we are concerned with the relation of ideas independent of actual existence, and moral reasoning, which concerns matter of fact and existence.

Of all the invariable relations, only the relation of quantity or number is strictly demonstrable. The others are intuited in that they are discoverable at first sight. Nevertheless, Hume refers to all of these scientific relations as demonstrative. He claims that these four relations "can be the objects of knowledge and certainty" (*Treatise*, p. 70), and that these same four relations are "the foundation of science" (*Treatise*, p. 73).

The following chart is a summary of Hume's view on relations.

A. Natural Relations

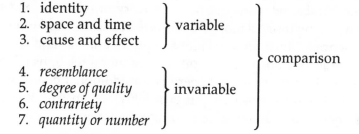

      1. resemblance
      2. contiguity in time and
         space   } association
      3. cause and effect (moral reasoning)

B. Philosophical Relations

      1. identity
      2. space and time   } variable
      3. cause and effect

                             } comparison

      4. *resemblance*
      5. *degree of quality*   } invariable
      6. *contrariety*
      7. *quantity or number*

"Ought" As A Relation

How is the foregoing account of relations relevant to Hume's moral theory? We have already seen in Chapter Two how Hume's critique of the notion that moral distinctions are based upon reason involved a denial of the existence of moral relations.

Hume's argument is, you will recall, that reason operates generally in one of two ways, forming relations of ideas or inferring matter of fact. Moral distinctions are not relations of ideas because moral relations are unintelligible, and if they were intelligible they would apply to animals and to inanimate objects; and finally because such alleged relations could not influence human conduct.

Let us examine in some detail the first point, namely, that moral relations are unintelligible. Returning to Book III, Part I, section 1, paragraph 17, Hume notes "There has been an opinion very industriously propagated by certain philosophers, that morality is susceptible of demonstration" (*Treatise*, p. 463). We have reason to believe, as we saw, that Hume is referring to Locke and Clarke among others. Hume continues: "If you assert, that vice and virtue consist in relations susceptible of certainty and demonstration, you must confine yourself to those *four* relations, which alone admit of that degree of evidence" (*Ibid.*), and those four relations are identified by Hume as "*Resemblance, contrariety, degrees in quality, and proportions in quantity and number*" (*Treatise*, p. 464). These are exactly the four demonstrable relations in Hume's theory of relations, and they are the same four relations he has referred to as "the foundation of science." Since these relations apply to animals and to inanimate objects, none of these four can be moral relations (*Treatise*, p. 464). Is it possible that there is an additional demonstrable relation? Hume considers this possibility and specifically denies that there is an additional or new moral relation.

> Should it be asserted, that the sense of morality consists in the discovery of some relation, distinct from these, and that our enumeration was not compleat, when we comprehended all demonstrable relations under four general heads: To this I know not what to reply, till some one be so good as to point out to me this new relation. 'Tis impossible to refute a system, which has never yet been explain'd. (*Treatise*, p. 464)

Hume then states that there are two insurmountable objections to the existence of moral relations: First, "it is impossible to shew those relations" (*Treatise*, p. 466) and second we cannot relate such relations to human conduct because "we cannot prove *a priori*, that these relations, if they really existed and were perceived, would be universally forcible and obligatory" (*Ibid.*). As Hume made clear, "'tis not sufficient to shew the relations upon which they [right and wrong] are founded: We must also point out the connexion betwixt the relation and the will" (*Treatise*, p. 465).

In effect, Hume first denies the intelligibility of moral relations and then argues that even if such relations did exist the obligatoriness of them upon the will is incomprehensible. This corresponds to Clarke's two assertions that the relations exist and that they "ought" to influence our conduct. Hume denies both the existence of such relations and the connection between them and the will.

Is there any evidence that for Hume in this section of the *Treatise* the word "ought" is being used in the sense of obligation as it would be understood in the theories of those who advocate the existence of moral relations? The answer is that Hume does use the word "ought" one other time in that section of the *Treatise*, in the twenty-fourth paragraph. The word appears there in italics *"ought"* (*Treatise*, p. 467), just as it does in the is-ought paragraph, and finally it has the meaning in that context which it must have for those who advocate the existence of moral relations.

> Ask anyone why incest in the human species is criminal, and why the very same action, and the same relations in animals have not the smallest moral turpitude and deformity? If it be answered, that this action is innocent in animals, because they have not the reason sufficient to discover its turpitude; but that man, being endowed with that faculty, which *ought* to restrain him to duty, the same action instantly becomes criminal to him; should this be said, I would reply, that this is evidently arguing in a circle....if the essence of morality consisted in these relations, Their [i.e. animals'] want of a sufficient degree of reason may hinder them from perceiving the duties and obligations of morality, but can never hinder these duties from existing. (*Treatise*, pp. 467-68)

Hume's Critique of "Ought" as a Moral Relation

The is-ought paragraph on pp. 469-70 summarizes what Hume has been saying all along between pages 463 and 468. To show this, let us return to the schema. In (b₃) Hume asserts that "ought" expresses a "new relation". First, Hume has denied that moral distinctions are relations of any kind. If "ought" expresses a relation, and if morality does not consist of relations, then the so-called moral "ought" is unintelligible. Second, Hume has called it a "new relation". In this, Hume is once again being polemical. Hume has already rejected the existence of additional or "new" relations. In the earlier context in which Hume rejected "new" relations, he challenged his opponents to produce the alleged relation, to have it "pointed out" and "explained" (*Treatise*, p. 464). What does Hume require in (b₄)? He requests that the new relation of "ought" be "observed" and "explained" (*Treatise*, p. 469). Clearly this is an almost identical repetition of the same point on p. 464.

In (b₅), Hume challenges his opponents to show how "this new relation can be a deduction from others, which are entirely different from it" (*Treatise*, p. 469). What does "others" mean in this context? To begin with, grammatically and syntactically it must mean 'other relations'. Since "others" is a plural, there must be a set of relations which Hume has in mind. I suggest that it is the four demonstrable relations of science that Hume has in mind. Further, I suggest that what Hume is saying is that one cannot deduce or demonstrate the alleged "ought" relation by inferring it from the four relations of science. It should be clear that (b₅) is a repetition of an earlier point now made explicitly about the word "ought".

In (b₆) Hume claims that the demonstration is "inconceivable". He does not say 'problematic' or 'difficult' but inconceivable. The word "inconceivable" is strong, but it too is a repetition of an earlier statement in which Hume declared twice that it was "impossible" to meet his two conditions: namely, to show that these relations existed and that they would be obligatory. "Inconceivable" is, I submit, synonymous here with "impossible". Hume's rejection of moral relations will be repeated in *An Enquiry Concerning the Principles of Morals*: "In these sentiments then, not in a discovery of relations of any kind, do all moral determinations consist" (*EPM*, p. 291).

The Critique of "Ought" and the Vulgar

If what I have said about (B) in our schema is correct, then how does (B) relate to both (A) and (C)? That is, how does the change from (A) to (B) prove the three points of (C)? First, asserts Hume, the rejection of the claim that moral distinctions are relations or perceived by reason would also subvert the vulgar systems of morality (c_1).

What does Hume mean by the "vulgar"? For an explanation of this term we must go back to Book I of the *Treatise*. This too should remind us of Hume's contention "that our reasonings concerning *morals* will corroborate whatever has been said concerning the *understanding*" (*Treatise*, p. 455).

In Part IV of Book I of the *Treatise*, Hume raised the problem "concerning the continued and distinct existence of body" (*Treatise*, p. 188). Hume did not question the existence of body, rather his question concerned the nature of the belief we have in the continuous and distinct existence of body. "We may well ask, *What causes induce us to believe in the existence of body?* but 'tis in vain to ask, *Whether there be body or not?* That is a point, which we must take for granted in all our reasonings" (*Treatise*, p. 187). I should note in passing that this quotation reinforces a point I made in the first chapter, namely, that Hume never challenged common sense beliefs, rather he questioned alternative philosophical accounts of our common sense beliefs.

According to Hume, there are three possible sources of the "opinion of a *continued* or of a distinct existence," and they are "the senses, reason, or the imagination" (*Treatise*, p. 188). Which of these is the correct source of our belief?

We may rule out the senses, for it would be a contradiction to speak of the senses informing us of the existence of objects when the senses were not operating; and even when the senses are operating they do not convey any information about a distinct existence. Distinct existence is conveyed only if the impressions are images or representations, and our senses "never give us the least intimation of any thing beyond" (*Treatise*, p. 189).

Reason is also incapable of producing our opinion about the continuous and distinct existence of body. If we directly identify our perceptions with objects, then we cannot infer, or reason to, the latter from the former. Only a causal argument can establish the desired conclusion. One possibility is to distinguish the perception from the object, and then to infer the latter from the former. Hume rejected this possibility (*Treatise*, p. 193). A causal inference can go beyond present experience only when the inferred perception is closely associated in past experience with a perception closely resembling the present perception. Our past experience has only been of perceptions and never of objects. Therefore, causal reasoning does not permit us to infer the object from the perception (*Treatise*, p. 212).

Hume's conclusion is that the imagination is the source of our opinion concerning the continued and distinct existence of body (*Treatise*, p. 193). In addition, the imagination is responsible for the distinction which we make among the three kinds of impressions we perceive. "The first are those of the figure, bulk, motion and solidity of bodies. The second those of colours, tastes, smells, sounds, heat and cold. The third are the pains and pleasures, that arise from the application of objects to our bodies, as by the cutting of our flesh with steel, and such like" (*Treatise*, p. 192). With regard to these three sets of qualities, traditionally called primary, secondary, and tertiary qualities, there are two conflicting opinions. The opinions involved are those of the *vulgar* and those of the philosophers. "Both philosophers and the vulgar suppose the first of these to have a distinct and continued existence. The vulgar only regard the second as on the same footing. Both philosophers and the vulgar, again, esteem the third to be merely perceptions, and consequently interrupted and dependent beings" (*Ibid.*).

The *vulgar* (*Treatise*, pp. 192, 209), or the "vulgar system" (*Treatise*, p. 213), believe in the continuous and distinct existence of the immediate objects of perception.[11] "The vulgar confound perceptions and objects, and attribute a distinct continued existence to the very things they feel or see" (*Treatise*, p. 193). They therefore attribute a distinct and continued existence to the secondary qualities as well as to the primary ones. Moreover, "children, peasants, and the greatest part of mankind" subscribe without argumentation to this position.

On the other side we have the *philosophers* (*Treatise*, p. 192), or "philosophy" (*Treatise*, p. 193), or "the modern philosophers" (*Treatise*, p. 192), or the "philosophical system" (*Treatise*, p. 213). The philosophers recognize the difficulties of the vulgar view and seek to remedy these difficulties through the "opinion of the double existence of perceptions and objects" (*Treatise*, p. 211). They recognize that "every thing, which appears to the mind, is nothing but a perception, and is interrupted, and dependent upon the mind" (*Treatise*, p. 193). To avoid the vulgar view of confounding perceptions and objects, philosophers distinguish between perceptions and objects. Perceptions are interrupted, perishing, and variable, whereas objects are supposed to be uninterrupted, and, therefore, continuous and distinct in their existence (*Treatise*, p. 211). Finally, the philosophers seek to infer the existence of the object from the existence of the perception of primary qualities. Hume, following Berkeley, criticized the distinction between primary and secondary qualities, but Hume also denied the possibility of inference from any qualities to an object of any kind.

Now it should be clear that Hume has no intention of denying the existence of body and therefore no intention of rejecting outright the vulgar view. The vulgar view is precisely what he has sought to explain (*Treatise*, p. 209). What Hume does deny or reject is the vulgar assumption that our perceptions have a continued and distinct existence. Hume offered his famous experiment of pressing his eyeball to show that our perceptions are dependent. Hence, Hume accepted the philosophers' contention that our perceptions are "dependent on the mind" (*Treatise*, p. 193).

At the same time, Hume rejected that part of the philosophical view that claims we can infer objects from perceptions. Hume's own position consisted then of three contentions. First, he accepted the vulgar view that there is a continuous and independent existence (i.e. external objects). Second, even though there is an independent existence, all perceptions are still "in the mind". Finally, he proposed to resolve the two contentions by appeal to the process of the imagination (*Treatise*, p. 209).

My concern is not with the subtleties and cogency of Hume's own solution but with what that solution does to clarify Hume's moral philosophy. Hume believed that moral distinctions are impressions. If moral distinctions are impressions, then we must know if they have a continuous and distinct existence. It would seem that if all perceptions are "in the mind" then moral perceptions must likewise be in the mind. Second, we would expect Hume to reject any philosophical attempt to infer the existence of independent moral objects from moral perceptions. Third, we have already seen that Hume maintained that moral impressions are analogous to secondary qualities. If moral impressions are like secondary qualities, then we should expect a head-on conflict with the vulgar view which mistakenly attributes an independent existence to moral distinctions.

The foregoing are precisely the conclusions which Hume has drawn. Recall that the major argument against treating moral distinctions as *relations* of ideas is that such relations "must antecedently exist, in order to their being perceived" (*Treatise*, p. 468). Because they would exist independently of perception, such relations are applicable to animals and inanimate objects. Analogously, if moral distinctions referred to primary qualities "in the object", then they would be referring to entities existing independently of perception and would also be applicable to animals and inanimate objects. The argument is the same in both cases, and that is why Hume considers it a decisive argument.

The vulgar[12] believe in the continuous and distinct existence of whatever they perceive. This includes secondary as well as primary qualities. If the vulgar are correct, then moral distinctions are applicable to animals and inanimate objects. By rejecting the contentions that moral distinctions are either relations or perceived by reason, where both of these views commit one to the belief in the existence of moral distinctions which are totally independent of the observer or the agent, Hume is also able to "subvert all the vulgar systems of morality" (*Treatise*, p. 470). Of course the vulgar do not believe that moral distinctions are applicable to animals and inanimate objects. Nevertheless, the uncritical acceptance of the vulgar view has this unwelcome consequence. It could be argued that Hume, the champion of common sense, saves the vulgar systems from themselves. Recall that for Hume philosophy is common sense methodized and corrected.

We must be careful to see to what extent Hume actually subscribes to the philosophical view. The philosophical view not only distinguishes between perceptions and objects, but it also seeks to infer the object from the perception. This particular inference Hume would not permit. And this is the second reason why morality "consists not in any *matter of fact*, which can be discovered by the understanding" (*Treatise*, p. 468). To deny Hume's contention one must produce the inferred object, hence Hume's challenge and his conclusion that "you can never find it" (*Ibid.*). The perception must be similar to what we have experienced or are experiencing, and hence it would have to be some kind of impression. If it is an impression, then inference would be superfluous. The moral distinction or quality is already present in the form of a feeling. In conclusion, we may say that Hume only accepts that part of the philosophical view which makes all perceptions dependent upon the mind, and in that important sense moral distinctions are comparable to secondary qualities.

At the same time that Hume is subscribing to one part and one part only of the philosophical system and rejecting another part of that system, Hume recalls that the vulgar attitude is practically inescapable. "Vice and virtue, therefore, may be compared to sounds, colours, heat and cold, which, according to modern philosophy, are not qualities in objects, but perceptions in the mind: And this discovery in morals, like that other in physics, is to be regarded as a considerable advancement of the speculative sciences; tho', like that too, it has little or no influence on practice" (*Treatise,* p. 469). The vulgar are correct, of course, in believing in the reality of moral distinctions, but the moral distinctions must now be understood as partly dependent upon the observer or agent.

The foregoing analysis has shown the continuity of argument from Hume's theory of the understanding to his theory of morals. Two points should be emphasized. Since moral distinctions are mind-dependent, they are not independent of human perception and therefore do not apply to animals and inanimate objects. Furthermore, since moral distinctions are like secondary qualities, they, like other kinds of secondary qualities, are a special kind of fact and not an inferior reality. "Nothing can be more real, or concern us more, than our own sentiments of pleasure and uneasiness" (*Ibid.*). Moral distinctions are not *sui generis*, rather they are like other perceptions. This continuity also makes clear what Hume meant in the Introduction to the *Treatise* when he argued that "all the sciences have a relation, greater or less, to human nature" (*Treatise,* p. xix), and when he claimed further that the recognition of the science of man as basic allowed us to recognize that when we "explain the principles of human nature, we in effect propose a complete system of the sciences, built on a foundation almost entirely new, and the only one upon which they can stand with any security" (*Treatise,* p. xx). This is not, as Kemp Smith had maintained, the mere extension of an ethical theory to epistemology and to metaphysics, it is an entirely new conception of what constitutes philosophy, namely, the Copernican Revolution.

The foregoing interpretation of what Hume means by the "vulgar system of morality" is compatible with Hume's general epistemology, with what he says in the section of the *Treatise* with which we are dealing, and with the immediately preceding paragraph where he mentioned the "modern philosophy" (*Treatise*, p. 469). Our contention that Hume had Clarke specifically in mind when he discussed "ought" is perfectly compatible with the claim that Hume intended his argument to have a wider application, i.e. to serve as an indictment of vulgar systems of morality. This could be a case of Hume extending the original Hutcheson argument. Recall that Hume said in (A) that he was speaking of all previous moral systems.

The connection with "ought" can perhaps be brought out in yet another way. If moral distinctions referred to entities completely independent of man, then we could perhaps find ourselves employing the expression that we "ought" to conform ourselves or our conduct to those allegedly independent entities. But if moral distinctions are not independent of mankind, then it is meaningless to set up an opposition between what *we* feel and do on the one hand and what we are supposed to feel and do. Recall Hume's contention in his discussion of the passions (*Treatise*, p. 413, quoted above) that all ancient and modern moral systems are unable to account for the link between approbation and motivation.

MacIntyre[13] has suggested that "vulgar" refers to eighteenth century religious systems. That suggestion is compatible with my interpretation. This would also reinforce the claim that Hume is denying the intelligibility of the alleged moral "ought", for in his rejection of the conflict of reason and passion and the fallacy of arguing that we "ought" to conform to reason, Hume did mention "popular declamations" of the "supposed preeminence of reason above passion" and the alleged "divine origin of the former" (*Treatise*, p. 413).

(c_2) and (c_3) are even more obvious. If Hume has successfully argued that we cannot explain moral distinctions in terms of moral relations, then vice and virtue are not relations (c_2).

Specifically the connection between the rejection of the moral or normative "ought" and vice and virtue can be explained by once more returning to Hume's major argument. There are two objections to the notion that moral distinctions of any kind and specifically vice and virtue are perceived as relations. First, Hume directly argued that these moral relations are unintelligible. Second, he argued that if they were intelligible, they could not be proven *a priori* to be obligatory (*Treatise*, p. 466). In showing the unintelligibility of the alleged moral relation of "ought", Hume merely reinforces indirectly the contention that the original distinctions of vice and virtue are not relations.

Having shown that an immediate perception of a moral distinction is not a matter-of-fact inference to a mysterious quality, and having shown that there is no demonstrative moral relation, and having defined reason as being either demonstrative or matter-of-fact inference, Hume concludes that moral distinctions are not "perceived by reason" (c_3). (c_3) is simply the conclusion to a section whose very title is almost a *verbatim* repetition of the conclusion, "Moral Distinctions not derived from Reason".

Hume's Theory of Obligation

One of Hume's opponents who saw what Hume was up to was Thomas Reid. Reid correctly summarized Hume's argument and then attempted to answer it by counter assertion.

First, Reid saw that Hume wished to reject the moral or normative "ought". He rightly claimed that Hume wished to "discard from morals the words *ought* and *ought not*."[14] Reid then went on specifically to answer the demands made by Hume in (b_4), (b_5), and (b_6). To Hume's demand that "ought" be explained, Reid replied that everyone knew what these words meant. He then quoted Dr. Johnson's definition of 'ought' as "being obliged by duty".[15] Second, to Hume's claim that "ought" is inexplicably deduced from a different relation, Reid replied that moral truths are deduced "from the first principles of morals".[16] Reid admitted that "ought" is to be classified among the relations. As he put it, "ought....expresses the moral obligation", and "moral obligation....belongs to the category of relation".[17]

What did Reid mean by a relation? A relation, he claimed, is *indefinable*, something of which we have a clear conception, and dependent upon the ideas related.[18] Reid compared moral relations to equality and proportion (i.e. a relation, for Reid, is what Hume would call an invariable relation capable of demonstration). "Equality and proportion are relations between qualities, which every man understands, but no man can define".[19] "Moral obligation is a relation of its own kind, which every man understands, but is, perhaps, too simple to admit of logical definition. Like all other relations, it may be changed or annihilated by a change in any of the two related things".[20]

To Hume's objection that relations would apply to animals, Reid claimed that moral principles do not apply to animals "because it contradicts every man's notion of moral obligation".[21] I submit that this is hardly an adequate reply to Hume, for the question is not what people think but to what their theory commits them. Reid has said nothing to show how such relations would not apply to animals. Second, and more important, Reid has not answered the overriding Humean objection that the influence of such alleged relations on human conduct is inexplicable. Failure to explain this merely reduces Reid's view to bald counter assertion.

The foregoing discussion of Reid was meant to show that Hume is not arguing against a straw man but against a position that was actually articulated and defended. Second, it reinforces my claim that Hume was rejecting the moral "ought". Third, it raises the question of how we are to understand obligation in Hume. So often, a critique on someone's conceptualization of an issue is taken as a rejection of the existence of the issue.

If Hume rejected the moral or normative "ought", then what Hume is declaring is that previous theories of moral obligation are unintelligible. In itself this charge is not new since it was made, as I have already shown, by Hutcheson as well. More-over, this charge follows from the distinction between questions of virtue (approbation) and questions of obligation (election), and it follows from the insistence that reason cannot overrule the passions. Both of these distinctions are, as we have seen, found in Hutcheson and Hume.

How would we expect holders of the major alternative theo-ries to react to a charge that one of their concepts is unintelligi-ble? Given the usual philosophical ploys, the expected reaction is to charge that one's opponent fails to make an important dis-tinction or fails to account for something important. One never admits, and we hardly ever see, that one's premises are chal-lenged. So the reaction to Hume's rejection of "ought" directly or indirectly is to assert that Hume failed to account for moral obligation.

Reid was the first to assert that in discarding "ought" Hume was discarding moral obligation because that is what "ought" meant. This charge in varying forms is repeated throughout the subsequent secondary literature. In his analysis of Hume's the-ory of obligation, T.H. Green noted that Hume "completes the assimilation of the moral to the natural".[22] As Norman Kemp Smith expressed it:

> There is, on Hume's theory of morals, no such thing as *moral* obligation, in the strict sense of the term. There is, that is to say, no intrinsically self-justifying good that with *authority* can claim approval. The ultimate ver-dict rests with the *de facto* constitution of the individual.[23]

In his article on Hume's account of obligation, Bernard Wand makes the same claim in two ways. "First, moral obligation on this view [Hume's] has no distinctively moral function".[24] "And to accept the view that every act of moral obligation must be due to the influence of others upon us is to deny the fundamental moral fact of responsibility".[25]

For Hume the fundamental facts of human nature and the in-fluence of moral rules upon conduct make it necessary to deny that there are moral facts or relations in the sense in which his opponents assert that there are. Hume, of course, has an account of moral obligation, but we must note that such an account differs fundamentally from all previous accounts, except in part from Hutcheson's. Although there is no fundamental dichotomy between the moral and the natural for Hume, the moral evolves from the natural.

As Hutcheson had expressed the view, obligation means one of two things, and only these two things. Obligation may mean prudence, the relation of means to ends. Obligation may mean that the omission of an action causes us to feel pain.

> When we say one is obliged to an Action, we either mean, 1. That the action is necessary to obtain Happiness to the Agent, or to avoid Misery: Or, 2. That every Spectator, or he himself upon Reflection, must approve his Action and Disapprove his omitting it, if he considers fully all its Circumstances. The former meaning of the Word Obligation presupposes selfish Affections, and the Senses of private Happiness; the latter Meaning includes the moral Sense.[26]

In Hume there is a corresponding distinction between a natural obligation and a moral obligation. The natural obligation is one of interest or prudence, what Hutcheson said presupposed the selfish affections. When a mother, e.g., tells her child "you ought to eat your vegetables", we are dealing with natural obligation or what Kant would call a hypothetical imperative.[27] The moral obligation is strictly limited to those cases involving the feeling of pain resulting from the omission of an action. This sense of obligation may be present independently of or simultaneously with the contingent motivational state of the person. The statement in which Hume makes this clear also distinguishes between virtue on the one hand and obligation on the other.

> All morality depends upon our sentiments; and when any action, or quality of the mind, pleases us *after a certain manner*, we say it is virtuous; and when the neglect, or non-performance of it, displeases us *after a like*

manner, we say that we lie under an obligation to perform it. (*Treatise*, p. 517)

Finally, we should note that for Hume the connection between obligation, now understood as a special kind of moral sentiment, and our consequent conduct is a causal connection. We discover the existence and operation of moral obligations just as we discover all other connections of cause and effect and that is "by experience" (*Treatise*, p. 466). We shall elaborate on Hume's theory of moral obligation later, but for the moment it was important to note that he had one and that the invoking of a moral "ought" on the part of Hume's opponents reflects difficulties in their understanding of both moral insight and its connection with moral motivation. Hume faced no such difficulties.

Alternative Interpretations[28]

With the exception of Reid and Green, there has come down to us a traditional way of reading the is-ought paragraph. According to that tradition, even where those who subscribe to the tradition differ on their interpretation of other issues in Hume's moral philosophy, Hume is supposed to be discussing the question of how "ought" is deduced from "is". In other words, it is assumed that Hume is questioning in some way the relationship between propositions with the "is" copula and propositions with an "ought" copula. Specifically, it is said that Hume is questioning how the relation of "ought" is deduced from the relation of "is". A sampling of this way of interpreting Hume's is-ought paragraph is the following:

1. "When I am fully cognizant of the non-ethical relations I cannot infer from them, and them alone, the ethical relations" (C.D. Broad).[29]

2. "Reason is concerned with positive knowledge or with relations of ideas and matters of fact; and it is impossible to de-

rive from such knowledge the conception of good and bad or of obligation" (B.M. Laing).[30]

3. "Many British moralists of the present time would agree with Hume's short but pregnant criticism (469sq.) that his opponents in this matter had illegitimately attempted to deduce *ought* from *is*" (J. Laird).[31]

4. Hume "insists that an 'ought' cannot be deduced from an 'is'" (D.D. Raphael).[32]

5. "Hume's demand....to show how ethical propositions may be deduced from non-ethical ones" (A.N. Prior).[33]

6. "Hume's point is that ethical conclusions cannot be drawn validly from premises which are nonethical" (W.K. Frankena).[34]

7. "He is asserting that the question of how the factual basis of morality is related to morality is a crucial logical issue" (A. MacIntyre).[35]

8. "Hume makes ought-propositions a sub-class of is-propositions" (G. Hunter).[36]

9. "For any ethical h and factual e, $P(h/e)<1$." (D.C. Stove).[37]

10. "Hume says that this derivation of an *ought* from an *is* only seems inconceivable (469)" (Jonathan Harrison).[38]

11. "...the stronger claim that *ought* cannot be derived from *is* is controversial" (J.L. Mackie).[39]

The traditional interpretation is that Hume is discussing the deduction or inference between "is" and "ought".[40] In terms of the three issues we have specified as crucial to modern British moral philosophy, the traditional interpretation is that in the is-ought paragraph Hume is discussing either (a) the source of moral insight or apprehension or (b) the relationship of moral insight or apprehension to motivation. These two issues must not be confused. We have maintained that although Hume discussed both of these issues throughout this section of the *Treatise*, in the is-ought paragraph Hume is specifically discussing the issue of the source of moral apprehension. In addition, we maintain that Hume is denying the intelligibility of a moral relation of "ought". Hence, there is no sense in which Hume is discussing the relationship of apprehension to motivation within the is-ought paragraph.

Beyond that common point not all subscribers to the traditional view will agree. Before discussing the differences, let us first discuss the basic claim of the traditional view.

In the interpretation which I have given above, I claimed that what Hume was saying was that "ought", if it expressed an alleged moral relation, could not be deduced or inferred from the other four relations of science. In short, Hume was not in the least concerned with any purported deduction between "is" and "ought". My arguments in support of my interpretation fell into two classes: (a) textual support from the entire section in which the is-ought paragraph occurs and other parts of the *Treatise*; (b) reference to the immediate historical context in which Hume was working. The latter included the assertion that Hume was repeating a point previously made by Hutcheson, the references to Clarke, and the fact that Thomas Reid took Hume to be saying precisely what I have attributed to Hume.

I might also add as a supporting note the fact that T.H. Green in his interpretation of this point did not take Hume to be speaking about the deduction between "is" and "ought". In his discussion, Green noted that Hume was rejecting "ought" by discussing the "intrusion" of "ought statements" into moral discourse. According to Green, Hume is attempting to account "for the intrusion of the 'ought and ought not' of ethical propositions upon the 'is and is not' of truth concerning nature."[41] Green rightly notes that this is part of Hume's more general attempt to complete the "assimilation of the moral to the natural."[42] Without having to accept everything in Green's interpretation, it is nevertheless clear that Green does not see any deduction of "ought" from "is".

I turn now to a rebuttal of the tradition in general. The is-ought passage will not sustain the view that Hume is even discussing the deduction or inference of "ought" from "is". A look at the paragraph and the schema shows that the transition from (A) to (B) in other writers is, according to Hume, a "change" and "imperceptible". Second, the specific "is" statements made by Hume in (a_1) are statements about God and human affairs. Such statements are matter of fact in form, or alleged matters of fact. Since for Hume it is not possible to demonstrate matters of fact,[43] Hume could not be talking about "deduced" with reference to what he says in (a_1). Hence, Hume could not be discussing the deduction from "is" to "ought". One could counterargue that perhaps Hume was using "deduction" in a loose sense in this context, but no one has ever been able to support this view.

It is much more plausible and consistent to interpret Hume as discussing the "deduction" of "ought" as a relation from the other four relations of science, which according to Hume are the only demonstrable relations. Of course, the four demonstrable relations capable of deduction do not include matters of fact at all. Hence, Hume could not be concerned with discussing the deduction of "ought" from "is". Keep in mind that relations are complex ideas and that Hume's main contention throughout this section of the *Treatise* is that moral distinctions are apprehended as impressions and not ideas.

It has also been suggested that the antecedent of "others" could be 'affirmation' as well as relation. If the antecedent of "others" is affirmation, then "others" refers to the being of a God or observations concerning human affairs. This suggestion is based on the appearance of the word 'affirmation' in the same context where Hume declared "ought" to be a new relation. Hume said "...new relation or affirmation..." The obstacle to accepting this reading, in addition to everything else which has already been said, is that in the specific context where Hume uses "others" he only talks about 'relation' and not affirmation. One would have to explain why Hume failed to repeat the word 'affirmation' in the key context. In addition, if Hume were trying to contrast two different kinds of relational modes of discourse, then he would have said 'another' and not "others".

Having shown the implausibility of the traditional interpretation in general, we may turn our attention to specific variations of the traditional view.

First variation: Morality for Hume, it is sometimes said, is completely a matter of feeling and not of reason, and therefore Hume must be *denying* that *inference of any kind* is at all relevant to morality. According to this variation, Hume is denying that morality is in any way dependent upon facts, that the "ought" in this context is symbolic of all morality and that morality cannot be inferred from "is".

What gives a semblance of plausibility to this view, specifically that "others" in (b_5) refers to "is" and that the "is" stands for causal relations, is a statement made by Hume in the paragraph immediately preceding the is-ought paragraph:

> Nor does this reasoning only prove, that morality consists not in any relations, that are the objects of science; but if examin'd, will prove with equal certainty, that it consists not in any *matter of fact*, which can be discover'd by the understanding. This is the *second* part of our argument; and if it can be made evident, we may conclude, that morality is not an object of reason. But can there be any difficulty in proving, that vice and virtue are not matters of fact, whose existence we can infer by reason? Take any action, allow'd to be vicious: Wilful murder, for instance. Examine it in all lights, and see if you can find that matter of fact, or real existence, which you call *vice*. In which-ever way you take it, you find only certain passions, motives, volitions, and thoughts. There is no other matter of fact in the case. The vice entirely escapes you, as long as you consider the object. You never can find it, till you turn your reflexion into your own breast, and find a sentiment of disapprobation, which arises in you, towards this action. *Here is a matter of fact; but 'tis the object of feeling, not of reason* [italics mine]. It lies in yourself, not in the object. So that

when you pronounce any action or character to be vicious, you mean nothing, but that from the constitution of your nature you have a feeling or sentiment of blame from the contemplation of it. Vice and virtue, therefore, may be compar'd to sounds, colours, heat and cold, which, according to modern philosophy, are not qualities in objects, but perceptions in the mind: And this discovery in morals, like that other in physics, is to be regarded as a considerable advancement of the speculative sciences; tho' like that too, it has little or no influence on practice. Nothing can be more real, or concern us more, than our own sentiments of pleasure and uneasiness; and if these be favourable to virtue, and unfavourable to vice, no more can be requisite to the regulation of our conduct and behaviour. (*Treatise*, pp. 468-69)

This paragraph is interpreted by some readers to mean that moral distinctions are not matters of fact. From this it is but a short step to conclude that Hume must also be saying that moral distinctions cannot, therefore, be inferred from matters of fact.

However, the foregoing interpretation completely misses the mark, and this can be seen especially when the entire paragraph and context are taken into account. To begin with, Hume does not deny that moral distinctions are matters of fact; he specifically says that they are facts. What kind of facts are they? They are facts in precisely the same way that "sounds, colors, heat and cold" are facts. That is, they are secondary qualities. Second, what Hume is denying is that the perception of a moral distinction is an inference, specifically a causal inference. Moral distinctions are perceived as impressions and not as inferred ideas. The important and key word in this context is "discover". If we directly perceive smoke, then we may and do infer the existence of fire even if we do not at present see the fire. The inference is true if we can confirm the existence of the fire at a future or later time by direct observation. It is the actual confirmation which Hume calls a "discovery".

That Hume uses "discover" as a technical term can be seen by noting the following statement:

Having found in many instances, that any two kinds of objects – flame and heat, snow and cold – have always been conjoined together; if flame or snow be presented anew to the senses, the mind is carried by custom to expect heat or cold, and to *believe* that such a quality does exist , and will discover itself upon a nearer approach. (*EHU*, p. 46)

We "discover" moral distinctions in the same way that we discover that a tomato is red, that fire is hot, and that snow is cold. We discover moral distinctions as directly perceived secondary qualities. Of course, this in no way implies that moral distinctions or sentiments are not inferable from other elements when the distinction or sentiment is not itself immediately present. We do not infer that tomatoes directly present to us are red, rather we see that they are red. This does not exclude the possibility of inferring that presently unseen tomatoes are red.

That the foregoing is Hume's point can be seen again by a careful reading of the paragraph in question. It is perfectly clear from the context that what Hume is denying is that vice and virtue are "in the object". Vice and virtue are not hidden or mysterious qualities whose objective (i.e. "in the object") existence we infer from other qualities. Vice and virtue are secondary qualities which exist "in us" in the same way that colors exist "in us".

The further implausibility of the first variation can be seen from the following. If the first variation is correct, then Hume must be saying that we cannot infer moral distinctions from causal relations. But Hume never speaks about inferring one item from a causal relation. What we do in a causal relation is infer either the cause from the effect or the effect from the cause. We do not infer the relation as a whole or from the relation as a whole. From the cause I infer the effect; from the effect I infer the cause. Hume does not speak about inferring something from the causal relation as a whole.

Second variation: In this variation it is assumed that Hume identifies the moral domain with moral relations and that such moral relations cannot be inferred from non-moral relations.

This is a view which had been asserted by Platonists, e.g. Ralph Cudworth in his critique of Hobbes. Cudworth argued that moral relations are given a priori and hence cannot be inferred from a posteriori events. Hume's position is also seen in this variation as analogous to that of those who argue that the moral domain is *sui generis* even though given in experience. That is, the moral domain cannot be inferred from other kinds of experience. Certain contemporary forms of intuitionism (e.g. Prichard)[44] and non-naturalism (e.g. Moore) exemplify this view. Hume, it appears to some, is asserting the noninferability of the moral order independently of the issue of whether the moral order is factual or nonfactual.

Although Hume would be sympathetic to the view that there is a moral domain, it is implausible to attribute the second variation to him. What Hume specifically has denied is that moral distinctions of any kind are relations. That is, Hume did not identify the moral domain with relations. If Hume denies that moral distinctions are relations, then it would be pointless to argue that moral relations are not derivable from something else. Hume rejected the very intelligibility of moral relations both in the is-ought paragraph and throughout the section as a whole. Finally, I do not see how one can plausibly interpret Hume as making a merely logical point when the is-ought paragraph, as we have argued in Chapter One, appears in a section devoted to the issue of how we apprehend the moral domain.

It could be argued by adherents of the second variation that Hume is just tacking on as an extra argument the non-derivability of moral relations. I have agreed with this, but this does not show that the deduction of which Hume speaks is between "is" and "ought". In fact, Hume's entire previous argument is against those who seek to derive moral relations from demonstrable relations, the four so-called relations of science, and not causal judgments. Finally, aside from the implausibility of attributing this view to Hume, if this variation were correct it would serve to refute the more widely held variations which I discuss below.

Third variation: It is most commonly held that what Hume is denying is that moral judgments, however interpreted, are derivable or inferable from non-moral judgments. Presumably this follows from the fact, or alleged fact, that moral judgments are different in kind from non-moral judgments. More specifically, it is asserted that non-moral judgments are factual or matter of fact, and that moral judgments are not. Hence, one cannot infer the latter from the former.

Aside from what has already been said, we should note the following. If variation two is correct then variation three is not. That is, if the moral domain is sui generis but factual then it is incorrect to say that Hume denies the factual nature of morality. Moreover, if Hume's point is that moral relations do not exist, then it does not follow that moral judgments as understood by Hume are not inferable. One would have to establish this independently of the is-ought paragraph. I shall consider this view in the next chapter.

Second, in the is-ought paragraph and generally in all of section one, Hume is not discussing moral judgments primarily but moral sentiments. The exact relationship between the two will be made clear in the next chapter, but some points can still be made here. Hume is discussing moral distinctions, i.e. moral sentiments, and this seems to be the case throughout section one, which is entitled "Moral distinctions not derived from Reason". It is also clear that Hume is discussing moral sentiments from the fact that in the is-ought paragraph the conclusions, that is part (C) of the schema, are all about moral distinctions or sentiments. A moral distinction or sentiment is an impression, not an idea. No impression by its very nature is inferable. Only ideas may be inferred. Hume's denial of the inferability of moral distinctions, and that is what is alleged in variation three, would be a trivial point. Not only is it the case that moral distinctions as impressions are not inferable but it is also the case that the impressions of color, sounds, heat and cold are not inferable. Since the latter are always classified as matter of fact, it follows from this variation that matters of fact cannot be inferred. Not only is this conclusion ludicrous, but this would be a preposterous contradiction of Hume's entire philosophy. Moreover, the fact that impressions cannot be inferred in no way shows that the ideas which are based upon those impressions are not inferable. In short, if the is-ought paragraph is about sentiments and not judgments, then either variation three is trivially true or it is preposterous.

The final rebuttal of variation three is that interpreters of Hume are forced to admit that in many contexts Hume makes moral judgments a special class of factual judgments, and that in some contexts Hume himself infers moral judgments from non-moral factual judgments. One can get around this rebuttal but it would be a pyrrhic victory. One may argue that Hume has simply contradicted himself and violated the very rule he has articulated. However, if there are several interpretations of a text, and at least one interpretation makes the text consistent while the others must charge the author with inconsistency, then standard scholarly procedure demands that we discard those interpretations which must resort to the charge of inconsistency. If we do not adopt this rule, then exegesis would be hopeless.

Fourth variation: According to this view, Hume is not dealing with the general relationship between moral judgments and non-moral factual judgments. That is, variation four denies the generality of variation three. Closer adherence to the text, it is alleged, reveals that Hume is specifically concerned with questions of obligation and motivation. On the positive side, the fourth variation argues that Hume is asserting that obligation cannot be deduced from factual truths alone. For Hume, to have an obligation involves having a motive not just being aware of truths, even moral truths.[45]

This variation is much closer to the text than any of the others. However, there are difficulties with it. First, it is not clear whether Hume is allegedly discussing the relationship between statements of some kind and statements of obligation, or whether Hume is allegedly discussing the relationship between statements on the one hand and obligations as events, not statements of obligation, on the other. There are, therefore, three possibilities to discuss: the relationship among statements, the relationship among events, and the relationship of a statement to an event.

A full treatment of Hume's theory of moral judgments will follow in the next chapter, but some remarks can be made here. First, I do not think, as I have already indicated, that Hume really has propositional statements in mind in the is-ought passage. When Hume discussed obligation he noted, as we have already seen, that obligation either appealed to natural, pre-moral motives of self-interest or prudence, or obligation in the moral sense referred to feelings of shame: "when the neglect, or non-performance of" an action "displeases us *after a like manner*, we say that we lie under an obligation to perform it" (*Treatise*, p. 517). The latter feeling, like any moral sentiment, is connected, as we have seen in Chapter Two, with the indirect passions that can motivate us. Therefore, it is correct, and important, to note that for Hume obligation is connected with motivation. The circumstances under which we feel moral sentiments of all kinds are precisely what Hume's moral theory is designed to show. Therefore, it should be possible to infer from one set of circumstances another set about our feelings of obligation. Hence, it is possible, and we shall show actually is the case, that statements of moral obligation can be inferred from other kinds of statements, precisely because obligations as feelings and motives exist under specified circumstances. The real question is what kinds of circumstances. Clearly for Hume, as we have shown and as variation four admits, those circumstances are not alleged moral relations.

If, however, we understand obligations as actual motives or events, as variation four admits, then 'ought' is equivalent to 'is obliged', where the latter expression refers to a factual state of affairs. If 'ought' is now understood in this sense, then we may ask from what states of affairs 'ought' in this sense is derivable. As Hume himself says in the same section, obligations are cause and effect relationships (*Treatise*, p. 466), and surely cause and effect is matter of fact. If causation is factual, and if obligation is causal, then obligation for Hume is factual. If obligation is factual, then surely obligation is inferable from other facts. Hence, variation four is incorrect.[46]

Finally, we come to the question of how knowing a moral truth (i.e. believing a moral judgment) can be related to action, i.e. the relationship of a statement to an event. The answer to this question is that the mechanism of sympathy, as an analogue to belief, explains how believing the truth of certain moral judgments leads directly to action. This will be dealt with in detail in the next few chapters. On Hume's theory there is no gap between belief and action in both the moral and non-moral spheres.

It is only Hume's opponents and not Hume who have difficulties with obligation. Thus, the only way to save variation four is to turn it into variation five, wherein it is argued that Hume does think we can have an "is-ought" relation if properly understood.

Fifth variation: Some scholars who have examined Hume with care have noted that Hume on many occasions derived moral judgments from non-moral factual judgments. Hence, they have recognized the inadequacy of the previous variations. As a response to this situation, MacIntyre has suggested that what Hume was dramatizing for us was the necessity for deriving "ought" from "is".[47] We should therefore look in Hume for a special kind of inference from facts to moral concepts. This variation still assumes that Hume is discussing inference from "is" to "ought".

There are three objections to this variation. First, not only must we assume that Hume is not to be taken literally, but we must also assume that Hume did not really mean "deduction" when he used that word in (b_5). There is no independent support for these assumptions. Second, however inadequate variation four might have been, it is correct to say that Hume specifically talked about "ought" and not about morality in general when he said there could be no deduction. One would have to show that "ought" is being used in a symbolic sense for all of morality. There is no support for this. Further, Hume specifically distinguished between judgments of virtue and judgments of obligation: "these two are evidently distinct. 'Tis one thing to know virtue, and another to conform the will to it" (*Treatise*, p. 465). Third, and most important, in this section of the *Treatise* as well as in the rest of his philosophy, Hume specifically denied that there was a third mode of inference.

> As the operations of human understanding divide themselves into two kinds, the comparing of ideas, and the inferring of matter of fact; were virtue discover'd by the understanding; it must be an object of one of these operations, nor is there any third operation of the understanding, which can discover it. (*Treatise*, p. 463)

Variation five, having recognized that Hume does permit inference from non-moral factual judgments to moral judgments, should have then reconsidered whether the whole tradition was not based upon a more fundamental misreading of the is-ought paragraph. Having come this far, one should simply and openly challenge the whole tradition of interpreting Hume as dealing with "is" and "ought".

If I were to try to explain the history of this misinterpretation of Hume, I would note the following considerations. There is always a tendency to confuse (a) what an author said, and (b) what he should have said in order to be correct, i.e. more like us. Thus, there is always a tendency on the part of a sympathetic reader to attribute to an author what we want to find. The retrospective adoption by twentieth century positivists of Hume, coupled with their desire to ban morality from the realm of rational consideration, reinforced a certain reading of Hume. If the rest of what Hume said appeared inconsistent with that reading, then so much the worse for Hume or the text. At the same time Hume's general philosophical orientation and his derivative view of moral philosophy were so different from what preceded him and from what largely followed, that it was to be expected that his critics should either miss some of his points or be scandalized by the points they did not miss. In a remarkable way, people of diverse persuasions and sympathy could agree on the traditional reading. This even lent a certain specious plausibility to the reading.

I cannot forbear adding to my comments the observation that the distinction between the *I Think* and the *We Do* perspectives is crucial here. All those who have missed the point of the is-ought paragraph have viewed the issue discussed as a purely theoretical one. Consequently, it becomes problematic for them as to how we connect moral insight with moral motivation. In the larger context of Hume's moral philosophy this is no problem at all, as the succeeding chapters will argue. It is no special problem for Hume because he began with a perspective that was both rooted in action, as opposed to thought, and social, not atomistically individual. More will be said about this in the last chapter. Long after contemporary meta-ethical disputes stop focussing on a misunderstood paragraph in the *Treatise*, the issue addressed by that paragraph will remain alive. That is why it is so important to get the text right.[48]

A second general problem suggested by the traditional misreading is that of seeing Hume in his historical context. Those more careful about the text and the historical context have been least guilty of the foregoing misinterpretation. Whether one agrees with the rest of what they say or not, Green and Kemp Smith did not perpetrate or perpetuate the misreading. Kemp Smith did not even discuss the paragraph. The problem of ignoring historical context is compounded by those who consciously dismiss the relevance of the history of their subject. This is especially regrettable in Hume's case since, if I am correct, he has been way ahead of everyone in the radical nature of his *We Do* Copernican Program and his proposals. More specifically, that Hutcheson anticipated Hume's questioning of "ought" is missed by those who fail to read Hutcheson or who fail to read all of his ethical writings. The same can be said of Reid, who despite his disagreement with Hume at least recognized that Hume was rejecting the traditional moral "ought". It goes without saying that both Hutcheson and Reid should be taken more seriously in their own right.[49]

Finally, I wish to call attention to a current tendency among some philosophers to represent issues as purely logical without consideration of the metaphysical presuppositions. It is easy to read the is-ought paragraph as a purely logical point about not being able to deduce "ought" from "is" as if it were merely the logical point that nothing could be in the conclusion which was not already in the premises. Hume's paragraph served this purpose admirably, especially if the paragraph is quoted in an incomplete manner. The part of the paragraph that is routinely omitted is the last part, what our schema identifies as (C).

> But as authors do not commonly use this precaution, I shall presume to recommend it to the readers; and am persuaded, that this small attention would subvert all the vulgar systems of morality, and let us see, that the distinction of vice and virtue is not founded merely on the relations of objects, nor is perceiv'd by reason. (*Treatise*, pp. 469-70)

Among those who have quoted the paragraph with the omission, I note Basson, Broiles, Chappell, Foot, Pears, Kydd, Laing, Nowell-Smith, and Weldon.[50] The most relevant statement made in part (C) is that moral distinctions are not relations. If the traditional moral "ought" is alleged to express a relation, and if moral distinctions are not relations, then it is clear that "ought" in the traditional sense does not express a moral distinction. The argument here is so clear and convincing that to disregard (C) is to miss the entire point.

Summary

Our interpretation of the is-ought paragraph has revealed the following:

1. Hume had Clarke specifically in mind as his target, but Hume was addressing himself to a fundamental orienta-

tion in Western moral theorizing, one with which he disagreed.

2. Hume was in no way discussing the relationship between "is" and "ought".

3. Hume was questioning the intelligibility and status of "ought". Hume did not deny the existence of an internal sanction or moral obligation, rather he rejected the traditional conceptualization of moral obligation.

4. In doing (3), Hume was following Hutcheson's lead.

5. Hume rejected the notion that "ought" signified a special moral relation, and

6. He rejected the view that one could infer "ought" from the four demonstrable relations of science.

7. The rejection of "ought" undermines the vulgar because it reinforces Hume's positive doctrine that moral distinctions are sentiments "in the mind" and not representations of entities totally independent of human beings.

8. Hume's views on the nature of moral judgment and on obligation must be established independently of the is-ought paragraph.

CHAPTER FOUR

HUME'S THEORY OF MORAL JUDGMENT

Does Hume Have a Theory of Moral Judgment?

Contemporary discussions of moral theory are often posed in terms of questions and answers about moral judgments, where the 'judgment' is a linguistic or logical entity. Hume did not pose the issues of moral philosophy in such linguistic or logical terms, and neither did his predecessors or contemporaries. Instead, Hume tended to speak about our moral experience and our moral conduct. He is said, by many contemporary readers, to have been concerned with moral psychology rather than moral language. Some, but not all, of these readers view this state of affairs in Hume as regrettable, but it is nevertheless the case that Hume's idiom was not ours.

At the same time, many contemporary moral theorists who refer to Hume's moral theory do attempt to attribute a theory of moral judgment to Hume and thereby make reference to Hume's alleged position or positions on moral judgments as linguistic or logical entities. I would agree that although Hume does not use the idiom of moral judgment as a linguistic entity as a central part of his concern, he does so use it occasionally, and it is therefore possible to reconstruct and to extract from Hume's writings both a theory of language in general and a theory of moral judgment as a linguistic entity. At the same time, I note that the failure to spell out in detail such a reconstruction has led commentators to attribute to Hume a wide variety of confused and contradictory positions. Ironically, many readers have not been careful to see the precise sense in which Hume used his language.

In what follows, I shall present Hume's theory of language in general, the relationship between his theory of language and human psychology, and his specific theory of moral language. I shall then show that such a general position is not merely implicit in what he says but explicitly made in a wide variety of contexts. As a result, a consistent theory of moral judgment emerges from Hume's writings. The key to understanding such a theory is Hume's distinction between moral sentiments and moral judgments. Finally, I shall show that the failure to make such a distinction accounts in large part for the misinterpretations of, and conflicting views attributed to, Hume.

Language

Briefly, Hume's theory of language was the commonly accepted one among British philosophers of his time, that language in general and words in particular stood for our ideas. In this sense, language in general and most words in particular make linguistic reference to mental entities, specifically our ideas. In the *Treatise*, Hume stated clearly that words stand for ideas:

> ...an observation, which may be made on most of their [metaphysicians'] own discourses, viz. that 'tis usual for men to use words for ideas, and to talk instead of thinking in their reasonings. We use words for ideas, because they are commonly so closely connected, that the mind easily mistakes them. (*Treatise*, pp. 61-62)

It is assumed by Hume that linguistic uniformity across languages is a reflection of certain uniform mental operations.

> As all simple ideas may be separated by the imagination, and may be united again in what form it pleases, nothing would be more unaccount-

able than the operations of that faculty, were it not guided by some universal principles, which render it in some measure, uniform with itself in
all times and places.–...This uniting principle among ideas...is the cause
why, among other things, languages so nearly correspond to each other.
(*Treatise*, p. 10)

The same point about language is made in the *Enquiries*. In
An Enquiry Concerning the Principles of Morals, Hume outlined his
method for uncovering the general principle of morals. This included beginning with linguistic distinctions and then trying to
determine to what extent these linguistic distinctions point to
mental distinctions.

The very nature of language guides us almost infallibly in forming a
judgment of this nature; and as every tongue possesses one set of words
which are taken in a good sense, and another in the opposite, the least
acquaintance with the idiom suffices, without any reasoning, to direct us
in collecting and arranging the estimable or blameable qualities of men.
(*EPM*, p. 174)

Notice that Hume said "almost" infallibly, for later he qualified
his earlier remarks and explained why a moral philosopher must
go beyond language.

Nothing is more usual for philosophers to encroach upon the province of
grammarians; and to engage in disputes of words, while they imagine
that they are handling controversies of the deepest importance and concern. It was in order to avoid altercations, so frivolous and endless, that I
endeavoured to state with the utmost caution the object of our present
enquiry...I do not find that in the English, or any other modern tongue,
the boundaries are exactly fixed between virtues and talents, vices and
defects, or that a precise definition can be given of the one as contradis-
tinguished from the other....A moral, philosophical discourse needs not
enter into all these caprices of language, which are so variable in different
dialects, and in different ages of the same dialect....But, *secondly*, it is no
wonder that languages should not be very precise in marking the
boundaries between virtues and talents, vices and defects; since there is
so little distinction made in our internal estimation of them. (*EPM*, Appendix iv, pp. 312-14)

It has become a commonplace to recognize, and perhaps to overemphasize, one of the critical weapons in Hume's arsenal. When Hume wished to test the legitimacy of philosophical language or a specific term, he analyzed the idea to which the term allegedly referred. The idea, in turn, is analyzed by trying to locate the impression to which the idea corresponds.

> When we entertain, therefore, any suspicion that a philosophical term is employed without any meaning or idea (as is but too frequent), we need but enquire, from what impression is that supposed idea derived? (*EHU*, p. 22)

On the surface this appears to be the old naive and unsophisticated empiricist theory of language. But what usually goes unnoticed is that a far more sophisticated theory and set of distinctions appears in Hume but in a different format, namely, in his ontological and psychological theories about the relationships among impressions and ideas.[1] Nevertheless, for our purposes, it remains clearly the case that words stand for ideas.

Before discussing that relationship, one important point needs to be emphasized.[2] The difference between Hume and later empiricists such as A.J. Ayer is that whereas later empiricists have been concerned with the empirical referent of sentences, Hume was concerned with the empirical referent of a specific term. Hume did not challenge the meaningfulness of, let us say, statements about necessary connection, rather he asked for the specific referent or origin of the term "efficacy" or the expression "necessary connection". Hence, when Hume engaged in an analysis of key issues he was apt to seek for the referent or origin of a specific term or word, not the sentence. Thus, Hume did not concern himself with all the special problems of dealing with different kinds of sentences.

Ideas and Impressions

In order to discuss the nature and properties of moral judgments, I shall employ the distinction between an experience and the description of that experience. This traditional distinction is important for an understanding of Hume's moral theory because of the manner in which it is formulated by him. In general, we have all had the experience of heat, but we do not expect the word "hot" to be accompanied by a burning sensation. We do not expect a map to duplicate in every respect a geographical entity, for if it did we would have two identical entities and not a map. Nevertheless, the general acceptance of this distinction between an experience and the description of that experience does not guarantee for us that everyone will assign the same set of properties to the experience and that everyone will agree upon what properties are to be assigned to the description of the experience.

There is one property, however, which is usually assigned to the description of experience but which is not assigned to the experiences themselves. That property is truth value. Without committing ourselves to any particular theory of truth most of us would agree that descriptions, or judgments, or statements, or sentences, or propositions, etc., are true or false in a way that experiences are not. Immediate experience is not taken to have reference to anything else; it does not call for confirmation; and it does not constitute knowledge in the usual sense. Statements, or logical-linguistic entities, whatever they may be called, which make assertions or ascribe properties to the objects of experience make reference to immediate experience. Statements, judgments, or descriptions imply a reference to standard conditions; they are capable of confirmation; and they constitute knowledge.

Now that the difference between an experience and a description of experience has been explained, we may proceed to formulate that distinction within Hume's theory. The corresponding distinction in Hume is between impressions and ideas.

Impressions correspond to immediate experiences and ideas correspond to descriptions of experience. In short, most propositional properties are assigned by Hume to ideas.

Hume first introduced the distinction between impressions and ideas in terms of vivacity.[3] Impressions strike the mind with great force and vivacity, whereas ideas are weak and languid. The criterion of vivacity, however, fails to cover instances in which impressions are more like weak images. Moreover, Hume himself stresses that in fever and madness our ideas may acquire a degree of vivacity which far exceeds even the most forceful impressions. Vivacity is an extremely important concept in Hume's philosophy in the *Treatise*, but by Hume's own admission it is not the crucial distinguishing factor between impressions and ideas.

Hume made a second distinction between impressions and ideas by calling attention to the temporally derived character of ideas. Ideas are derived from impressions in the sense of being temporally posterior to impressions. But even this distinction is not definitive. Impressions of reflection, which include passions and desires among other things, are not derived from unknown causes as in the case of the impressions of sensation. Impressions of reflection are derived from ideas. After a sensation or impression of pleasure, for example, we have an idea of pleasure. If the idea is recalled by memory, it produces the impression of desire. Temporal posteriority, therefore, is not an unfailing mark of the distinction.

It is not force, not liveliness, nor temporal posteriority which can absolutely distinguish ideas from impressions. The crucial distinction between ideas and impressions is the *referential* nature of ideas as opposed to the non-referential nature of impressions. Reference is not a distinction capable of empirical identification such as force or vivacity. As it stands, reference is a concept presupposed and introduced by Hume for the purposes of analysis. Those who insist upon a narrow empiricist or phenomenalistic reading of Hume will miss it. Those who understand that Hume begins from a social and historical common sense perspective will have no trouble in seeing this point. The referential nature of ideas is best seen by noting the sense in which ideas are said to "copy", "represent", or make "reference" to impressions.

> Every one will readily allow, that there is a considerable difference between the perceptions of the mind, when a man feels the pain of excessive heat, or the pleasure of moderate warmth, and when he afterwards recalls to his memory this sensation, or anticipates it by his imagination. These faculties may mimic or *copy* the perceptions of the senses; but they never can entirely reach the force and vivacity of the original sentiment. The utmost we say of them, even when they operate with greatest vigor, is that they *represent* their object. (*EHU*, p. 17) [*italics mine*]

It was precisely because he wished to emphasize the referential nature of ideas as opposed to impressions that Hume criticized Locke's use of the term 'idea'.

> I here make use of these terms, *impression and idea*, in a sense different from what is usual, and I hope this liberty will be allowed me. Perhaps I rather restore the word, idea, to its original sense, from which Mr. *Locke* had perverted it, in making it stand for all our perceptions. (*Treatise*, p. 2n)[4]

Since the distinguishing characteristic of an idea is that it is referential, ideas may be true or false. Impressions, being non-referential, are not capable of being either true or false. This is why, for example, passions as impressions cannot be true or false.

> Reason is the discovery of truth or falshood. Truth or falshood consists in an agreement or disagreement either to the *real* relations of ideas, or to *real* existence and matter of fact. Whatever, therefore, is not susceptible of this agreement or disagreement, is incapable of being true or false, and can never be an object of our reason. Now 'tis evident our passions, volitions, and actions, are not susceptible of any such agreement or disagreement; being original facts and realities, compleat in themselves, and implying no reference to other passions, volitions, and actions. 'Tis im-

possible, therefore, they can be either pronounced true or false, and be either contrary or conformable to reason. (*Treatise*, p. 458)

As he had put it even earlier:

A passion is an original existence, or, if you will, modification of existence, and contains not any *representative* quality, which renders it a *copy* of any other existence....'Tis impossible, therefore, that this passion can be opposed by, or be contradictory to truth and reason; since this contradiction consists in the disagreement of ideas, considered as *copies*, with those objects which they *represent*. (*Treatise*, p. 415)[5]

In the *Abstract*, Hume further elaborated the distinction between impressions and ideas as a distinction between feeling and thinking.[6] Impressions are feelings, whereas ideas are the contents of our thoughts. All thinking, therefore, is concerned with ideas. To form a judgment in the mental sense of having a thought is for Hume to conceive of an idea in a particular manner.

We may here take occasion to observe a very remarkable error....This error consists in the vulgar division of the acts of the understanding, into *conception, judgment*, and *reasoning*, and in the definitions we give of them. Conception is defined to be the simple survey of one or more ideas: Judgment to be the separating or uniting of different ideas: Reasoning to be the separating or uniting of different ideas by the interposition of others, which show the relation they bear to each other. But these distinctions and definitions are faulty in very considerable articles. For *first*, 'tis far from being true, that in every judgment, which we form, we unite two different ideas; since in the proposition, *God is*, or indeed any other, which regards existence, the idea of existence is no distinct idea, which we unite with that of the object, and which is capable of forming a compound idea by the union. *Secondly*, as we can thus form a proposition, which contains only one idea, so we may exert our reason without employing more than two ideas, and without having recourse to a third to serve as a medium betwixt them. We infer a cause immediately from its effect; and this inference is not only a true species of reasoning, but the strongest of all others, and more convincing than when we interpose another idea to connect the two extremes. What we may in general affirm concerning these three acts of the understanding is, that taking them in a proper light, they all resolve themselves into the first, and are nothing but particular ways of conceiving our objects. Whether we consider a single object, or several; whether we dwell on these objects, or run from them to others; and in whatever form or order we survey them, the act of the mind exceeds not a simple conception; and the only remarkable difference, which occurs on this occasion, is, when we join belief to the conception, and are persuaded of the truth of what we conceive. (*Treatise*, pp. 96-97n)

The analogy between the experience-description of experience distinction and the impression-idea distinction has been upheld. Ideas, for Hume, perform those functions we nowadays assign to linguistic entities. Furthermore, there seem to be several different kinds of judgments: judgments of existence which concern one idea, and judgments of causality covering two ideas. Finally, since ideas may have truth value, and since judgments consist wholly of ideas, judgments must also have truth value. Thus, the distinguishing characteristic or property of judgments is that they are either true or false.

So far we have seen how Hume is able to formulate the distinction between experience and the description of experience, and how he is able to account for judgments, as ideas, which are referential and capable of being either true or false. The distinctions appear in Hume's philosophy as the distinction between impressions and ideas. It follows that if we can show the existence in Hume of moral ideas, then there can be such things as moral judgments. Finally, such judgments could presumably be either about existence or causal relationships, and as judgments they could be either true or false.

Can there be and are there moral ideas in Hume's moral philosophy? As we have already seen, moral distinctions or moral sentiments are impressions (*Treatise*, p. 470). For every simple impression there is a corresponding idea:

The rule here holds without any exception, and that every simple idea has a simple impression, which resembles it; and every simple impression a correspondent idea. That *idea of red* [*italics mine*], which we form in the dark, and that impression, which strikes our eyes in sunshine, differ only in degree, not in nature....the case is the same with all our simple impressions and ideas,...But if any one should deny this universal resemblance, I know no way of convincing him, but by desiring him to show a simple impression, that has not a correspondent idea. (*Treatise*, pp. 3-4)

All of this applies to Hume's moral philosophy. Recall that Hume compared moral impressions to colors (*Treatise*, p. 468). Recall as well that relations are complex ideas, and that in denying moral distinctions are relations, Hume would be denying that moral ideas are complex. Hence, if they exist, they must be simple ideas. Once more we see how important it was for Hume to deny the existence of moral relations.

Hume makes one other important point about simple impressions and ideas, and that is that "simple perceptions or impressions and ideas are such as admit of no distinction nor separation" (*Treatise*, p. 2). What this means is that in order to define simple impressions and ideas we cannot break them down into constituent parts, rather we must describe their accompanying circumstances. That is why Hume said that moral perceptions are like pleasures and pains which must be further distinguished by their circumstances (*Treatise*, p. 472).

One source of confusion for readers in Hume's classification of ideas and impressions is that the division between simple and complex is not the same as the division between impressions of sensation and impressions of reflection, but there is an overlap. The division between simple and complex is an analytical one, whereas the division into sensation and reflection is genetic. Impressions of reflection can be subdivided into simple and complex, and impressions of sensation can be subdivided into simple and complex. If we are to locate simple ideas of morals we must first locate simple impressions of morals, and this requires that we locate them as either impressions of sensation or impressions of reflection.

Among the impressions of reflection, Hume distinguished between the calm and the violent. The calm impressions include the impressions of vice and virtue (*Treatise*, p. 276). Notice that this information appears first and most clearly in the earlier discussion of the passions, probably the least read part of the *Treatise*. The violent impressions include the passions. Later Hume argued that the ideas derived from the calm and simple impressions of reflection (including vice and virtue) give rise to the passions which are also simple impressions of reflection but violent. It is important to realize that vice and virtue are not themselves passions but give rise to the passions.[7]

We may conclude, then, that moral ideas are simple ideas corresponding to simple moral impressions, with the reminder that such impressions are impressions of reflection. *See the chart on the next page.* This conclusion indicates what Hume must say if he is to be consistent with what he has already said throughout the *Treatise* about the relationship between impressions and ideas. Now we may raise the question does Hume actually speak about moral ideas? The answer is that he does.

> Let us proceed to examine the causes of pride and humility; and see whether in every case we can discover the double relations [of impressions and ideas], by which they operate on the passions....To begin with [the ideas of] VICE and VIRTUE, which are the most obvious causes of these passions....The virtue and vice must be part of our character in order to excite pride and humility. What further proof can we desire for the double relation of impressions and ideas? (*Treatise*, pp. 294-96)

The exact mechanism by which the ideas of virtue and vice cause the indirect passions will be discussed in the next chapter when we deal with the passions and with the sympathy mechanism.

In Book III of the *Treatise*, in the discussion of justice, Hume raised two questions. The second question was the following: "*Why we annex the idea of virtue to justice, and of vice to injustice*" (*Treatise*, p. 498). And a few pages later, Hume made the following point about moral ideas:

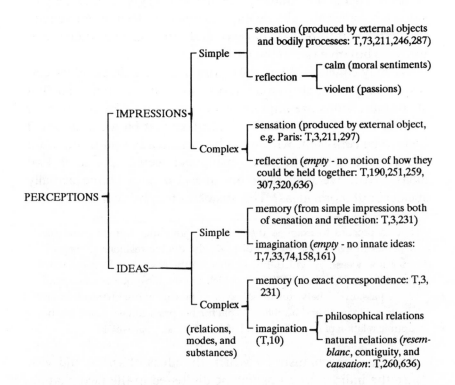

PERCEPTIONS

IMPRESSIONS

Simple
- sensation (produced by external objects and bodily processes: T,73,211,246,287)
- reflection
  - calm (moral sentiments)
  - violent (passions)

Complex
- sensation (produced by external object, e.g. Paris: T,3,211,297)
- reflection (*empty* - no notion of how they could be held together: T,190,251,259, 307,320,636)

IDEAS

Simple
- memory (from simple impressions both of sensation and reflection: T,3,231)
- imagination (*empty* - no innate ideas: T,7,33,74,158,161)

Complex (relations, modes, and substances)
- memory (no exact correspondence: T,3, 231)
- imagination (T,10)
  - philosophical relations
  - natural relations (*resemblanc*, contiguity, and *causation*: T,260,636)

Moral Sentiments

For if nature did not aid us in this particular, 'twould be in vain for politicians to talk of *honourable,* or *dishonourable, praiseworthy* or *blameable.* These words wou'd be perfectly unintelligible, and wou'd no more have any idea annex'd to them, than if they were of a tongue perfectly unknown to us. (*Treatise,* p. 500)

At the very beginning of the *Enquiry Concerning Human Understanding,* Hume offered an example of a moral idea in order to show the relationship between impressions and ideas:

When we think of a golden mountain, we only join two consistent ideas, *gold,* and mountain....A virtuous horse we can conceive; because, from our own feeling, we can conceive virtue; and this we may unite to the figure and shape of a horse, which is an animal familiar to us....all our ideas or more feeble perceptions are copies of our impressions or more lively ones. (*EHU,* p. 19)

The reader might well ask at this point whether or not Hume has contradicted himself. The initial question formulated at the beginning of Book III was "*whether 'tis by means of our ideas or impressions we distinguish betwixt vice and virtue*" (*Treatise,* p. 456). The answer Hume gave was that moral distinctions or sentiments are impressions and not ideas. If so, how can Hume have also said that there are moral ideas?

The contradiction is only apparent. When Hume raised the initial question, he was asking, as we saw in Chapter Two, whether our discovery or immediate perception of a moral distinction was either an idea or an impression. He maintained that our immediate perception was an impression and not an idea. This in no way excludes the possibility that there are moral ideas which result from or copy the immediate perception of an impression. On the contrary, Hume must insist that if there is an impression then there is a later corresponding idea. Hume was concerned with the immediate apprehension or discovery when he raised or formulated the initial question.

The reader may now ask why did Hume formulate the question in such a manner, a manner which certainly misleads a good many readers. There are two rather important reasons for Hume's having formulated the question in that particular manner. To begin with, Hume began each of the three books of the *Treatise* with the distinction between impressions and ideas and then proceeded to restate each issue in terms of that distinction. As we have already seen, this kind of beginning is a reflection of the Newtonian program in which analysis begins by first identifying and isolating the elements of analysis, and then proceeds to study the causes or general principles which explain the interactions among the identified elements. The elements for Hume are moral sentiments, which are impressions. The general principle, as we shall see, is sympathy. The whole point of Hume's analysis is to show that what worked for the analysis of the understanding and the passions will also work for the analysis of morals. Failure to note this continuity undermines a good many analyses of Hume's moral philosophy. One should not read his moral theory without reading the rest of his philosophy.

Second, Hume formulated the initial question in the manner he did because of what he was arguing against. Hume's opponents had maintained that reason was the source of moral apprehension. Reason has as its object, according to Hume's philosophical system, ideas and only ideas. Therefore, if Hume was to refute his opponents he must show *not* that there are no moral ideas, but rather that moral distinctions are not initially and immediately apprehended as ideas. If the immediate apprehension of moral distinctions is in the form of impressions, not ideas, then reason is not the source of moral apprehension. It should be noted, however, that denying reason to be the initial source of moral apprehension in no way excludes the possibility that we can reason about something which is not initially apprehended by an act of reason. None of our sensations is apprehended by reason, rather they are impressions gained through sensation and from internal sources of feeling. Of course we can later reflect upon or reason about them. But Hume insists that we not confuse the initial apprehension or discovery with the temporally posterior reflection.

In the great controversy of his age, Hume sided with those who had argued that moral distinctions were discovered as sentiments, not as objects of reason. But like the others who had argued for this position, Hume allowed that there might be reflection on the sentiments, that is, in his terminology, moral ideas. It also follows that if there are moral ideas then there must be moral judgments.

There is one statement which seems to contradict this:

> The mind can never exert itself in any action, which we may not comprehend under the term of *perception*; and consequently that term is no less applicable to those judgments, by which we distinguish moral good and evil, than to every other operation of the mind. To approve of one character, to condemn another, are only so many different perceptions. (*Treatise*, p.456).

Calling a 'moral judgment' a perception would seem to imply that such judgments are impressions and not ideas. But by the time Hume completed his analysis, he concluded that "Morality, therefore, is more properly felt than judg'd of" (*Treatise*, p. 470). What Hume was saying in the contexts quoted above was that the immediate apprehension of a moral distinction is a feeling, not an intellectual act or a judgment. This conclusion in no way controverts the existence of a later reflection on something originally apprehended as a feeling, and that later reflection may be a judgment. We may make judgments about our feelings or even to report our feelings, but our feelings are obviously not themselves judgments. That is all Hume meant in this context.

Let us now return to the full context in which Hume raised the initial question to see just how clear and self-conscious Hume was about the distinction between the immediate apprehension and the subsequent judgment. According to Hume, there are really two issues to be distinguished, not just one:

> *Whether 'tis by means of our* ideas *or* impressions *we distinguish betwixt vice and virtue, and pronounce an action blameable or praise-worthy?* (*Treatise*, p. 456)

There are two issues to be distinguished, although they are clearly related. There is the initial issue of *distinguishing* between vice and virtue, that is discovering or perceiving or apprehending virtue and vice. The apprehension is in the form of impressions. Hence, reason is not the initial source of moral distinctions. There is the second issue of *pronouncing* an action to be virtuous or vicious. Pronouncing is a linguistic activity, it is the public verbalizing of a propositional entity. It is what we would call a moral judgment. According to Hume, every meaningful verbal expression stands for an idea. Thus, a judgment when verbalized stands for an idea or set of ideas. A judgment as a mental act is in the form of ideas.

This raises two questions. First, does this mean that every pronouncement or verbalized moral judgment must stand for an idea? Second, since moral sentiments or distinctions are impressions does that mean that there can be no moral judgments?

The answer is the following. Every moral judgment as verbal stands for a moral judgment which is mental. Every judgment, including moral judgments, which is mental is in the form of an idea. Thus, if there are to be moral judgments there must be moral ideas. But the real question for Hume is whether moral ideas refer to or are derived from other ideas or whether they refer to and are derived from impressions. Hume's answer is that moral judgments or pronouncements refer ultimately to impressions. Moral judgments are ultimately about impressions and not other ideas. The distinction between form and content can be useful here. An idea in form may have as its content or referent an impression or another idea. To say that an idea refers to an impression hardly disqualifies the idea from being an idea.

The sequence is as follows:

t_1 a moral impression
t_2 a moral idea (which copies the moral impression)
t_3 a moral judgment (mental activity of judging in the form of an idea or ideas)

t_4 *a moral judgment as a pronouncement (as a publicly verbalized or propositional form of what exists at t_3)*

What Hume insists upon is that ultimately the reference of the moral judgment is an impression and not an idea. The stress should be on the word 'ultimately'. Hume's opponents had argued that what occurs at t_1 is an idea, either in the form of an a priori insight or an a posteriori inference about how one thing is related (hence the ambiguous term 'relation') to another. No one, at the time, seems to have argued that we apprehend a simple moral quality. In the parlance of Hume's time, his opponents could argue that the original apprehension is a judgment, whereas Hume would and did deny that the original apprehension is a judgment. None of this means that in Hume's account there cannot be a subsequent judgment about an original apprehension that is not itself a judgment.

The foregoing shows that Hume was aware of the distinction between the initial discovery of moral distinctions and our pronouncements about what we initially discovered. He was, of course, interested primarily in the former. Since Hume made the distinction, and since contemporary moral philosophers are interested in the latter, we must be careful when we reformulate Hume's position on moral judgment with reference to contemporary discussions. That is, we must distinguish those contexts in which Hume is discussing the immediate apprehension of moral distinctions and those contexts in which he is discussing moral pronouncements or what we refer to as moral judgments.

Within Hume's writings we may formulate the foregoing distinction as *the distinction between moral sentiment (the initial apprehension of moral qualities) and moral judgment (the verbalization of a moral idea which copies the moral sentiment or impression)*. The following expressions are used by Hume to speak about the former, that is, moral sentiment:

a. "distinguish moral good and evil" (*Treatise*, p. 456)
b. *"distinguish betwixt vice and virtue"* (*Ibid.*)

c. the *discovery* of "vice and virtue" (*Ibid.*, p. 470)
d. having "the sense of virtue" (*Ibid.*, p. 471)
e. the "sentiment of blame or approbation" (*EPM*, p. 291)

The expression 'moral sentiment' is synonymous in Hume with the expressions 'moral distinction', 'morals', 'approbation', 'morality', and the 'sense of virtue'.

The following expressions are used by Hume to speak about moral judgment in the contemporary linguistic sense:

a. "*pronounce an action blameable or praiseworthy*" (*Treatise*, p. 456)
b. "pronounce an action or character to be vicious" (*Ibid.*, p. 469)
c. "pronounce the action criminal or virtuous" (*EPM*, p. 291)
d. "ascribe virtue" (*Treatise*, p. 472)
e. "apply the terms expressive of our like or dislike" (*Ibid.*, p. 582)
f. "express that this man possesses qualities whose tendency is pernicious to society" (*EPM*, p. 272)
g. "The very nature of language guides us almost infallibly in forming a judgment of this nature; and as every tongue possesses one set of words which are taken in a good sense, and another in the opposite" (*Ibid.*, p. 174)

Judgment, or 'moral judgment', is thus to be understood as synonymous with the words 'pronouncement', 'ascription', and 'expression'. Any attempt to attribute some theory of moral judgment to Hume must make clear what contexts are used to support that attribution and why that context is taken to embody exactly what Hume meant by a 'moral judgment'.

The Structure of Moral Judgments

For Hume, moral judgments fall into two main categories: judgments of virtue and judgments of obligation.[8] Let us examine judgments of virtue first.

To begin with, judgments of virtue are of the subject-copula-predicate form. That is, they are of the form "X is virtuous" or "X is vicious". We must now identify the subject, the copula, and the predicate of moral judgments.

The grammatical subject of a moral judgment is the action or character of a human being. The following statements make clear that the subject of a moral judgment refers to a human action. Hume says that we *"pronounce an action blameable or praiseworthy"* (*Treatise*, p. 456); later he speaks of judging "our passions, volitions, and actions" (*Ibid.*, p. 458), and the fact that "actions may be laudable or blameable" (*Ibid.*); he speaks of our being able to "blame any action" (*Ibid.*, p. 464n.); he challenges us to "take any action allow'd to be vicious" (*Ibid.*, p. 468); and finally he says that "an action, or sentiment, or character is virtuous or vicious" (*Ibid.*, p. 471).

Later, Hume clarified and qualified his original assertion that actions are the objects (referent) of our judgment, or the grammatical subjects of the judgment. Although the immediate object of a moral judgment is an action, the ultimate object (or referent) of the judgment is a motive on the part of the agent.

> 'Tis evident, that when we praise any actions, we regard only the motives that produced them, and consider the actions as signs or indications of certain principles in the mind and temper. The external performance has no merit. We must look within to find the moral quality. This we cannot do directly; and therefore fix our attention on actions, as on external signs. But these actions are still considered as signs; and the ultimate object of our praise and approbation is the motive, that produc'd them. (*Treatise*, p. 477)

Therefore, one must exercise caution in the ascription of virtue or vice to an act in view of the fact that an action is an abstraction. We still ultimately judge the agent performing the act. This point is related to another Hume makes, namely, that animals and inanimate objects cannot be the objects of our moral judgments. Moral sentiments as we have seen give rise to the indirect passions, and the indirect passions can only involve beings similar to ourselves, that is, other human beings.

The copula of moral judgments involving virtue and vice is 'is'.

What is the predicate of a moral judgment? So far Hume has spoken mainly of 'virtue' and 'vice' and words synonymous with the foregoing such as 'blameable' and 'praiseworthy'. Our question concerns the reference of the predicates 'virtuous' and 'vicious'. Like any other term Hume finds meaningful, the meaning is clarified by finding what the term makes reference to, that is to what impression the idea signified by the term refers. The moral predicates refer to the moral sentiments. Thus, the presence of a moral sentiment can serve to confirm the moral judgment. "An action, or sentiment, or character is virtuous or vicious: why? because its view causes a pleasure or uneasiness of a particular kind" (*Treatise*, p. 471).

The outline of a moral judgment, specifically in the case of virtue, is now clear. Moral judgments attribute moral qualities to an action. "So that when you pronounce any action or character to be vicious, you mean nothing, but that from the constitution of your nature you have a feeling or sentiment of blame from the contemplation of it" (*Treatise*, p. 469). Moral sentiments are distinguished, discovered, apprehended, confirmed, or perceived as impressions. The moral judgment, which is an idea or a set of ideas, refers to these moral sentiments.

Let us now turn to judgments of obligation. Judgments of obligation are of the form "X is obliged to do y" where X is the name of a person or human being and y is some human action. There are two kinds of obligation, natural and moral. A natural obligation, according to Hume, is an action, y, to be performed as a means to some end, where the end is something that we already desire or are motivated to achieve. It is what we would call a prudential action, or what Kant called a hypothetical imperative. Thus, if I wish to avoid getting wet in a rainstorm then I am obliged to raise my umbrella. Raising my umbrella is not something I want as an end in itself, in fact it may be something of a nuisance. On the other hand, I do wish to avoid getting wet. Thus, I am obliged to raise my umbrella.

In the case of moral obligation, the action in question, namely y, is something I am actually motivated to perform, yet my motivation is not to perform it as a means to some other end. Rather, I am actually motivated to perform y because I have or will have a feeling of uneasiness if I do not perform it. Y is not something I wish to do in some natural or ordinary sense, rather it is the omission of y which will cause my discomfort. Thus, the correct translation of the judgment "X is obliged to do y", where the obligation is moral, is that "X will feel discomfort if he does not perform act y" and where the feeling of discomfort is a moral sentiment. Hume put it as follows, with special contrast to judgments of virtue:

> All morality depends upon our sentiments; and when any action, or quality of the mind, pleases us *after a certain manner*, we say it is virtuous; and when the neglect, or non-performance of it, displeases us *after a like manner*, we say that we lie under an obligation to perform it. (*Treatise*, p. 517)

There are several conclusions to be drawn here. First, the distinction between natural and moral obligation is not only a customary one, but as Hume drew it the distinction is identical to the way in which Hutcheson had drawn it. "When we say one is obliged to an action, we either mean, 1. that the action is necessary to obtain happiness to the agent, or to avoid misery: Or, 2. that every spectator, or he himself upon reflection must approve his action, and disapprove his omitting it, if he considers fully all its circumstances. The former meaning of the word Obligation presupposes selfish affections, and the senses of private happiness: The latter meaning includes the moral sense."[9] Second, it follows that since Hume speaks of moral obligation,

Hume has a theory of moral obligation, although it is not the same as the kind of theory that Hume's rationalist opponents had. Third, since moral obligation or judgments of moral obligation are statements about moral sentiments that exist under certain circumstances, judgments of moral obligation like judgments of virtue are purely factual judgments in Hume's theory. Fourth, if one uses the word 'ought' as a synonym for the phrase 'is obliged' and is referring to moral obligation as opposed to natural or non-moral obligation, then the word 'ought' would be descriptive of a particular moral sentiment and not a reference to an alleged relation. We can now understand Hume's rejection of the alleged moral "ought", like Hutcheson's rejection, to be the rejection of the notion of moral relations. Hume's and Hutcheson's rejections are not denials of the existence of moral obligation but the affirmation of a very different kind of understanding of moral obligation. Nor was Hume attempting in any way to draw a distinction between factual judgments and moral judgments. Fifth, again we see that moral sentiments confirm the moral judgment.

We may take this opportunity to summarize Hume's account of moral obligation:

1. Hume has an account of moral obligation.

2. Hume's understanding that moral obligation refers to a sentiment, a feeling of pain if we do not perform an action, is very close to common sense notions of moral obligation.

3. The sentiment is clearly distinguished from the pleasure of performing an action, and this too is part of the common sense notion.

4. Hume's own account has none of the difficulties of his rationalist opponents who spoke of the existence of alleged moral relations.

5. Hume's account of moral obligation is clearly distinguishable from accounts of legal obligation.

6. Hume's account of moral obligation allows us to make empirical generalizations about moral obligation, for the kind of uniformity in human nature and man's social condition that Hume recognized allows us to study the conditions under which the feeling might exist and might not exist.

One of the most interesting points made by Hume is that in the case of the artificial virtues, the natural obligation to adhere to such virtuous acts is a matter of interest, but that "afterwards a sentiment of morals concurs with interest and becomes a new obligation upon mankind" (*Treatise*, p. 523). The process by which a natural obligation based upon interest is converted into a moral obligation based upon a moral sentiment is explained by Hume in the *Treatise* by reference to the theory of sympathy.

The Properties of Moral Judgments

Moral Judgments in Hume's theory are made under standard conditions. Hence, moral judgments are publicly confirmable, they provide us with knowledge, and are either true or false. Since one can specify the conditions under which moral judgments tell us something both about ourselves and the world, it is possible to reason about morality in the narrow sense of the term 'moral'. Finally, if we can reason about morals, it is possible to draw inferences from conditions which are non-moral to conditions under which moral sentiments exist. In short, we can infer moral judgments from non-moral judgments in Hume's theory. Given Hume's analysis of moral sentiments to which the moral judgment makes reference, it will also become clear how moral judgments can influence our action.

Hume makes abundantly clear that moral judgments are made under standard conditions. In the case of all perception, it is necessary to specify standard conditions. Standard conditions insure confirmation and the communication of information through the uniformity of perspective.

> Such corrections are common with regard to all the senses; and indeed 'twere impossible we could ever make use of language, or communicate our sentiments to one another, did we not correct the momentary appearances of things, and overlook our present situation. (*Treatise*, p. 582)

Here again we should be reminded of Hume's drawing the comparison between moral sentiments and secondary qualities. If all perceptions can be corrected, then it is the case that moral perceptions which are akin to secondary qualities can be corrected as well.

There are two ways in which moral sentiments involve standard conditions. To begin with, it is part of the definition of a moral sentiment that it is a sentiment which exists under special conditions. "Tis only when a character is considered in general, without reference to our particular interest, that it causes such a feeling or sentiment, as denominates it morally good or evil" (*Treatise*, p. 472). In addition, Hume specifies that the moral judgment must make special reference to the perspective from which it is made. He distinguishes between the "mere view" which is immediate and the "general view" which specifically makes reference to standard conditions.

> Thus we are still brought back to our first position, that virtue is distinguished by the pleasure, and vice by the pain, that any action, sentiment or character gives us by the mere view and contemplation. This decision is very commodious; because it reduces us to this simple question, *Why any action or sentiment upon the general view or survey, gives a certain satisfaction or uneasiness*, in order to shew the origin of its moral rectitude or depravity... (*Treatise*, p. 475-76)

Elsewhere in the *Treatise* Hume says that "when we receive those feelings from the general consideration of any quality or character, we denominate it vicious or virtuous" (*Treatise,* pp. 608-09). And "every thing, which gives uneasiness in human actions, upon the general survey, is called Vice, and whatever produces satisfaction, in the same manner, is denominated Virtue" (*Treatise,* p. 499).

In the *Enquiry Concerning the Principles of Morals*, the same point is stressed, especially its importance for language.

> The distinction, therefore, between these species of sentiment (humanity and personal ambition) being so great and evident, language must soon be moulded upon it, and must invent a peculiar set of terms, in order to express those universal sentiments of censure or approbation, which arise from humanity or from views of general usefulness and its contrary. (*EPM,* p. 274)

So important is the existence of standard conditions for the confirmation of moral judgments that Hume can stress that "it is the nature, and indeed, the definition of virtue, that it is a quality of the mind agreeable to or approved of by everyone who considers or contemplates it" (*EPM,* p. 261n).

The capacity to be influenced by standard conditions or what Hume calls the general view is the result of a phenomenon Hume had discussed in Book I of the *Treatise*, where he invoked the presence of general rules.

> Should it be demanded why men form general rules, and allow them to influence their judgment, even contrary to present observation and experience, I should reply, that in my opinion it proceeds from those very principles, on which all judgments concerning causes and effects depend. (*Treatise,* p. 147)

> This difficulty we can remove after no other manner, than by supposing the influence of general rules. We shall afterwards take notice of some general rules, by which we ought to regulate our judgment concerning causes and effects; and these rules are form'd on the nature of our understanding, and on our experience of its operations in the judgments we

form concerning objects. By them we learn to distinguish the accidental circumstances from the efficacious causes.... The general rule is attributed to our judgment; as being more extensive and constant. The exception to the imagination; as being more capricious and uncertain. (*Treatise*, p. 149)

The application of these general rules to moral judgments is made clear by Hume in Book III.

Where a character is, in every respect, fitted to be beneficial to society, the imagination passes easily from the cause to the effect, without consider-ing that there are still some circumstances wanting to render the cause a compleat one. *General rules* create a species of probability, which some-times influences the judgment, and always the imagination.... The case is the same, as when we correct the different sentiments of virtue, which proceed from its different distances from ourselves. The passions do not always follow our corrections; but these corrections serve sufficiently to regulate our abstract notions, and are alone regarded, when we pro-nounce in general concerning the degrees of vice and virtue. (*Treatise*, p. 585)

When discussing the nature of knowledge, Hume consistently adopted the position that there were three types of knowledge: demonstrations, proofs, and probabilities. Knowledge in the strict or traditional sense corresponds to what Hume would call demonstrable knowledge, where the latter is concerned with the relations of ideas. According to Hume, there are no such things as moral relations (i.e. moral relational ideas). Hence, moral knowledge, if it exists, cannot be about anything demonstrable or certain. Proofs concern matters of fact about which we can be psychologically certain, because we have a perfect past record. Probable knowledge, in the strict sense, is knowledge that is based upon or conformable to past experience but not with a perfect record. Hume sometimes uses the expression 'probable knowledge' to cover both proofs and probabilities in order to distinguish them from demonstrations. There is also a fourth kind of knowledge about which Hume sometimes speaks, and that is intuitive knowledge. In intuitive knowing we cannot be mistaken about our immediate experience, although we can draw mistaken inferences from immediate experience to something outside of it.

Moral knowledge is, for Hume, knowledge of matter of fact. To begin with, there are judgments of virtue about our immediate experience, judgments about which we cannot be mistaken. Note, however, that these are not causal judgments.

> The distinction of moral good and evil is founded on the pleasure or pain, which results from the view of any sentiment, or character; and as that pleasure or pain cannot be unknown to the person who feels it, it follows...that there is just so much vice or virtue in any character, as everyone places in it, and that 'tis impossible in this particular we can ever be mistaken. And tho' our judgments concerning the *origin* of any vice or virtue [i.e. causal judgments], be not so certain as those concerning their *degrees*; yet, since the question in this case regards not any philosophical origin of an obligation, but a plain matter of fact, 'tis not easily conceiv'd how we can fall into an error. (*Treatise*, p. 546-47)

In addition, moral judgments can be causal matter of fact judgments which involve considerations of probability.[10]

> Where a character is, in every respect fitted to be beneficial to society, the imagination passes easily from the cause to the effect, without considering that there are still some circumstances wanting to render the cause a compleat one. *General rules* create a species of probability, which sometimes influences the judgment, and always the imagination. (*Treatise*, p. 585)

The totally factual nature of moral judgments in Hume's account is brought out in a number of places, but no where better than in *An Enquiry Concerning the Principles of Morals*: "The hypothesis which we embrace is plain. It maintains that morality is determined by sentiment. It defines virtue to be *whatever mental action or quality gives to a spectator the pleasing sentiment of approbation*; and vice the contrary. We then proceed to examine a plain matter of fact, to wit, what actions have this influence" (*EPM*, p. 289). We are now in a position to recall that the same view animated Hume's analysis from the very beginning. In Book I of the *Treatise*, he had proclaimed that:

> ...two objects are connected by the relation of cause and effect, when the one produces a motion or any action in the other, but also when it has a power of producing it. And this we may observe to be the source of all relations of interest and duty, by which men influence each other in society, and are plac'd in the ties of government and subordination. (*Treatise*, p. 12)

In the *Enquiry Concerning Human Understanding* a similar point is made: "Where would be the foundations of *morals*, if particular characters had no certain or determinate power to produce particular sentiments, and if these sentiments had no constant operation on actions?" (*EHU*, p. 90)

The matter of fact nature of moral judgments is now clear. Moral judgments concern either the existence of moral qualities (qualities of virtue or of obligation) or causal relationships between those moral qualities and other objects of our experience. If moral judgments are matter of fact judgments, then there are two senses in which moral judgments may be reasonable or unreasonable, true or false. Moral judgments are false when founded on a false supposition about the existence of moral qualities or when founded on misinformation about means and ends, or cause and effect. In either case it is the judgment which is mistaken.

The point was first made by Hume in a general way:

> A person may be affected with passion, by supposing a pain or pleasure to lie in an object, which has no tendency to produce either of these sensations, or which produces the contrary to what is imagin'd. A person may also take false measures for the attaining his end, and retard, by his foolish conduct, instead of forwarding the execution of any project. (*Treatise*, p. 459)

But Hume also makes the same point with specific reference to moral judgments.

> Moral good and evil are certainly distinguish'd by our *sentiments*, not by *reason*: But these sentiments may arise either from the mere species or appearance of characters and passions, or from reflexions on their tendency to the happiness of mankind, and of particular persons. My opinion is, that both these causes are intermix'd in our judgments of morals; after the same manner as they are in our decisions concerning most kinds of external beauty: Tho' I am also of opinion, that reflexions on the tendencies of actions have by far the greatest influence, and determine all the great lines of our duty. (*Treatise*, pp. 589-90)

A further property of moral judgments is the fact that moral judgments may be inferred from non-moral judgments. What does this mean? To begin with, moral judgments are moral in the sense that they are about moral qualities or moral sentiments, both in the case of judgments of virtue and in the case of judgments of moral obligation. They are moral because of their content. Moral sentiments are facts which exist under certain circumstances, and once we know those circumstances we can infer things about those moral facts. The circumstances are also factual conditions, but they are not moral. By this I mean that the judgments which embody descriptions of the circumstances do not themselves refer to moral sentiments. Nevertheless, the judgments which factually describe the conditions and the judgments which describe the moral sentiments are both classes of factual judgment. Moreover, *these two classes are causally connected*. Hence, one may make inferences from one class, namely the non-moral, to the other class, the moral, and *vice versa*. As thus stated, it seems a rather obvious point, but I make it in order to be able in the last chapter and elsewhere to relate Hume's position to other moral theories and to other ontological and epistemological positions.

A specific example of how this property of moral judgments appears in Hume's treatment can be taken from the *Enquiry Concerning the Principles of Morals*. There Hume said that a certain class of moral judgments may be inferred from factual considerations regarding utility.

Usefulness is agreeable, and engages our approbation. This is a matter of
fact, confirmed by daily observation....Here is a principle, which accounts,
in great part, for the origin of morality...(*EPM*, pp. 218-19)

Further, Hume went on to suggest how even this fact could
be explained, and thus provide another factual level from which
judgments of utility could be inferred: "We need be at no loss to
account for the influence of utility, and to deduce it from principles the most known and avowed in human nature" (*EPM*, p.
213).

The final property of a moral judgment that we shall note is
the influence of that judgment upon conduct. Only passions,
according to Hume, can motivate us. Reason can guide our
conduct, but it can never motivate conduct or oppose the course
of the passions. In order to explain how moral judgments can
influence or guide conduct, we must go back to the relationship
between moral judgment and moral sentiment. Moral judgments are factual judgments about moral sentiments. One of
the properties of moral sentiments or impressions is that, like all
impressions, they give rise to ideas, in this case moral ideas.
Among the properties of moral ideas, the ideas of virtue and
vice, is that they give rise to the indirect passions. By giving rise
to the indirect passions, action can be produced. The moral
judgment which embodies the moral idea thus influences action
by informing us of matters in which we are predisposed to action. We recall that:

...reason, in a strict and philosophical sense, can have an influence on our
conduct only after two ways: Either when it excites a passion by informing us of the existence of something which is a proper object of it; or
when it discovers the connexion of causes and effects, so as to afford us
means of exerting any passion. These are the only kinds of judgment,
which can accompany our actions, or can be said to produce them in any
manner. (*Treatise*, p. 459)

It is important to distinguish between directly motivating action and guiding action. Hume never claims that any judgment,

126

including moral judgments, can directly motivate us. In fact, he specifically denies such a possibility. "The impulse arises not from reason, but is only directed by it" (*Treatise*, p. 414). On the other hand, Hume does account for how judgments can guide our action, action to which we are predisposed by our passions. In fact, Hume specified cases where the moral judgment in particular may fail to guide action. It all depends upon our passions. There are cases where "our passions do not readily follow the determination of our judgment. This language will be easily understood, if we consider what we formerly said concerning that *reason* which is able to oppose our passion" (*Treatise*, p. 583).

The crucial distinction in Hume's theory that accounts for all of these distinctions and qualifications is the original distinction between idea and impression, or more specifically in this context between moral sentiments, which are impressions, and moral judgments which are ideas, articulated or unarticulated. Technically speaking, only a moral sentiment can actually move us. It is not the judgment but "Morals" [i.e. moral sentiments] which "excite passions, and produce or prevent actions" (*Treatise*, p. 457). The moral idea constituting the judgment must become a moral sentiment in order for it to incite the indirect passions. The exact mechanism of this excitation will be described in the next chapter. Here it is important to note the difference between the two points we are making.

First, every judgment contains an idea which refers in a general way to an impression. When we make the judgment, the impression need not necessarily be present. For example, I might describe the color of a shirt which I am not now wearing but which is at home in a closet. The impression of color is understood although one need not have the impression at present in order to comprehend my meaning. The same holds true for a moral judgment. Second, for the judgment I make actually to influence my conduct at the time I make it, it is, strictly speaking, necessary for the idea in the judgment to be enlivened so as to become an impression. It is thus necessary for Hume to provide in his moral theory a device or mechanism by which an idea may be enlivened so as to become an impression and thereby influence my conduct. In Book I of the *Treatise*, Hume described this process with respect to belief. In Books II and III, Hume provides an analogous mechanism by which an idea, only this time a moral idea, may become enlivened so as to take on the properties of an impression and thereby influence our conduct. That analogous process is the sympathy mechanism. Once more this reinforces Hume's point that one continuous argument holds the *Treatise* together, and once more this undermines any contention that Hume is making a special case for moral judgments.

Failure to grasp the distinction between sentiments which can motivate and judgments which influence us by providing relevant information leads to apparent contradictions. On the one hand, Hume can say that "'tis one thing to know virtue, and another to conform the will to it" (*Treatise*, p. 465); on the other hand, he can say that "Morals excite passions, and produce or prevent actions" (*Treatise*, p. 457). If we were to treat both statements as being about moral judgments, then we would find that moral judgments both motivate and that they do not motivate us.[11] The contradiction disappears when we notice that the first quoted statement does apply to moral judgment whereas the second quoted statement is about moral sentiment.

Moral Judgment and Sympathy

A moral judgment is an idea. A moral sentiment is an impression. The transition from the moral idea to the moral impression must be accounted for if the belief in moral judgments is to result in action. The transition from the moral judgment (idea) to the moral sentiment is accomplished through sympathy.

> The bare opinion of another, especially when inforc'd with passion, will cause an idea of good or evil to have an influence upon us, which wou'd otherwise have been entirely neglected. This proceeds from the principle of sympathy or communication; and sympathy, as I have already ob-

serv'd, is nothing but the conversion of an idea into an impression by the force of imagination. (*Treatise*, p. 427)

There are three stages in the sympathy process. First, we have an impression or we form an idea of a person or his situation. From this impression or from the first idea we infer a second idea which is associated with the person or his situation. Finally, the second or inferred idea is converted into an impression (*Treatise*, pp. 317-19). In this manner, a moral judgment can be said to be believed. This process is, moreover, completely analogous to the manner in which causal inferences come to be believed and acted upon. There are three stages in which we come to believe in a causal inference. First, an object is present to the memory (idea) or senses (impression). Second, by the force of custom we infer a commonly associated object. Third, such a conception is attended with the belief feeling (*EHU*, p. 48). Finally, we note that the feeling of belief is important because it influences action.

> I have already observ'd that belief is nothing but a lively idea related to a present impression. This vivacity is a requisite circumstance to the exciting all our passions, the calm as well as the violent. (Treatise, p. 427)

> An idea assented to *feels* different from a fictitious idea....belief....is something *felt* by the mind, which distinguishes the ideas of the judgment from the fictions of the imagination....and renders them the governing principles of all our actions. (*Treatise*, p. 629)

Sympathy operates for moral judgments in precisely the same manner as belief operates for the other judgments of the understanding. Hume enunciates the similarity.

> What is principally remarkable in this whole affair is the strong confirmation these phenomena give to the foregoing system concerning the understanding....when we sympathize with the passions and sentiments of others, these movements appear at first in our mind as mere ideas, and are conceiv'd to belong to another person, as we conceive any other matter of fact. 'Tis also evident, that the ideas of the affections of others

are converted into the very impressions they represent, and that the passions arise in conformity to the images we form of them....– sympathy is exactly correspondent to the operations of our understanding... (Treatise, pp. 319-20)

Summary

Moral judgments are factual judgments, they are capable of truth or falsity, they are confirmable or disconfirmable, and they are made with standard conditions in mind. Moral judgments are not mere reports of personal feelings but descriptions of moral qualities and of the causal relations of actions to which we ascribe moral qualities. Such descriptions are themselves inferable from other descriptions which are factual but not necessarily moral. Finally, moral judgments do not motivate human action, but they can guide human action like any other judgment.

The summary of this analysis of Hume's theory of moral judgment may be presented as an argument in the form of a series of interlocking syllogisms:

1. All simple impressions have corresponding ideas.
   Moral sentiments are simple impressions.

   ∴ Moral sentiments have corresponding moral ideas.

2. Any idea may be formed into a judgment.
   There are moral ideas.

   ∴ There are moral judgments.

3. Judgments are ideas.
   Ideas are either true or false.

   ∴ Judgments are either true or false.

4. Moral ideas form moral judgments.
    Judgments are either true or false.
    _____
∴   Moral judgments are either true or false.

5. Moral ideas form moral judgments.
    Judgments may be either existential or causal.
    _____
∴   Moral Judgments may be either existential or causal.

6. All causal judgments involve inference from one
        quality or event to another.
    Some moral judgments are causal judgments.
    _____
∴   Some moral judgments involve inference from one quality
    or event to another.

7. From the existence of a particular quality or event we
        can infer the existence of a moral quality or event.
    These particular qualities or events may be non-moral.
    _____
∴   From the existence of non-moral qualities and events we
    can infer the existence of a moral quality or event.

The Historical Treatment of Hume's Theory of Moral Judgment

In this chapter we have outlined Hume's theory of moral judgment. We have shown that Hume does have a clear and self-conscious view of language in general and of moral language in particular. Those views may only be peripheral to Hume's main focus, but that does not mean that the views are not there. Those views may not be acceptable to other theorists, but again that does not prevent those views from being present in Hume's writings. Those views may even be *in some respects* unsophisticated, but that does not mean that Hume did not hold such views, and it does not eliminate the presence of some very subtle points. In addition to Hume's holding of a theory of language, we have shown that all of the distinctions we are accustomed to making in purely linguistic fashion can be made within Hume's writings as distinctions between impressions and ideas. Thus, *the distinction between moral sentiments and moral judgments becomes crucial to understanding Hume's moral theory.* If Hume's theory is misunderstood, then such misunderstandings are the result of either (a) carelessness, or (b) the confusion between what Hume says about moral sentiment with what he says about moral judgment, or (c) a misunderstanding generated by basic philosophical disagreement with Hume's approach to moral theory.

Let us trace the history of the misinterpretation of Hume's theory of moral judgment. *Thomas Reid* was the first to take Hume's theory to task. Reid was well aware of the difference between having a feeling and making a judgment. He knew that judgments affirmed propositions, that judgments connected a subject with a predicate, and that they were either true or false. A word, as opposed to a judgment, expressed a feeling but not a judgment. For example, 'toothache' expresses a feeling but does not affirm a proposition. However, Reid acknowledged that to report the presence of a feeling under specified circumstances is to affirm a proposition.[12] Not only are these distinctions clear, but they are distinctions that would be acceptable to Hume. Hume himself made such distinctions. In short, there is no disagreement in the foregoing respects between Reid and Hume about the functions of language.

Not only do Reid and Hume agree on the functions of language, but they also agree on what constitutes the context of moral approbation. Reid quotes with approval Hume's description of the circumstances under which moral approbation takes place: "I think it unnecessary to follow him [Hume] through all the accounts of ingratitude which he conceives may be given...because I agree with him...that the crime of ingratitude is not any particular individual *fact*; but arises from a complication of circumstances, which, being presented to the spectator excites the sentiment of blame, by the particular structure of his mind."[13]

If Reid and Hume agree on language, and if they agree on what constitutes the context of moral approbation, wherein do they disagree? The disagreement is on the nature of moral apprehension. Both agree that such apprehension is in the form of a moral sentiment, but they differ as to their analysis of that sentiment. We already know that Hume analyzed moral sentiments to be impressions, not ideas, and to be analogous to secondary qualities. According to Reid, however, the sentiment is quite literally a judgment accompanied by a feeling.[14] This judgment about which Reid is speaking is not to be confused with the linguistic utterance reporting what is going on in our mind. The judgment of which Reid speaks is a mental event, an intellectual apprehension which he claimed is part of the moral approbation itself.

Hume, as we have seen, was more than willing to admit that the actual sentiment is preceded by intellectual judgments about means-ends relationships and the consequences of certain actions, etc. But Hume steadfastly insisted that these intellectual determinations were not part of the moral sentiment itself.

The real issue of disagreement was over the nature of the moral sentiment itself. For Reid the moral sentiment is the apprehension of what Hume would call a moral relation. Reid, in fact, believed in the existence of moral relations in Locke's sense. The moral sentiment for Reid is a feeling combined with the recognition of the relation which exists among the elements in the moral situation. It is as such an intellectual act, an act of reason. It is not a mere impression as Hume would maintain.

The Reid-Hume debate, at this point, is not a misunderstanding but a difference of philosophical perspective. The remainder of the debate between them has to be grasped as flowing from these basic differences in philosophical outlook. It was certainly not a disagreement on the nature of language.

Reid made no attempt to answer Hume's objections against the existence of moral relations. That is, Reid did not really respond to the charge that such relations being independent of our apprehension are applicable to animals and inanimate objects. Reid merely denied the charge. Nor did Reid respond to the difficulty of relating the apprehension of such alleged relations to action. One might charge Reid with evading Hume's main criticisms. For Reid, the objectivity of moral qualities, in the sense of independence of mankind, had to be maintained no matter what difficulties it encountered.

Instead of answering Hume's specific objections, Reid was content to state his own case and to defend it on other grounds. First, Reid appealed to common sense.

> Authors who place moral approbation in feeling only, very often use the word *Sentiment*, to express feeling without judgment....the word *sentiment*, in the English language, never, as I conceive, signifies mere feeling, but *judgment accompanied with feeling.*[15]

An examination of the *Oxford English Dictionary* does reveal the acceptability of Reid's usage, however, it also reveals that in Reid's time the word 'sentiment' was widely used to refer to a feeling alone. No moral sense theorist can thus be dismissed simply by appeal to common sense, for common sense in the form of common linguistic usage supports both cases.

A second linguistic appeal by Reid concerns moral judgments as statements. According to Reid, a moral judgment as a propositional entity does not refer to the speaker's feelings, nor does it refer to the speaker.[16] Since Hume's analysis does refer to the speaker, Hume's analysis, according to Reid, must be incorrect. At the very least, Reid recognized what Hume was maintaining.

Here it must be admitted that Reid is correct in maintaining that common usage does not recognize reference to the speaker's feelings or presence. But that does not mean that Hume failed to deal with this issue. Let us first see how Hume might rebut Reid's case, and let us see if this rebuttal was made prior to Reid having presented his case. Moral sentiments for Hume are like secondary qualities. Feeling virtue is like sensing redness. As science had shown, by Hume's time and Reid's, col-

ors are not properties solely of objects but the result of the interaction of objects with the human nervous system. This was
substantiated in the work of Galileo, Boyle, Descartes, and the
incomparable Newton. The sentence "the tomato is red" does
not directly or overtly refer to the human nervous system, but
surely a properly scientific and philosophical analysis of the sentence would bring out the reference to the perceiver. One could
hardly reject that analysis purely on the grounds of common
linguistic usage. The same can be said for the statement that
"The Sun rises". Technically we would have to say that the sentence is false, but we have maintained the usage and the truth of
the sentence by now understanding it or analyzing it in a different way. Common usage does not even have to be modified as
long as we all understand the new proper analysis or meaning
of the statement.

The foregoing line of defense is exactly the one taken by
Hume as early as the *Treatise*.

> Vice and virtue, therefore, may be compar'd to sounds, colours,...which
> according to modern philosophy, are not qualities in objects, but percep-
> tions in the mind: And this discovery in morals, like that other in physics,
> is to be regarded as a considerable advancement of the speculative sci-
> ences; tho', like that too, it has little or no influence on practice. (*Treatise*,
> p. 469)

This does not prove that Hume was right, but it does show
that his position cannot be dismissed simply by appeal to
ordinary usage.

Lest one get the notion that Reid is championing common
sense and Hume is not, it is worth while recalling that Hume
claims his analysis to be consistent with common sense. Recall
that in Hume's distinction between the vulgar and the philosophical, a distinction he employed in his discussion of the double existence theory of perception as well as in his discussion of
the is-ought paragraph,[17] Hume conceived of his analysis as a
more refined version of the vulgar or common sense position. It
should also be remembered that if we are going to take common

sense seriously then Hume's constant relating of his moral theory to practice and to action is much more consistent with common sense than Reid's analysis. Again, this does not prove that Hume is correct, but it does show that common sense is no enemy to Hume's position. As Prior so aptly put it, Hume accepted the common sense view of his time "that the rightness of an act is a motive for performing it, and its wrongness a motive for the contrary."[18]

We come now to a final point made by Reid, a point which is clear enough in its context, a point which shows the deep philosophical divisions between Reid and Hume, and a point that reflects the special challenge to those modern moral theorists who seek standards internally. According to Reid, if moral judgments were expressions of the speaker's feelings, then it would not be possible to contradict someone else's judgment because "every man must know his own feelings."[19] This is another way of Reid's saying that the moral sentiment is not simply a feeling but a feeling and a judgment about some purely objective relation of the conduct of a particular person. Any misunderstanding is avoided by noting that 'express' means here to report in a propositional sense. Reid is, in short, denying that moral judgments are reports about speaker's feelings, even feelings as caused by events outside the speaker.

A Humean response to this objection by Reid should be obvious. We do in fact challenge the judgments that other speakers make about their feelings, for example, in the case of colors. Such *intersubjective* judgments are made from the perspective of standard conditions, and such standard conditions can be invoked in the case of moral judgments as in any other. It is thus possible to respond to Reid by noting that he failed to take heed of Hume's discussion of the general point of view.

As we have shown, Hume was well aware of the foregoing kind of criticism and of the appropriate answer that he could make. In the first section of *An Enquiry Concerning the Principles of Morals*, a work written in part as an answer to Reid, Hume noted:

> It must be acknowledged, that both sides of the question are susceptible of specious arguments. Moral distinctions, it may be said, are discernible by pure *reason*: else, whence the many disputes that reign in common life....Truth is disputable; not taste: what exists in the nature of things is the standard of our judgment; what each man feels within himself is the standard of sentiment. (*EPM*, p. 171)

Hume's answer to this specious charge is to recall the role of the general view or standard conditions.

> But in order to pave the way for such a sentiment and give a proper discernment of its object, it is often necessary, we find, that much reasoning should precede, that nice distinctions be made, just conclusions drawn, distant comparisons formed, complicated relations examined, and general facts fixed and ascertained....a false relish may frequently be corrected by argument and reflection. (*EPM*, p. 173)

Reid's criticism of Hume's theory of moral judgment is like Kant's criticism of Hume's analysis of our habits of mind. Even if it is the case now that human beings are so constructed that consensus and convergence on all matters is achievable, can Hume and other modernists who opt for internal standards rule out the possibility that in the future different human beings might develop with conflicting natures? If so, how could we moralize with them? On what basis could we claim that our perspective, as opposed to some alternative one, is the right perspective? This is a serious possibility, but such a possibility in no way shows the correctness or incorrectness of either Hume's or his opponents' position.

It is also interesting to recall what was said in Chapter Three about Reid's recognition of Hume's rejection of the normative "ought". Reid attributed Hume's discarding of "ought" to Hume's more basic contention that moral approbation is a feeling and not an intellectual apprehension. Of course, Reid was correct. In Hume's theory there is no special problem of relating moral apprehension to human action. In Hume's theory it makes no sense to say that we ought to do what our feelings direct us to do; that is already what, according to Hume, we do, and must do. In short, Reid saw the connection between Hume's rejection of "ought" and Hume's theory of both moral approbation and moral judgment.

The foregoing discussion of Reid's critique shows both to what extent criticisms or objections of a philosophical nature can meaningfully be made of Hume's theory and to what extent some criticisms are misguided. On the one hand, when Reid claimed that Hume denied the existence of moral judgment what Reid meant was that Hume had an alternative theory of moral sentiment! That is, Reid and Hume disagreed about moral apprehension. This disagreement has nothing to do with denying the cognitive status of linguistically articulated moral pronouncements. On the other hand, when Reid claimed that Hume had no way to correct or challenge linguistically articulated moral pronouncements, Reid simply missed the intersubjective dimension of Hume's account as provided for by the general view or standard conditions. Later readers anxious to classify Hume as the upholder of some noncognitive theory of moral judgment have carelessly taken both of Reid's objections and treated them as if they were the same.

Although he did not raise the issue of the status of moral judgments, *T.H. Green* gave an analysis of Hume's theory that was similar to Reid's. Both Green's analysis of what Hume meant by virtue and the analysis of what Hume meant by obligation ("ought") interpreted these phenomena as feelings excited under certain circumstances. The analyses also make reference to the spectator or observer and to general tendencies. Although he disagreed with Hume's analysis, Green attributed to him a view which came very close to what Hume was saying.[20]

The first symptom of ambiguity about the cognitive status of Hume's theory of moral judgment can be found in the Selby-Bigge index to the *Enquiries*. There, *Selby-Bigge* makes reference to a statement found on pp. 172-73 of *An Enquiry Concerning the Principles of Morals*:

> The final sentence, it is probable, which pronounces characters and actions amiable or odious, praiseworthy or blameable; that which stamps on them the mark of honour or infamy.–..it is probable, I say, that this final sentence depends on some internal sense or feeling, which nature has made universal in the whole species.

Selby-Bigge paraphrases this statement as: "...the final sentence is pronounced by some internal sense..."[21] Now it is clear that Hume's statement does not say that the statement or sentence is pronounced by an internal sense. Such a view would turn the moral judgment into an expression and not a report, something like "Ouch!". What Hume actually says is that the sentence *depends upon* the feeling but is not identical to the feeling. Notice as well how quick Hume is to add something about the universality of the feeling. This interpretation is also borne out by another statement made by Hume in the same work.

> In these sentiments, then, not in a discovery of relations of any kind, do all moral determinations consist. Before we can pretend to form any decision of this kind, everything must be known and ascertained on the side of the object or action. Nothing remains but to feel, on our part, some sentiment of blame or approbation; *whence* [*italics mine*] we pronounce the action criminal or virtuous. (*EPM*, p. 291)

It should be clear in this context that the sentiment is one thing and the judgment or pronouncement is another thing, that the judgment is temporally posterior to the sentiment, and that the judgment is a report of the existence of the sentiment under certain conditions. Selby-Bigge's misleading summary remains as an ongoing encouragement to treat Hume's theory of moral judgment as noncognitive.

In his 1921 article in *Mind*, "Hume's Ethical Theory and Its Critics", F.C. Sharp stressed the point that Hume's theory of moral judgment involved reference to standard conditions. Sharp mentions that there were already those who accused

Hume of subjectivism, but Sharp does not name anyone in particular.

In 1930, C.D. *Broad* published *Five Types of Ethical Theory*, and devoted one chapter to Hume. With respect to moral judgment, Broad attributed to Hume the view that there may be objective agreement on ethical matters. Broad recognized the distinction between judgment and sentiment in Hume's theory and the importance of intersubjectivity, although Broad is critical of Hume's representation of this objectivity in a way reminiscent of Reid's critique.

The serious misrepresentation of Hume's moral theory began in the 1930's as a result of the claim that Hume was a forerunner of positivism. In *Language, Truth, and Logic* (1936), A.J. *Ayer* claimed general inspiration from Hume, but Ayer did not specifically single out Hume when Ayer presented his own ethical theory. It was left to *Hedenius* in his 1937 *Studies in Hume's Ethics* to charge Hume with holding that "moral judgments, being determined by sentiments, cannot be true or false."

Hedenius attempted to substantiate this claim by referring to the *Treatise* (p. 458), where Hume said "'Tis impossible, therefore, they [passions, volitions, actions] can be pronounced either true or false, and be either contrary or conformable to reason." But what Hume is saying in this context is that in calling an action virtuous or vicious we are not saying that the action is either true or false, reasonable or unreasonable. What we are being told is that 'virtue' is not synonymous with 'truth'. This hardly amounts to saying that the moral judgment which ascribes virtue or vice to an action is not true or false. Analogously, the word 'red' is not synonymous with the word 'truth', but that does not mean that ascribing colors results in judgments that are neither true nor false. I suspect that Hedenius was mislead by not being familiar with the historical context including other writers like Wollaston against whom Hume had to make the point that 'virtue' and 'truth' are not synonymous.

The crucial development in the widespread misinterpretation of Hume came with the publication in 1944 of *C.L. Stevenson's*

Ethics and Language.[22] There Stevenson suggested that "Hume has most nearly asked the questions that here concern us, and has most nearly reached a conclusion that the present writer can accept." Stevenson recognized the important difference between a moral theorist who argues that the moral judgment reports a feeling and a theorist who argues that a moral judgment expresses in a non-reportorial way a moral feeling. Moreover, Stevenson conceded that Hume was the former and not the latter. A consistent emotivist view would interpret moral judgments as (a) expressions of feelings where the expression is not a report but a venting of feeling, (d) deny truth value to moral judgments, and (c) deny the objectivity of moral judgments even in the sense of intersubjectivity.

Stevenson claimed that he was inspired by Hume, but Stevenson was also very careful not to attribute emotivism to Hume. Later emotivists, readers, and even critics did not hesitate to attribute emotivism to Hume. Some seemed to accept the view that where earlier theorists suggest the views of later theorists, then the earlier theorists must hold an incipient view of the later theorist. Some even saw this as a way of complementing Hume and immediately proceeded to single out contexts in Hume which they claimed suggested emotivism. Those who were critical of Hume's philosophy in general found comfort in the attribution of emotivism to Hume as a kind of reductio ad absurdum of Hume's philosophy as a whole.

We might point out that when emotivists use the word 'express' to convey what they mean by a judgment which is not a report and therefore neither true nor false, they are using the word in a special technical sense. The *Oxford English Dictionary*, on the other hand, shows that there is a clear sense of 'express' (9b and 9c) current during Hume's time and since in which 'express' is a verb equivalent to 'describe'. Moreover, there are two contexts in Hume's writings where he used the word 'express', and in both cases Hume was talking about a description or report made from a general point of view.

But these variations we regard not in our general decisions, but still apply the terms expressive of our liking or dislike, in the same manner, as if we remain'd in one point of view. Experience soon teaches us this method of correcting our sentiments, or at least, of correcting our language, where the sentiments are more stubborn and inalterable. (*Treatise*, p. 582)

But when he bestows on any man the epithets of *vicious* or *odious* or *depraved*, he then speaks another language, and expresses sentiments, in which he expects all his audience are to concur with him. He must here, therefore, depart from his private and particular situation, and must choose a point of view, common to him with others; he must move some universal principle of the human frame, and touch a string to which all mankind have an accord and symphony. (*EPM*, p. 272)

There is no context in which Hume says or implies that a moral judgment is an expression of one's personal feelings.

Let us look at those interpreters who in the aftermath of Stevenson's work thought that they found some ambiguity or hint of emotivism in Hume. The first to suggest an ambiguity about emotivism, claiming that Hume was not an emotivist if you read some contexts but that Hume might be interpreted as an emotivist if you read other contexts, was *J.N. Findlay*.[23] Findlay's charge was repeated by his student Prior, later repeated and expanded by D.D. Raphael, and repeated once again by Paul Edwards.[24]

What made these interpreters of Hume think that Hume was ambiguous? The clearest and most extensive answer was given by Raphael who detailed the specific contexts in Hume's writings which in his reading justify attributing emotivism to Hume.

Let us examine those contexts as specified by *D.D. Raphael* and see if the charge of incipient emotivism can be sustained or discounted in Hume's ethical writings. Raphael singles out four quotations, three from the *Treatise* and one from the second *Enquiry*. According to Raphael, these four quotations show that at times Hume held to the view that statements of the form 'X is virtuous' are to be analyzed as giving expression to the moral emotions which the speaker feels on contemplating X.[25]

142

First:

> We do not infer a character to be virtuous, because it pleases: But in feeling that it pleases after such a particular manner, we in effect feel that it is virtuous. (*Treatise*, p. 471)

In rebuttal, I note, first, that this quotation does not even mention moral judgment. In fact, Hume's statement is not about moral judgment but about our moral sentiments. Further, the quotation itself and the larger context in which it appears make abundantly clear that what Hume was discussing was the immediate apprehension of moral qualities. Such qualities are apprehended as impressions and not as inferences. This in no way implies that under other circumstances we could not infer the existence of moral qualities. The analogy with secondary qualities, which Raphael himself concedes, also makes clear that if we were to accept Raphael's interpretation we would have to say that for Hume all judgments about secondary qualities are not reports but expressions and that such judgments could never be inferred. This would be absurd in general, there is no evidence that Hume ever held a theory like it, and there is abundant evidence that Hume believed just the opposite.

Second:

> The distinction of moral good and evil is founded on the pleasure or pain, which results from the view of any sentiment, or character; and as that pleasure or pain cannot be unknown to the person who feels it, it follows, that there is just so much vice and virtue in any character, as every one places in it, and that 'tis impossible in this particular we can ever be mistaken. (*Treatise*, pp. 546-47)

This quotation is supposed to show that Hume believed moral judgments expressed the emotion of a particular speaker as opposed to what all or most people would feel. But it is clear from the very quotation itself that Hume speaks of "every one" so that he could not have meant here just one speaker. Moreover, Hume made the same kind of statement about immediate certainty with respect to any impression including those that have nothing to do with morality. Questions of correctness aside, all that Hume was saying was that reports of our immediate experience are infallible, although our immediate experience may be based upon presuppositions which are quite wrong, and inferences beyond our immediate experience are certainly not infallible. This is something we discussed earlier in the chapter. Finally, the remainder of the statement, which Raphael omits, makes it quite clear that Hume claims to be dealing with a judgment of fact! "...since the question in this case regards not any philosophical origin of an obligation, but a plain matter of fact, 'tis not easily conceiv'd how we can fall into an error" (*Ibid.*).

Third:

> Vice and virtue, therefore, may be compar'd to sounds, colours, heat and cold, which, according to modern philosophy, are not qualities in objects, but perceptions in the mind. (*Treatise*, p. 469)

In rebuttal we should recall that the analogy between moral qualities and secondary qualities in no way implies that moral judgments are subjective. Objectivity for Hume is clearly objectivity in the sense of intersubjectivity. Raphael attempts to argue on the basis of this quotation alone that Hume's views are like Ayer's. But even Ayer himself clearly distinguished between expressions which are not subject to truth value and reports about feelings which are true or false on the grounds of intersubjective confirmation. Finally, it should be recalled that since for Hume all perceptions are dependent upon the mind, if we took this as a mark of subjectivity then the class of factual judgments would be an empty one. If the class is empty then the contrast between morality and matters of fact would be somewhat pointless.

Fourth:

...[moral or aesthetic taste] has a productive faculty, and gilding or stain-ing all natural objects with the colours, borrowed from internal senti-ment, raises in a manner a new creation. (*EPM*, p. 294)

In rebuttal, we note, first, that this quotation is about moral sentiment and not about moral judgment. The title of the sec-tion in which the quotation appears is "Moral Sentiment". Further, this quotation once more tells us that moral qualities, and aesthetic ones as well, are analogous to secondary qualities. This in no way implies that judgments about secondary qualities are not intersubjectively confirmable and subject thereby to truth and falsity.

Raphael has persistently failed to distinguish what Hume said about moral sentiment from what Hume said about moral judgment. At one point Raphael even claimed that for Hume "words like 'vice' and 'crime' do not describe facts of the kind de-scribed by such words as 'red' or 'angry'."[26] Yet it is clear from the very quotations that Raphael singles out that Hume does as-sert the similarity of 'vice" to 'red'. The whole point of Hume's analysis was to show that in the relevant respects they are the same.

Although Raphael thought that drawing an analogy between moral judgments and aesthetic judgments was a mistake and the result of Hutcheson's bad influence upon Hume, when Hume did discuss the analogy he frequently made clear that both kinds of judgments were made from a general perspective or standard conditions. Evidence that when Hume drew the analogy he had judgment in mind is the presence of words such as "say" instead of talking about immediate feelings.

In like manner, external beauty is determin'd merely by pleasure; and 'tis evident, a beautiful countenance cannot give so much pleasure, when seen at a distance of twenty paces, as when it is brought nearer us. We say not, however, that it appears to us less beautiful: Because we know

what effect it will have in such a position, and by that reflexion we correct
its momentary appearance. (*Treatise*, p. 582)

Further evidence that Raphael confuses what Hume says
about moral sentiment with what Hume says about moral judgment is the allegation that Hume began by denying that moral
judgment could be due to reason. Hume made no such denial.
What Hume denied was that moral qualities are perceived as
ideas, that is, as objects of reason. Moral qualities are perceived
as impressions. Moral sentiments are thus not objects of intellectual apprehension; this implies nothing about moral judgment. Raphael sees in Hume's writings a double theory: one
theory in which moral judgments are intersubjective, and one
theory in which moral judgments are expressions of private feeling. This double theory is the result of Raphael's confusion of
what Hume said about moral sentiment with what Hume said
about moral judgment. Each set of Hume's statements is taken
to be a different theory of moral judgment. Raphael never gives
a single reason why Hume had such an alleged double theory
and never employs the notion of a double theory to explain any
other aspect of Hume's moral theory.

By 1959, the emotivist interpretation of Hume seemed fairly
well established. In his 1959 textbook on *Ethical Theory*, R.B.
Brandt claimed that Hume had anticipated and suggested a form
of emotivism. In the same year, *Nowell-Smith* stated definitively,
that "Hutcheson and Hume, for example, tried to reduce moral
judgments to expressions of feeling."[27] And in 1961, M.J. *Scott-
Taggart* could assert without opposition that for Hume "moral
judgments are not judgments about, but expressions of, my
feelings."[28] Recently, MacIntyre has claimed that the elements of
practical reasoning in Hume are emotive utterances.[29]

Hume exegesis apparently went through three stages since
the 1930's. First there was a more or less correct understanding
of his views conjoined with the claim that emotivists could find
inspiration in Hume. Both Ayer and Stevenson were themsleves
careful not to attribute emotivism to Hume himself. In the sec-

146

ond stage, the opponents of emotivism claimed to find an ambiguity in Hume wherein he occasionally holds an intersubjective theory and occasionally holds an emotivist theory. I have explained this as a confusion between what Hume says about moral sentiment and what Hume says about moral judgment. In the third stage, it is asserted as a matter of canonical Hume exegesis that Hume is an emotivist.

Aside from textual and historical myopia, another element had entered to reinforce the emotivist reading of Hume. That element was the growing importance of the is-ought paragraph. In his 1939 article in *Mind*, W. *Frankena* identified Hume's is-ought paragraph as the first instance of the charge of a naturalistic fallacy, later made famous by G.E. Moore.[30] The stage was now set for someone to argue that if the is-ought paragraph was the first identification of the naturalistic fallacy then Hume could not hold an intersubjective factual account of moral judgments, as we have maintained throughout this book. Alternatively, one could hold that Hume was himself confused, sometimes seeing his own radical pre-emotivism and sometimes not. Frankena finds such a dual view about Hume in Broad. Raphael is the best example of someone who holds the double view.

I have heard speakers use the now suspect interpretation of the is-ought paragraph as the single piece of evidence to show that Hume was an emotivist who thereby denied the cognitive status of moral judgments. As the argument was expressed, if Hume denied that moral judgments (e.g. judgments with 'ought') could be inferred from factual judgments that is because moral judgments are not themselves factual or cognitive. All of those passages in Hume's writings where he says just the opposite and treats moral judgments as cognitive and does infer moral judgments from other factual judgments are to be reinterpreted to show that Hume was confused!

The transition from "suggesting" an ambiguity on moral judgment to the connection with the is-ought issue was made by *A. N. Prior*. In the introduction to his book, Prior specifically acknowledges his indebtedness to his teacher Findlay and to the work of Raphael.[31] Following Reid and Raphael, Prior claims that on the one hand "Hume is as eager as Reid to emphasize the difference in kind between a genuine judgment and a feeling", and that on the other hand Hume is ambiguous about whether moral judgments are intersubjective reports of feelings, in which case the reports are either true or false, or whether they are themselves feelings, in which case judgments are neither true nor false.[32] What is the explanation for why Hume would ignore a distinction he was at such pains to establish? According to Prior, it is Hume's formal adherence to a "ridiculous" theory about belief which accounts for this confusion. In addition, Prior claims that "in his detailed handling of the relation between feeling and judgment in the moral consciousness the theory is simply abandoned..."[33] Finally, this allegedly "ridiculous" theory of belief accounts in part for Hume's insistence that "ought" cannot be deduced from "is" since belief is connected in Hume with motivation.[34]

To begin with, Prior is correct in noting that Hume does understand the difference between feelings (impressions) and judgments about feelings (ideas, either thought or verbalized). Prior is also correct in seeing that there is some relation in Hume's theory between 'ought' (obligation) and questions of motivation. Prior is also correct in noting that Hume's moral theory is related to his theory of belief. What Prior has not understood is the actual connection.

Where Prior is fundamentally mistaken is in his interpretation of the is-ought paragraph. As we have been at such pains to make clear in Chapter Three, the discussion of the alleged moral "ought" has nothing to do with moral judgment but with moral sentiment or in this case the alleged state of affairs to which "ought" is supposed to make reference. Again we must not confuse what Hume said about moral sentiment or apprehension with what he said about moral judgment.

More important to note is that a better understanding of Hume's theory of belief would have made all of the foregoing clear. Part of the reason Prior finds Hume's theory of belief ridiculous is that Prior operates with an *I Think* perspective whereas Hume engages in philosophy from a *We Do* perspective. This is a point we suggested in the first chapter and it is a point we shall emphasize in the last chapter of this book. Moreover, the distinction between idea and impression remains crucial for Hume's theory in allowing him to make all of the distinctions that he does. In the detailed handling of his theory, rather than abandoning the distinction between idea and impression, Hume is completely dependent upon it. Any reader who fails to grasp this fails also to grasp Hume's position. The entire theory of sympathy is only intelligible on the grounds that there is a distinction between a judgment (idea) and a feeling (impression). Finally, it is Hume who insists that sympathy is analogous to belief so that Hume's moral theory must be understood as analogous to Hume's account of how beliefs cause actions. Hume's theory is far more subtle than his critics realize. That is why it will be so important to turn to his theory of sympathy in order to see how he works out the complicated relationships between sentiment and judgment. That is precisely what we shall do in the next chapter.

In his book *Hume's Moral Epistemology*, Jonathan Harrison claims both that Hume is the greatest of British philosophers[35], and that Hume is also repeatedly inconsistent.[36] As a result, it is impossible for Harrison to decide which of five theories Hume actually held: moral judgments are either (a) about the judger's feelings, or (b) about the feelings of mankind, or (c) a moral sense, or (d) a nonpropositional theory, or (e) judgments are a species of feeling.

Among its numerous errors, Harrison's book perpetuates the failure to distinguish those contexts in which Hume is speaking about moral sentiment and those contexts in which Hume is speaking about moral judgment. One glaring instance of this is Harrison's assertion that for Hume morality "consists not in any matter of fact..."[37]. The glaring ellipsis reveals the incomplete quotation on which mythical readings of Hume are established. Harrison's failure to make the necessary distinctions is the result of not understanding the historical context of Hume's writings. By the author's own admission, he was "more interested in the validity of Hume's arguments than in their historical setting."[38] Apparently, Harrison thought it was possible to identify the arguments without consideration of context. Finally, Harrison missed the subtleties of Hume's analysis of moral judgment because he did not take the theory of sympathy seriously. Harrison claims at one and the same time that the discussion of sympathy is "peripheral to an understanding of Hume's moral epistemology"[39], and that he finds Hume's theory of sympathy "virtually incomprehensible."[40] No wonder Harrison fails to grasp Hume's theory of moral judgment.

In his book *Hume's Moral Theory*, *J.L. Mackie* suggests that the most plausible interpretation of Hume's account of moral judgment is what he calls the 'objectification theory'. Moral sentiments, as Hume himself says, are like secondary qualities such as color, that is, not simply in the object but involving the presence of a subject. Thus says Mackie "we tend to project these sentiments onto actions or characters that arouse them."[41] Further, "this projection or objectification is not just a trick of individual psychology...,there is a system in which the sentiments of each person both modify and reinforce those of others; the supposedly objective moral features both aid and reflect this communication of sentiments, and the whole system of thought of which the objectification, the *false belief* [*italics mine*] in the fictitious features, is a contributing part, flourishes partly because...it serves a social function."[42] Mackie then applies this interpretation to Hume's views on the artificial and natural virtues. Mackie attributes to Hume the view that prudent self-interest accounts for the origin of the artificial virtues and that sympathy leads to the development of moral motivation. Mackie criticizes this view of Hume's as incomplete because it is in need of supplementation by a sociological theory of the development of convention. The sociological supplementation seems to be Mackie's main point in the book.

The most unnecessary paradox in Mackie's treatment is the suggestion that moral judgments are false because they involve a projection. Does anyone, on the contrary, think that judgments about color are false because they involve projections? What we are witnessing here is a more fundamental philosophical conflict between traditional realism (Mackie) in which it is insisted upon that truth results only from structures independent of human beings and intersubjectivism (Hume's Copernican Revolution perspective, e.g.). Mackie believes there are contexts in which Hume slurs the distinction between judgment and sentiment. On the contrary, Hume offered the first serious distinction and analysis of the distinction. Finally, Mackie never fully grasps the sympathy process in which the confluence of sentiment, judgment, social context, and the influence on action is made clear. All of this reinforces why it is necessary that we move to a detailed treatment of Hume's theory of sympathy.

A much more sympathetic approach to Hume's theory of moral judgment and one that attempts to rescue Hume from his detractors is to be found in *David F. Norton's David Hume: Common-Sense Moralist, Sceptical Metaphysician*.[43] We have already had occasion to mention that Norton attributes to Hume, and Hutcheson, a moral realist position in opposition to those who usually attribute some kind of subjectivism to Hume. Norton goes to great lengths to show that for Hume and Hutcheson moral terms are not wholly the product of artifice but represent something real. He also stresses the importance of the corrective role of general rules.[44] Unfortunately, Norton's defense of Hume is marred by a serious confusion about realism.[45] What Norton shows, and rightly so, is that Hume and Hutcheson are subscribers to intersubjectivism and not realism. The realist thesis collapses when we begin to realize that the perspective is controlled by general *social* rules which are not grounded in the structure of the external objective world but reflect the interests of society over time. That is why, among other things, Hutcheson went to such trouble about God's guarantee of the uniformity of the moral sense. By concentrating on the *Treatise*, Norton misses all of the changes Hume introduced in *An Enquiry Concerning the Principles of Morals*, changes that deal specifically with the social perspective. Finally, Norton sharply distinguishes between Hume as practical philosopher and Hume as speculative philosopher thereby missing completely the *We Do* perspective of Hume's approach to philosophy.[46] It is intersubjectivity which unites Hume's moral philosophy with Hume's epistemology, and all of this is a reflection of Hume's Copernican Revolution in Philosophy. When we turn in the next chapter to Hume's discussion of the passions we shall see just exactly how Hume relates thought to action.

CHAPTER FIVE

THE PASSIONS AND SYMPATHY

The Significance of the Passions

At the end of Chapter One, we saw how Hume's program could be characterized as Newtonian. In addition, we have argued that Hume's moral theory reflects an extension of Newtonian analysis into the moral realm. As part of that Newtonian analysis, Hume postulated the existence in the mental world of an analogue to Newton's theory of gravitation, namely the principle of the communication of vivacity. The communication of vivacity is used in Book I of the *Treatise* to explain belief, it is used in Book II to explain the passions and sympathy, and finally sympathy as the communication of vivacity is used in Book III to explain moral judgments. At the end of Chapter Two, we showed that Hume formulated his special concern in morals in terms of the question, "What is the general principle of morals?" We asserted there that the answer would be sympathy. It is, therefore, necessary to show just how sympathy can be the general principle of morals. Finally, at the end of Chapter Four, we argued that most of the misunderstandings surrounding Hume's moral theory were rooted in the failure both to distinguish and to understand the relationship between moral sentiment and moral judgment. The key to understanding the relationship between moral sentiment and moral judgment is sympathy. In the *Treatise*, therefore, the keystone of Hume's moral theory is sympathy. These promissory notes must now be honored.

Hume's first and most crucial discussion of sympathy comes in Book II of the *Treatise*, within the discussion of the passions. In what follows in this chapter we shall be concerned to outline Hume's discussion of the passions and to show how sympathy fits in with that discussion. In the next chapter, Chapter Six, we shall show how sympathy functions in the moral theory of Book III of the *Treatise*.

Most interpretations of Hume either ignore or underestimate the importance of the passions.[1] Without understanding the theory of the passions one cannot understand the structure and main theme of the *Treatise*, one cannot understand Hume's analysis of belief, one cannot understand the function of the discussion of scepticism, one cannot understand the sympathy mechanism and hence the whole of Hume's moral theory, and one cannot understand Hume's conception of the self. In short, the failure to comprehend fully the theory of the passions detracts from any attempt to comprehend many of the most significant issues in Hume's philosophy. Hence, we shall concern ourselves with explicating Hume's theory of the passions both narrowly and as it operates within the broader context of his entire philosophy.

My suspicion is that the failure to appreciate the significance of Hume's discussion of the passions is part of the failure to see the Copernican Revolution in Hume's philosophy, specifically the *We Do* perspective. A good deal of the secondary literature on Hume's philosophy is written by philosophers and commentators who hold to an *I Think* perspective. Consequently, these readers either fail to see what Hume is driving at, or they think that Hume is confused about what he is doing, or they disagree outright with any approach which takes action or practice as the primary context of analysis.

Present State of the Literature on the Passions[2]

The oldest and most unsympathetic view of Hume is to be found in the work of Thomas Reid.[3] Among other things, it was Reid who first accused Hume of advocating a form of irrational hedonism. According to Reid, "Mr. Hume gives the name of passion to every principle of action in the human mind; and, in consequence of this maintains, that every man is and ought to be led by his passions."[4] In one form or another, this view has been echoed by others.

T.H. Green, for example, assumed that Hume was a psychological hedonist. Therefore, when Green came across Hume's statement about some of the direct passions not operating on the anticipation of pleasure and pain, Green accused Hume of being inconsistent.[5] It never occurred to Green that Hume might not be a psychological hedonist after all. On reflection, most of the traditional contradictions attributed to Hume's work turn out to be conflicts between some pre-established conception of what Hume's philosophy is supposed to be and what Hume should have said if he were to remain consistent with his commentator's preconceptions.

In his book on Hume, B.M. Laing offered a useful summary of the historical influences on Hume's treatment of the passions, including the influence of Descartes, Malebranche, and Crousaz. Laing was also among the first, but not the first if we count Kemp Smith's 1905 article, to point out that Reid had misrepresented Hume. Finally, Laing raised the issue, without developing it, of whether Hume's treatment of the passions was consistent with what Hume had said in Book I of the *Treatise* about the self.[6]

John Laird's treatment of Hume, published in the same year as Laing's, 1932, reverted to the position of T.H. Green. Laird charged Hume with being an inconsistent hedonist.[7] He also repeated Reid's charge that Hume's position on the relationship between reason and passion is trivially true in that it follows from the definitions Hume gave to both reason and passion.

Laird construes Hume's position as sheer affirmation and not argument. "Hume's opponents affirmed that the apprehension of duty and the fitness of things pertained to reason and *did* affect conduct."[8] Further, Laird charged that the discussion of the relationship between ideas and impressions at the beginning of Book II is in conflict with the discussion at the beginning of Book I.[9] In fact, this is part of the more general charge that Hume's phenomenalism and associationism understood in a phenomenalistic sense are inconsistent with some of the things Hume says about the passions.[10] Finally, in noting Hume's discussion of sympathy, Laird claimed that, on Hume's view, sympathy with someone else's toothache required us to feel a toothache as well.[11] It is tacitly assumed that this constitutes a *reductio* of Hume's position.

The most influential discussion of Hume's philosophy has been Norman Kemp Smith's. It is to Kemp Smith's credit that he challenged the Reid-Green interpretation of Hume and for recognizing that Hume was not a hedonist. Nevertheless, Kemp Smith perpetuated one of Reid's worst errors. Specifically, Smith reasserted that for Hume "reason is and ought to be the slave of the passions."[12] Like Reid, Kemp Smith incorrectly quoted Hume by omitting the crucial word "only" (*Treatise*, p. 415). That this misleading quote of Hume gives rise to or exemplifies a distorted view of Hume on the relation of reason to passion had already been pointed out in 1932 by Laird,[13] who was then criticizing Kemp Smith's original article in *Mind* in 1905. A much more extended critique of the same point was later given by Glathe and by Popkin.[14]

More interesting, Kemp Smith restates the charge, originally made in his 1905 article and repeated by Laing, that Hume's treatment of the passions contradicts earlier statements in the *Treatise* about the self. Kemp Smith's own elaborate interpretation of the *Treatise*,[15] including speculation about the order of composition of the Books of that work, hinges upon this alleged contradiction. If there is no such contradiction, then Kemp Smith's major theses are vitiated. Finally, Kemp Smith claimed that the treatment of the passions, difficulties aside, is largely irrelevant to what he considers to be the main argument of the *Treatise*.

In 1950, Albert Glathe published a pioneering serious treatment of Hume's discussion of the passions.[16] Glathe attempted to summarize carefully the main doctrines in the order in which they appeared. His main positive contribution was in detailing the importance of the transfer of vivacity. His main target of attack was Kemp Smith's thesis about the Hutchesonian origin of Hume's moral philosophy. Glathe also settled once and for all the importance of the missing "only" in the discussion of the relation between reason and passion. Nevertheless, Glathe's main concern was still with Book III, not Book II, and hardly at all with Book I. As a result, important elements about the passions were overlooked.

Passmore, writing in 1952, acknowledged the influence of Kemp Smith, Green, and Laird, but apparently had not read Glathe. Although he recognized that Hume was not a hedonist, Passmore repeated the charges that (a) Hume had contradicted himself on the nature of the self, (b) associationism was compromised as well as Hume's alleged phenomenalism, and (c) sympathy with someone else's toothache required us to have a toothache as well. Passmore also claimed that what Hume did with sympathy violated the argument about the existence of other minds. That Hume "had a quite extraordinary insensitivity to consistency"[17] was Passmore's general conclusion.

In 1963, P.L. Gardiner wrote a brief essay on Hume's theory of the passions in which he noted, perceptively, that Hume did not seek to derive all passions through association,[18] as James Mill had done. But Gardiner went on to repeat the recurrent criticism of Hume, namely, that "Hume's entire treatment of the passions as the isolable contents of a direct introspective awareness"[19] was problematic. The same kind charge has been repeated lately by MacIntyre who claims that for Hume the passions are pre-conceptual.[20]

The most serious treatment of the passions to date remains Pall Ardal's.[21] Whereas Passmore had stressed the connection between Book I and II, Ardal, like Glathe, emphasized the connection between Books II and III of the *Treatise*. Ardal rightly took Kemp Smith to task for claiming that the discussion of the passions was inconsequential. Ardal also made clear that Hume was not an egoist and that Hume's theory of sympathy did not require the sympathizer to have an analogous toothache. Rather, we pity someone who has a toothache. What neither Ardal nor anyone else provided was an interpretation of the passions which related Book II to both Book I and Book III in one coherent theory.

Crucial Issues in Hume's Theory of the Passions

The foregoing survey raises a number of issues on which Hume's commentators either do not agree or which appear problematic in Hume's theory of the passions. Those issues may be summarized as follows:

1. What is the overall relationship of Book II of the *Treatise*, in which Hume specifically discusses the passions, to both Books I and III? Do we need an overall theory about Hume's philosophy in order to understand properly the theory of the passions? More specifically, is there a rationale for the order in which Hume presents his theory in the *Treatise*?

2. In what way or ways did Hume identify the passions, and how are the passions related to the other entities in Hume's ontology?

3. Did Hume give a purely phenomenalistic analysis of the passions, and does this analysis lead to contradictory remarks about the functioning of the passions?

4. What is the precise role of associationism in the theory of the passions? How is this role related to Hume's alleged phenomenalism?

5. What is the role of the self in Hume's theory of the passions, and does the discussion in Book II contradict the discussion in Book I of the *Treatise*?

6. How is sympathy related to the passions?

7. What is the relationship of reason to passion?

8. How are the passions related to moral sentiments and to moral judgments? In short, what is the precise relationship between the passions and Hume's moral theory?

Hume's Method

In the *Treatise*, Hume presents a unified interpretation of human nature in terms of three principles. Before we can discuss these three basic explanatory principles, we must say something about Hume's method. Inspired by the success of Newton in explaining the physical world, Hume adopted the Newtonian precepts of universality, simplicity, the empirical criterion, and the rejection of occult hypotheses. Consequently, we should expect Hume to offer a theory which is general, simple, experimentally confirmable and which stops short of going beyond what is *presently* observable. At the same time Hume believes in a public and social world, the common sense world of physical objects, bodies, and physiological processes. He was as aware as everyone else in the seventeenth and eighteenth centuries that external stimuli on the bodily organs in some way accounts for a large part of our experience.[22] Hence, Hume was not reconstructing the whole of reality in phenomenalistic terms.[23] At the same time, Hume knew that the exact nature of the physiological process was still a matter of speculation so that immediate empirical confirmation could not be expected from the discipline of physiology.[24] Nevertheless, Hume was confident that *we* could still empirically confirm the presence of certain operations of the human mind. Hence, we may describe Hume's method as an appeal to introspection (i.e. what he calls his *'experiments'*), duly supplemented by the observation of other people and animals. The introspection is alleged to *confirm* the presence of universal principles which operate, originally, on the physiological level. Hume was optimistic about the future possibility of physiological confirmation, but he never confused the present introspective confirmation with the actual physical-biological process. He fully expected his own principles to be confirmed more directly eventually, but not in the present state of knowledge. In short, Hume's experiments are invitations to the reader to see whether the presence of these operations can be confirmed.[25]

The physiological basis of Hume's theory of the passions has not entirely escaped his previous readers. That Descartes and Malebranche had treated the passions with reference to the body is common knowledge. B.M. Laing has pointed out the similarity of Hume's treatment to that of Crousaz in the latter's *A New Treatise of the Art of Thinking* (translated into English in 1724). Crousaz had interpreted the mind as a mechanism "manifested in the train of ideas and in the succession of desires and passions."[26] This is precisely what Hume argued. John Laird, curiously, recognized that Hume's treatment of the passions had a tacit physiological basis somewhat similar to the psycho-physical dualism of Descartes and Malebranche,[27] but at the same time accused Hume of invoking the existence of "an impression, that secretly attends every idea" (*Treatise*, p. 375), an existence which Laird says should have been anathema to a sound phenomenalist.[28] Although it is true that secret impressions are inconsistent with sound phenomenalism, it is also perfectly clear that Hume's explicit physiological references show that Hume was no phenomenalist. Hume was not offering a phenomenalistic analysis but the conscious confirmation of processes believed to be essentially physiological.

It may very well be that psycho-physical dualism is an untenable epistemological and metaphysical position and that Hume himself was partly responsible for revealing its untenability, but it is still the case that Hume's own philosophy is based upon such a dualism.[29] At the same time, it should be noted that the problems of dualism do not vitiate everything that Hume said. Finally, once this dualism is noted and understood it will help to clarify much of what Hume said.

For example, Hume has been chastised for allegedly asserting that the passions can be identified as the "isolable contents of a direct introspective awareness."[30] Such a position seems not only artificial but incompatible with the common sense notion of the passions as dispositional. On the other hand, if we were to recognize that such feelings were only the conscious counterpart of a more basic physiological process, then Hume's analysis would be compatible with the dispositional presuppositions of common sense.

Let us now turn to the three principles which form part of Hume's basic account of human nature. First, Hume declared that impressions cause ideas, or more accurately that *every simple idea in its first appearance is caused by an impression*. This accounted for the representative function of ideas. Laird has challenged this first principle on the grounds that impressions of reflection, which include the passions, were derived from other impressions but were not said to be representative of them. According to Laird, this shows the "bankruptcy of the theory that whatever was derived from impressions necessarily 'copied' impressions."[31] In rebuttal of Laird's charge we note that it was never Hume's position to claim that what followed an impression always and necessarily copied an impression. Rather it was Hume's position that simple ideas in their first appearance copied impressions. This position requires some way or ways of identifying or distinguishing between ideas and impressions, and Hume provides several. The most important consideration is that impressions are caused by external objects or internal physiological processes operating upon the mind through the nervous system. Once more we see how the false presumption of phenomenalism obscures Hume's meaning. If we understand that impressions are perceptions either of the external world or of internal bodily operations and that ideas are the afterthoughts of these original perceptions, then the distinction between impressions and ideas is consistent with Hume's common sense position.

Second, Hume alleged that whatever the imagination finds distinguishable is capable of existing separately. Third, and most important, there is the *communication of vivacity* between impressions and ideas. It is this principle that explains belief in Book I, the passions and sympathy in Book II, and through sympathy the moral theory of Book III. This is the key explanatory principle in Hume's *Treatise*, and it is what holds the *Treatise* together. Failure to see this is the result of analyzing only Books I and II, as in Passmore, or just Books II and III, as in Glathe.

Since the communication of vivacity is best seen in the operation of the passions, and since impressions precede ideas, we may well ask why Hume began the *Treatise* with a discussion of ideas and belief before moving on to the passions.[32] Hume did answer the foregoing question at the beginning of the *Treatise*. Hume distinguished between impressions and ideas, between impressions of sensation and impressions of reflection, and it is among the latter that he finds the passions. He claimed that impressions of reflection deserve our greatest attention. Since ideas are the causes of the impressions of reflection, Hume proposed to study ideas first and then to see how ideas can give rise to these special impressions of reflection.[33] In short, *the discussion of belief is intended as a prelude to the discussion of the passions*, for it is the passions which constitute Hume's central concern in the *Treatise*. In addition, as we shall discuss below, the rationalist model of reason fails to account for how belief is related to passion and action. It will first be necessary to convince the reader of the failure of the rationalist model of reason before the reader can fully appreciate Hume's theory of the passions.

The greater part of Book I is concerned with Hume's analysis of causality and belief. Negatively, Hume argued that if causal reasoning functioned as a form of *a priori* conceivability, and if we could always conceive of the future not resembling the past, then we never have any reason to believe a causal inference. Positively, Hume offered a theory of belief in which causal inferences are believed because "when any impression becomes present to us, it not only transports the mind to such ideas as are related to it, but likewise communicates to them a share of its force and vivacity" (*Treatise*, p. 98). Even more important is the influence of belief, for "the effect, then, of belief is to raise up a simple idea to an equality with our impressions, and bestow on it a like influence on the passions. This effect it can only have by making an idea approach an impression in force and vivacity" (*Treatise*, p. 119). This mechanism of the transfer of vivacity, Hume tells us, will explain the whole rest of the *Treatise*.[34]

Causal reasoning is the most important kind of reasoning for human action, and it is also clear that Hume did not wish to challenge the common sense rules of causal reasoning. What he did wish to challenge was the explanation of those rules by the rationalist model. The influence of causal reasoning on conduct would be incomprehensible on the rationalist model. Hume pressed his case against the "several systems of philosophy" (*Treatise*, p. 263). If we take seriously the rationalist model or explanation of how reason operates, our belief in the external world and in ourselves would dissolve, and we would be paralyzed. The logical outcome of all forms of the rationalist model is extreme scepticism. But there is no question of whether an external world exists. Rather, the belief in an external world "is a point, which we must take for granted in all our reasonings" (*Treatise*, p. 187). The question is never how to refute scepticism, for logically that cannot be done. Rather, we must ask "*how it happens, that even after all we retain a degree of belief, which is sufficient for our purpose, either in philosophy or common life*" (*Treatise*, p.

185). The question is not do-we or should-we have those beliefs but why-do-we have these beliefs. This is a reflection of Hume's Copernican Revolution in philosophy, the so-called *We Do* perspective which it is the responsibility of the philosopher to explicate. Hume's deliberately paradoxical tone of voice is meant to drive home this point.

To sum up, Part IV, Book I of the *Treatise* is prelude to the passions in demolishing the rationalist interpretation of reason, in showing its failure to account for the world of common sense, in showing the standing contradiction between our actual behavior and the paralysis that model would inflict upon us. Hume has offered the only kind of refutation possible within his general philosophical framework by exposing the inability of the rationalist model to make sense of *our* practice. This is not how human beings operate. This is not how human beings ought to be said to function. Well, then, how do human beings function? This brings us to the passions in Book II.

Classification of the Passions

In Book I of the *Treatise*, Hume divided the impressions into two classes, those of sensation and those of reflection. In Book II, this same distinction is made and called a distinction between original impressions and secondary impressions.[35] Original impressions are impressions of the senses and internal or bodily pleasures and pains. They are purely physical in origin, and they are called original because they arise from these direct physical sources without any antecedent. Secondary impressions are secondary in the sense that they are preceded either by an original impression alone or by ideas which are themselves derived from original impressions. It is among the secondary impressions that Hume locates the passions.

The secondary impressions may also be divided into two classes, the calm and the violent. The calm impressions include both the moral sense, i.e. the sense of virtue and vice, and the aesthetic sense, i.e. the sense of beauty and deformity. Here we can anticipate a point in Hume's moral theory by noting that the moral sense comprises impressions which arise from or are caused to come into existence by previous original impressions and/or ideas. Clearly, then, when we discuss Hume's moral theory we shall be interested in the circumstances under which the moral sense is activated.

The violent impressions include the passions. Hume stresses that the distinction between the calm and the violent is relative. This, like the distinction of vivacity, is a tactical distinction used by Hume in his discussion of human motivation. The violent impressions or passions are subdivided into the direct and the indirect. The direct passions come in contrasting pairs and include desire and aversion, grief and joy, and hope and fear. They arise immediately from the original impressions of pleasure and pain. Later, Hume will argue that in some cases they arise without an antecedent. The indirect passions, which are Hume's major concern, include pride and humility as well as love and hatred. They arise from the original impressions of pleasure and pain in conjunction with other qualities. Hume's major concern can be focused more precisely as a concern with these other qualities.

In analyzing the passions, Hume distinguished between the cause of the passions and what he calls the object of the passions. With respect to the cause, he is concerned with what he calls the quality of the cause and the subject of the cause. True to his Newtonian program, Hume contended that "*'tis not by a different principle each different cause is adapted to its passion*" (*Treatise*, p. 282).

Hume discussed four passions in detail, the pairs pride and humility and love and hatred. Most of what he said can be grasped by concentrating on pride and humility. The objects of the passions are relatively easy to identify. Although otherwise different, pride and humility have the same object, namely, the self; the object of love and hatred is some other self. Whenever we feel pride or humility it is because of ourselves or something intimately related to ourselves. At the same time, it is not always the case that we feel pride and humility simply by reflecting upon ourselves. The passion has to be excited by some cause. The cause is that idea which excites the passion, whereas the object is that idea which follows or is caused by the passion. The indirect passions are, therefore, impressions which occur between two ideas.

The cause has both a quality and a subject. For example, if we are proud of the beauty of our house, then we can identify the house as the subject of the cause, and we can identify the beauty as that quality of the cause which excites our pride.

There are, according to Hume, three principles which account for the causes of the passions. The first principle is the association of ideas. The cause of a passion, at least an indirect passion, is always an idea. Therefore, resemblance, contiguity, and causation as associative relationships among ideas can cause a passion. The second general principle is the association of impressions. This is not to be confused with the association of ideas. Impressions may only be associated by resemblance, so that one passion, such as anger, which resembles envy, will easily allow us to feel the resembling passion. Hence, anger is often followed by envy. Third, and most important for the passions, is a *double association of ideas and impressions* wherein both previous principles unite and reinforce each other. For example, when one person is injured by a second person, the first person not only feels anger at the second person but the first person also feels uneasy whenever anything or any idea associated with the second person occurs.

A further example of the double association of ideas and impressions should make Hume's theory clear. Let us return to the example of pride felt because of our beautiful house. The beauty of the house (i.e.the quality of the cause of our passion of pride) is pleasurable independent of all other considerations. Therefore, the quality of the cause of the passion gives rise to a feeling of pleasure independent of all other considerations.

Second, in order to give rise to our passion, the subject of the cause of the passion, in this case our house, must be related to ourselves. In short, the causes of the passions have two properties: they are independently a source of either pleasure or pain, and they are related to ourselves. The passions, in turn, have two corresponding properties: each passion is itself either a pleasurable or a painful feeling or impression, and each passion gives rise to the idea of ourselves. This double impulse or coincidence explains why the indirect passions are so powerful.

As we shall see in our discussion of motivation, the passions are what motivate us. Hence, anything which can cause a passion is a potential source of human motivation.

Having loosened all of the components of our passional life, it is now time to raise the question of how these passions communicate with each other. This requires Hume's third great explanatory principle, the communication of vivacity. In fact, Hume's discussion of the double relations of ideas and impressions is a prelude to explain how vivacity is communicated.

The idea which is the cause of the passion gives rise to an impression of pleasure or pain. It may seem odd to some that Hume should be arguing that an idea can communicate vivacity to an impression since we had earlier been told that impressions cause ideas. However, what we were actually told was that passions are secondary impressions which in the case of pride and humility require a preceding idea. This preceding idea had its own original impression. Some may well ask how the idea could have retained this vivacity since impressions were supposed to be more vivid than ideas. But if we recall that there is a physiological mechanism at work, a mechanism of which we are not immediately conscious, and that in describing the passions Hume is merely describing the conscious counterpart of what is going on in the body, then we may well understand how vivacity as stored up momentum can be retained. This is crude but perfectly consistent, and reinforces how unintelligible Hume's theory appears unless we continually remind ourselves of its biological basis. "As these depend upon natural and physical causes, the examination of them would lead me too far from my present subject, into the sciences of anatomy and natural philosophy" (*Treatise*, pp. 275-76).

Let us return then to the main argument. There is an idea which gives rise to an impression of pleasure or pain. This impression of pleasure or pain is associated by resemblance with other impressions of pain and pleasure such as pride or humility. The impression of pride or humility in turn gives rise to the idea of the self. The transition or transfer of vivacity is thus from the first idea to the first impression; from the first impression to the second impression; from the second impression to the second idea. This transfer of vivacity, Hume reminds us, is analogous to the transfer of vivacity in the case of belief. "There is evidently a great analogy betwixt that hypothesis, and our present one of an impression and an idea, that transfuse themselves into another impression and idea by means of their double relation: Which analogy must be allowed to be no despicable proof of both hypotheses" (*Treatise*, p. 290). Hume also takes this opportunity to inform us that virtue and vice produce the indirect passions.

The Self

Hume believed in the existence of a self. As he made clear in Book II of the *Treatise*, the self is "that individual person, of whose actions and sentiments each of us is intimately conscious" (*Treatise*, p. 286), and he further described the self by reference to "the qualities of our mind and body" (*Ibid.*, p. 303). The self, then, for Hume consists of a mind and a body. Hume's last published statement on the self was in the dissertation on the *Passions* where he repeated this view by speaking of "qualities of our mind and body, that is, of self."[36]

If the self consists of a mind and a body, we must at some point raise the question of the relationship between the two. For the moment, it is important to stress that there are two dimensions to the self, a mind and a body, and we cannot assume that what Hume says about one of these dimensions, e.g. the mind, applies to the other dimension or to the whole which they comprise. So important is this point that Hume warns his readers in Book I that there are going to be *two different discussions of the self*, each designed to make a different point: "...we must distinguish betwixt personal identity, as it regards our thought or imagination, and as it regards our passions or the concern we take in ourselves. The first is our present subject [i.e. in Book I]..."(*Treatise*, p. 253).

What does Hume tell us about the mind? The mind is described as: (1)"a bundle or collection of different perceptions" (*Treatise*, p. 252); (2)"a kind of theatre, where several perceptions successively make their appearance" (*Ibid.*, p. 253); and (3)"a system of different perceptions or different existences, which are link'd together by the relation of cause and effect..." (*Ibid.*, p. 261).[37] It is the mind, therefore, which is a set of perceptions, not the self. It is not the self which is a set of perceptions but the idea of the self which refers to a set of perceptions. Since the self is a composite of body and mind, it is an error to assert that for Hume "people are nothing but bundles or collections of different perceptions."[38] People are composites of bodies and minds, but when they introspect their minds they find a set of perceptions. Hume always reminded us that ultimately all impressions are derived from sensation and that sensation has an anatomical or physiological basis.

So far we have seen that Hume maintains the self to be a composite of mind and body linked in some way. A further distinction which must be maintained is *the distinction between the self and the idea of the self*. As Butchvarov has expressed it, "the question of the existence of the self is prior to , and distinct from, the question of the identity of the self, although the possibility of the latter [question] presupposes an affirmative answer to the former [question]."[39] In explaining the idea of ourselves Hume finds that he must explain how we come to discover our continuous identity. It is precisely because the idea of the self does not refer to a simple and identical impression that the issue of identity arises.

This brings us to the question: what is the relationship of the idea of the self to the self? Since the self is a composite of mind and body it seems unlikely that Hume would maintain that the idea of the self is a simple one. Hume, in fact, denies that we have a simple idea of the self. The main point of the discussion in Book I is to expose the belief in a simple self and thereby a simple idea of the self as a myth.

> There are some philosophers, who imagine we are every moment intimately conscious of what we call our SELF; that we...are certain, beyond the evidence of a demonstration, both of its perfect identity and simplicity.... Unluckily all these positive assertions are contrary to that very experience, which is pleaded for them, nor have we any idea of *self*, after the manner it is here explain'd...there is no such idea. (*Treatise*, pp. 251-52)

The same point is reiterated in the Appendix: "...we have no impression of self or substance, as something simple and individual. We have, therefore, no idea of them in that sense" (*Treatise*, p. 633). What Hume is denying is that we have either the experience (i.e. impression) or the idea of a simple and identical self. He is not denying that there is a self, nor is he denying that we have an idea of the self. He is denying that we have a simple idea of a simple self.

If we have an idea of the self, but it is not a simple idea, then it must be a *complex idea*. The idea of the self is complex because the idea of the self "represents" (*Treatise*, p. 278) (a)"a succession of related ideas and impressions" or (b) "a connected succession of perceptions" (*Treatise*, p. 277). There are two questions to be raised about this complex. First, how is the idea acquired, and, second, what are the relationships integral to the parts of the set?

The answer to the first question is that the complex idea of the self emerges originally in action as the object of the indirect passions of pride and humility.[40] Hume's positive analysis of the self emerges in the second treatment of this topic, that is, in Book

II. The negative analysis is given first, that is, in Book I. The reason for this order is the now familiar pattern in Hume of first showing the inadequacy of any analysis of human nature which begins with an *I Think* perspective and then following with a positive analysis that is rooted in action, in the *We Do* perspective. The passions of pride and humility are impressions, and they have a preceding idea which causes or produces them. The indirect passions in turn produce or cause another idea. The second produced idea, called by Hume the object of the passions, is in the case of pride and humility none other than the idea of the self. The ideas which caused the passions are memories of past pleasures and pains. The subtlety and complexity of Hume's analysis is completely missed by those who begin with the presumption that every idea is derived from or copies a preceding impression. What Hume actually said, as we pointed out before, is that every simple idea in its first appearance copies a preceding impression. Complex ideas are not that simple and require a much more complicated account.

As an idea, the complex idea of the self must be preceded by an impression. The preceding impression is the passion either of pride or of humility. Some readers are bound to ask, shouldn't this produce the idea of pride or the idea of humility? Shouldn't the idea of the self come from an impression of the self? The answer, once again, is that it is *only* in the case of simple ideas that there is an original simple impression of sensation. Complex ideas do not have a one-to-one correspondence: "I observe, that many of our complex ideas never had impressions, that corresponded to them, and that many of our complex impressions never are exactly copied in ideas" (*Treatise*, p. 3). No complex idea, including and especially the complex idea of the self, need have a direct analogue in experience. Complex ideas, moreover, are formed through the creative activity of the mind's association of ideas.

What is even more important is that action is a fundamental category in Hume's analysis. Just as pure epistemology is incoherent and leads to scepticism when we try to understand our-

selves as if we were disembodied minds, so the concept of ourselves cannot be obtained in pure thought. It is the reference to
action that underscores the importance of the body as part of the
self. This rootedness in action is so fundamental that it cannot
be explained, rather it is the ground of explanation. "Unless nature had given some original qualities to the mind, it cou'd never
have any secondary ones; because in that case it wou'd have no
foundation for action, nor cou'd ever begin to exert itself"
(*Treatise*, p. 280).

We turn, now, to the second question about the complex idea
of the self, namely, what relationships hold the set together.[41]
The specific natural relations integral to the set are resemblance
and causation. Both resemblance and causation rely upon
memory.

> (a) ...the memory not only discovers the identity, but also contributes to
> its production, by producing the relation of resemblance among the per-
> ceptions. (*Treatise*, p. 261)

> (b) ...our identity with regard to the passions serves to corroborate that
> with regard to the imagination, by the making our distant perceptions in-
> fluence each other, and by giving us a present concern for our past or fu-
> ture pains or pleasures....Had we no memory, we never shou'd have any
> notion of causation, nor consequently of that chain of causes and effects,
> which constitute our self or person....In this view, therefore, memory does
> not so much *produce* as *discover* personal identity, by shewing us the rela-
> tion of cause and effect among our different perceptions. (*Treatise*, pp.
> 261-62)

These two functions of memory must be clearly distinguished.
The memory that *produces* is the memory of ideas of past pleasures and pains that give rise to the indirect passions. The indirect passions are simple impressions of reflection caused by
ideas. The memory that *discovers* the idea of the self is the memory of how the indirect passions give rise to the idea of the self
as their object. This shows clearly that Hume's discussion of
personal identity with regard to thought presupposes what he

says about personal identity with regard to the passions.[42] It shows, as well, that the complex idea of the self or personal identity is known only in *retrospect*. One cannot directly confront one's self or turn the self (as opposed to the idea of the self) into an object. One can remember its past or imagine its future. Moreover, memory does not reveal an unchanging self. Paradoxically, the self can be re-identified but never identified. Re-identification does not presuppose identification. This should not surprise us, for in Hume's ontology there are no universals, only the resemblances within an historical series.

Past Pleasures & Pains → Indirect passions → idea of the self

(Memory)   [Produces]   [Discovers]

Let us sum up this account of the complex idea of the self.

1. We must distinguish the self from the idea of the self. The self, as opposed to the idea of the self, is rooted in bodily action.

2. The idea of the self is a complex idea of the imagination and of the memory.

3. The imagination is the ideational analogue of sensory reflection. There are, however, no complex impressions of reflection to which complex ideas of the imagination can directly correspond. There is also, according to Hume, no notion of how such complexes of impressions could be held together. We are not dealing with a mirror image. Hence, memory cannot produce such a copy.

4. There is no simple impression of sensation of the self.

5. The complex idea of the self, therefore, must come from either complex impressions of sensation or simple impressions of reflection.

6. It cannot come from complex impressions of sensation alone because these are produced by external objects. At most, they would only be impressions of the physical body.

7. The complex idea of the self, therefore, must come from simple impressions of reflection (i.e., the passions).

In Book II of the *Treatise*, Hume presented his positive theory of personal identity and cleared up a number of issues. It is in action rather than in thought that we truly discover our personal identity. The implications of this discovery for moral theory will be momentous. Our passions, which are the important impressions of reflection, have causal connections both with our other perceptions and with the actions of our bodies. All of our perceptions are tautologically ours, but they are not all perceptions of ourselves. For an idea or impression to be *of* ourselves it must be causally related to our bodies. The connection among passions, action, and personal identity is brought out when Hume said of the will that it is *"the internal impression we feel and are conscious of, when we knowingly give rise to any new motion of our body, or new perception of our mind"* (*Treatise*, p. 399). The will is not itself a passion, but every passion which motivates us gives rise to the impression of the will. When we discover causal connections between our actions and our pleasures and pains we discover ourselves. This is personal identity with regard to the passions.

What is startling about the self as discussed within the context of the passions is that it becomes an impression. Hume spoke of "the idea or rather impression of ourselves" which is "always intimately present with us" (*Treatise*, p. 320). Does this contradict his earlier denial that there is a simple identical impression of self? The answer is no! Hume claimed that there was a transfer of vivacity from the original exciting ideas to the indirect passions of pride, humility, love and hatred. The indirect passion is experienced as an impression of reflection, getting its vivacity from an idea. As an impression it can and does pass along the

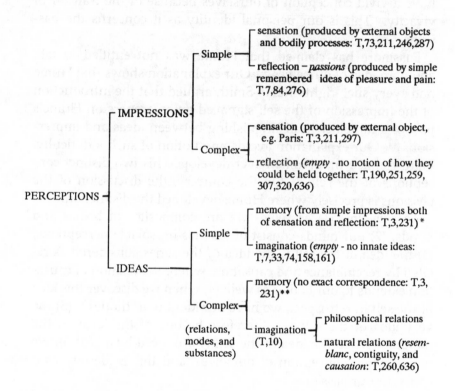

PERCEPTIONS

IMPRESSIONS

- Simple
  - sensation (produced by external objects and bodily processes: T,73,211,246,287)
  - reflection – *passions* (produced by simple remembered ideas of pleasure and pain: T,7,84,276)
- Complex
  - sensation (produced by external object, e.g. Paris: T,3,211,297)
  - reflection (*empty* - no notion of how they could be held together: T,190,251,259, 307,320,636)

IDEAS

- Simple
  - memory (from simple impressions both of sensation and reflection: T,3,231) *
  - imagination (*empty* - no innate ideas: T,7,33,74,158,161)
- Complex (relations, modes, and substances)
  - memory (no exact correspondence: T,3, 231)**
  - imagination (T,10)
    - philosophical relations
    - natural relations (*resemblanc*, contiguity, and *causation*: T,260,636)

* This is the memory that produces the idea of the self (T,253,261,277,280)

** This is the memory that discovers the idea of the self.

Idea of Self

vivacity to its object. In the case of pride and humility, the object of the indirect passions is the idea of the self. The transfer of vivacity allows the idea of the self to acquire the vivacity of an impression. When the idea of the self is produced by a passion, as opposed to being discovered in retrospect by the memory, we have a vivid conception of ourselves because of the transfer of vivacity. This is our personal identity as it concerns the passions.

Passmore has claimed that Hume was not entitled to talk about an idea of ourselves.[43] Our explanation shows that Hume had every such right. Kemp Smith argued that the introduction of the impression of the self signalled an awareness on Hume's part of a difficulty in distinguishing between ideas and impressions.[44] Our explanation avoids any notion of such a difficulty. Laird claimed that Hume never developed his two distinct conceptions of the self.[45] On the contrary, the discussion of the passions is precisely where Hume developed the distinction.

To *sum up*: (1) as selves we are composites of bodies and minds; (2) our minds consist of a series of isolable perceptions; (3) the idea of the self is the idea of the series considered as related by resemblance and causation, where the relation of causation extends to our bodies as well; (4) when we discover this idea of the self in retrospect, we have our identity in thought; (5) the very idea of the self can therefore be one of the ideas in the mind; (6) when the idea of the self is produced by a passion we have a vivid conception of ourselves, and this is identity as it concerns our passions.

I conclude that Hume's conception of personal identity and the self is dualistic. Once this is seen, all contextual difficulties about the self vanish, but alas to be replaced by the more fundamental difficulties of metaphysical dualism. However, these more fundamental difficulties do not themselves pose any immediate serious threat for the theory of the self as it operates either in Hume's discussion of the passions or of morality.[46]

Passions, Self, and Sympathy

An important element which Hume introduced into his discussion of the passions was the association of the passions. It should be recalled that ideas are associated by the imagination in three ways and that Hume also claimed that some ideas could cause passions. He also had claimed specifically that passions cause ideas and as such can transfer vivacity to these ideas. The passions, as impressions and not ideas, can only be associated with other passions by resemblance. In order for there to be movement from one passion to another we need either resemblance between the passions or an intervening idea. Hence, it follows that the idea of the self, which is caused by one passion, can itself be a cause of other passions.

This process is missed completely by Passmore who chided Hume by arguing that if the passions are to "be subject to the laws of association, the passions must stand to the imagination as raw material to an artificer."[47] But the imagination, as Hume made clear, deals only with ideas and not impressions. *As impressions, the passions cannot be material for the imagination, and this is why mere reason cannot move us to action.* What ideas influence us can only be discovered empirically by seeing which ideas trigger the mechanism of the passions, and under what sets of circumstances. There are definite limitations to this process, and Hume was attempting to show those limits and how they depend upon the transfer of vivacity.

Hume constructed his system of the passions by working out the laws of association and applying them to this important correspondence between the properties of the causes of the passions and the properties of the passions themselves. This correspondence accounts for the transition and mixtures which occur between the ideas as causes, and the passions as impressions by pointing back to the resemblances between the properties of the causes of the passions and the properties of the passions themselves. The direction which the cause of a passion takes is the same as the idea of the object toward which the passion itself is directed: the self or some other self. By the same token, the impression which is produced independently by the cause of the passion is pleasant or painful just as the passion itself is. These two associative bonds among all ideas and impressions, where the passions are impressions, mutually reinforce each other and account for the *double impulse* which the mind receives under such circumstances. Furthermore, this accounts for the passional strength of all objects which are pleasant or painful and which bear a reference to ourselves or others. Finally, we find that an easy transition can be made from one idea to another, once the idea in question acquires the vivacity of the associated impression, and thus a transition from one passion to the next. The arousal of a passion causes a whole series of similar ones to follow, especially when the mind considers the various aspects and relations of the causes and objects involved.

Hume next proceeded "to examine the causes of pride and humility; and see, whether in every case we can discover the double relations, by which they operate on the passions" (*Treatise*, p. 294). The last cause of pride and humility which he discussed was "our reputation, our character, our name" (Ibid., p. 316). In order to account for this cause, Hume employed the mechanism of sympathy. *Sympathy* is an instance of the double association theory of ideas and impressions. There is a self, and there are other selves (the objects of the passions); and there is an idea of pleasure or an idea of pain (the cause of the passions). In any case, it is to be noted that we are concerned with ideas that can arouse passions.

In the original description of the sympathy mechanism we find an observer, a subject, the subject's emotion, and the observer's idea of that emotion. The observer has an idea about a subject's emotion, an idea presented to the imagination of the observer as the result of a causal inference. The idea becomes so enlivened through the efficacy of the impression of self that the idea becomes an instance of the emotion or a resembling one, i.e. it becomes an impression. The process also involves the influence upon the imagination of certain pre-established relations such as contiguity and the resemblance between the observer and the subject. The influence involved is based upon the observation of customary concomitants of the emotion. At no time did Hume say or imply that the observer could directly inspect the emotion of the subject.

The process of sympathy begins with the belief about the affections of some other person, a belief resulting from an inference based on "those external signs in the countenance and conversation" (*Treatise*, p. 317). These signs are the customary effects of the affection in question. It is to be emphasized that what the inference establishes is only a belief about someone else's emotions. The belief constitutes an idea (*Treatise*, p. 97) which requires vivacity in order that it may be converted into an impression or an instance of that very emotion or affection. Thus sympathy may be defined as the process in which "the ideas of the affections of others are converted into the very impressions they represent" (*Treatise*, p. 319). The operation of sympathy requires a source of vivacity, and the source of vivacity is found by Hume in the impression of the self.

The idea that is the cause gives rise to an independent impression of pleasure or pain; this first impression is associated with other impressions which are pleasant or painful such as pride and humility; the impression of pride or of humility then gives rise to the idea of the self. The transition is from an idea to an impression; from the first impression to the second or resembling impression; from the second impression to a second idea. In sympathy, the second idea, namely the idea of the self, acquires the vivacity of the second impression, thereby arousing the corresponding affection within ourselves.

Hume gives the following example. Our fame or infamy, resulting from praise or blame, produces pleasure or pain in us. The exact relationship of this praise or blame to pride and humility can only be understood in terms of sympathy. When we are pleased by the praise of others, it is only because we observe the admirer and feel his pleasure, a pleasure produced by qualities in us and which are the object of his admiration. In other

words, our idea of his emotion produced by qualities in ourselves, becomes an emotion or impression directed toward the
same qualities. To experience one's own infamy is to feel,
through sympathy, the displeasure or pain of one's detractors.

Hume did not provide a definition of the indirect passions of
love and hatred. He claimed, instead, that these passions were
"sufficiently known from our common feeling and experience"
(*Treatise*, p. 329). Since there is an analogy between love and hatred on the one hand and pride and humility on the other,
Hume provided an explanation for love and hatred by means of
the double association theory. The object of love or hatred is
another person "of whose thoughts, actions, and sensations we
are not conscious" (*Treatise*, p. 329). Other people are the objects
of love and hatred because they resemble us. Since we do not
directly inspect the emotions of the resembling person, we must
depend upon inference. Thus far, the discussion of love and hatred corresponds to the discussion of pride and humility. At no
time did Hume derive love and hatred from pride and humility.

In the double association theory it is also necessary that the
cause of the passion produce pleasure or pain. Hume noted that
the causes of love and hatred are the same as the causes of pride
and humility. Since the causes of the latter passions "excite a
pain or pleasure independent of the passion" the same can be
said of the former passions. "The same qualities that produce
pride and humility, cause love or hatred" (*Treatise*, p. 332).

The importance of the impression of self is best seen in the experiments involving love and hatred. These experiments are designed to show that the causes of the indirect passions are pleasurable or painful independently of the indirect passions themselves. Hume's six experiments all involve the self, another person or self, and a cause or idea.

In the first experiment Hume showed that if the cause did not
produce pleasure or pain or if it was not related to either person
then there was no passion. In the second experiment, the cause
was related to both persons but produced no pleasure or pain.
The result again was no passion. In the third experiment there

was pleasure or pain, but since the cause was not related to either person no passion was produced. When all the conditions were met and all the elements were present, as in the fourth experiment, a passion did result. In the fifth experiment, Hume found a transition from love to pride and from hatred to humility.

The *sixth experiment* reveals some difficulties which arise in the transition of ideas when the causes of the passions conflict with certain properties of the imagination. In particular, the presence of certain qualities originally located in the self produce no transition from the pride or humility they produce to the love or hatred of a person closely related to the self. For example, "we never love or hate a son or brother for the virtue or vice we discern in ourselves; tho' 'tis evident the same qualities in him give us a very sensible pride or humility" (*Treatise*, p. 339). Why should no transition occur? "If a person be my brother, I am his likewise; But tho' the relations be reciprocal, they have very different effects on the imagination" (*Treatise*, p. 340). Is there a contradiction between the above phenomenon and the case of sympathy where the mind passes from the idea of ourselves to that of any other object related to us?

Hume explained the difference by appealing to two other features of the transfer of vivacity. First, the imagination passes easily from obscure to lively ideas, but the passage from lively ideas to obscure ones is made only with difficulty (*Treatise*, p. 339). Second, *the idea of the self has a greater vivacity, or rather acquires a greater vivacity, than the idea of another person because the impression of self is always present and takes precedence.* This is why the imagination can move from the idea of love to the idea of pride. This passage is obviously from the less vivid to the more vivid idea. The passage from pride to love or from humility to hate is much more difficult.

Passions, being impressions, pass more easily from the strong to the weak (*Treatise*, p. 341). When the passions and the imagination conflict, the law of the passions prevails: "...the affections are a more powerful principle than the imagination" and hence

181

it is "no wonder they prevail over it, and draw the mind to their side" (*Treatise*, p. 344). The foregoing accounts for the importance of the self.

> ...in sympathy our own person is not the object of any passion, nor is there any thing, that fixes our attention on ourselves; as in the present case, where we are suppos'd to be actuated with pride and humility. Ourself, independent of the perception of every other object, is in reality nothing: For which reason we must turn our view to external objects; and 'tis natural for us to consider with most attention such as lie contiguous to us, or resemble us. But when self is the object of a passion, 'tis not natural to quit the consideration of it, till the passion be exhausted; in which case the double relations of impressions and ideas can no longer operate. (*Treatise*, pp. 340-41)

The impression of self is absolutely essential to the process of sympathy because it provides the vivacity necessary to convert an idea into an impression. without a source of vivacity or a present lively impression there would be no sympathy, regardless of temporal, spatial, or interpersonal considerations.

Pity is problematic because it gives rise to a sympathetic hatred as well as a sympathetic love. From one point of view, the observer feels hatred because of the poverty and meanness of the victim. From another point of view, the observer feels love and a secondary sensation resembling benevolence (*Treatise*, p. 385). The problem is one of accounting for the presence of anything but benevolence or "why does sympathy in uneasiness ever produce any passion beside goodwill and kindness?" (*Treatise*, p. 385).

The answer to the present problem of pity has two parts. First, Hume explains that there is a second cause of the transition of passions, namely, the presence of additional desires having the same object or direction. This second cause of transition leads Hume to introduce a distinction between weak sympathy and strong sympathy.

The Passions and Sympathy

I have mention'd two different causes, from which a transition of passion may arise, viz. a double relation of ideas and impressions, and what is similar to it, a conformity in the tendency and direction of any two desires, which arise from different principles. Now I assert, that when a sympathy with uneasiness is weak, it produces hatred or contempt by the former cause; when strong, it produces love or tenderness by the latter. This is the solution of the foregoing difficulty... (*Treatise*, p. 385)

Weak sympathy is limited to the present moment. Strong sympathy gives us a broader perspective, "a lively notion of all the circumstances of that person, whether past, present, or future; possible, probable or certain" (*Treatise*, p. 386). In the former case, there is a sympathetically communicated feeling only of the unpleasant circumstances which afflict the subject, and this produces hatred by the now familiar mechanism of the double association of ideas and impressions. Here there is only a concern with the subject's bad fortune. In the case of a strong passion there is generated both a concern for bad fortune and for good fortune, where the added concern for good fortune is the result of benevolence, which functions as the desire having the same tendency and direction. Benevolence is an original pleasure arising from the pleasure of the person belov'd and a pain proceeding from his pain. "From which correspondence of impressions there arises a subsequent desire of his pleasure, and aversion to his pain" (*Treatise*, p. 387).

The main point to be noticed in the distinction between weak sympathy and strong sympathy, and the reason why I have dwelled so long on the intricacies of the sympathy mechanism, is Hume's attempt to explain all differences and to meet all objections by appealing to the transmission of vivacity. There are definite limitations to sympathy. These limitations, as well as the powers of sympathy are determined by vivacity. Thus, the primary difference we find between a limited and an extensive sympathy is determined by the vivacity of the sympathetically received impressions. "A strong impression, when communicated, gives a double tendency of the passions; which is related to benevolence and love by a similarity of direction" (*Treatise*, p. 387).

The major difference between pride and humility on the one hand and love and hatred on the other, aside from the difference of their respective objects, is that the former are "pure emotions in the soul, unattended with any desire, and not immediately exciting us to action" (*Treatise*, p. 367). Pride and humility do excite us to action, but they do not excite in the immediate manner of love and hatred. "Love is always follow'd by a desire of the happiness of the person belov'd, and an aversion to his misery: As hatred produces a desire of the misery and an aversion to the happiness of the person hated" (*Treatise*, p. 367). This explains in part why the sense of duty can function as a motive.

We have found that sympathy involves the conversion of an idea into an impression with the self serving as the source of vivacity. Like all of Hume's explanations in the *Treatise* we have been given an account of complex phenomena in terms of the relationship, usually association, between simpler elements.

Passion and Reason

We are now in a position to understand Hume's views on the relationship of passion to reason. Everyone is familiar with Hume's views as expressed in Book III of the *Treatise* and in the last part of Book II, specifically section iii of Part III (pp. 413-418). What is not generally recognized is that Parts I and II of Book II constitute the groundwork of what Hume will say in Part III.

A number of critics, beginning with Reid, have asserted that Hume's seemingly paradoxical conclusions about the relation of reason to passion are mere consequences of Hume's definitions of reason and passion. It is, of course, no crime to be consistent. There are, however, other important points to be noted about Hume's treatment. To begin with, we noted in Chapter One that Hume's position is a reflection of a widely held view in modern philosophy, a position shared not only by Hobbes but by Machiavelli and Spinoza among others. This new orientation was an attempt to bring theory closer to actual practice. Second, Hume's conclusions are offered only after an exhaustive introspective examination of our emotional life. Hume believed that his views could be empirically confirmed. Finally, the definition Hume gave of reason was not invented by Hume but taken from his rationalist opponents.

As Laird contended, "Hume's opponents affirmed that the apprehension of duty and fitness of things pertained to reason and did affect conduct."[48] Hume showed that on the analysis of reason given by various rationalists it was impossible to see how reason alone could move us. Scepticism is the only consistent position available to those who follow out the implications of the rationalist account of reason. Whatever they may advocate or claim on behalf of reason, their account of reason cannot make clear how reason alone can move us. Actually, when we examine the very words of Hume's rationalist opponents we find that they qualify their claims about reason's power in such ways that the qualifications undermine their position. Reid, for example, did assert that reason influences our action by making us see our long range interest. This is, of course, perfectly compatible with Hume's position. But Reid also admitted that "passions and appetites too often draw men to act contrary to their cool judgment and opinion of what is best for them."[49] If the passions can divert us sometimes then reason does not always and automatically move us. Either the passions are really what moves us or there is a third faculty which adjusts passion and reason. These possibilities Reid neither considered nor made consistent with the view that reason is supreme.

Hume's position, on the other hand, has the virtue of plausibility as well as consistency. There is no third faculty or self-consciousness that sits in judgment on the rest of our faculties. There are direct passions that do not respond to expectations of pleasure and pain, rather they are the original drives on which all subsequent action is based. All subsequent action depends upon ideas that trigger the indirect passions. Is it any wonder that Hume concluded that reason is and ought only to be understood as the slave of the passions?

When we morally blame others it is not only because they sometimes failed to see what was moral, but also because they may have seen what was morally right and ignored it. In their endeavor to deal with this phenomenon, rationalist moralists invoked (Hume would say "invented") the alleged moral "ought". Hume's position is that if the most reason can do is to tell us what we "ought" to do, and if this "ought" is not tied in some intelligible or plausible manner to the passions, then morality as thus understood is useless. "Ought" becomes a mysterious category which masks the inability to bridge the gap between apprehension and action. Common sense, on the other hand, tells us that we go to a great deal of trouble to inculcate moral principles because such principles can and do influence us. Any explanation of morality must make sense of this. Hume's account of the passions does this whereas his rationalist opponents cannot. We all presume a link between thought and action, but an adequate theory must make the link intelligible. Hume's conclusions with respect to the relationship between passion and reason are not the mere consequences of his definitions but follow from his critique of rationalist moral theories, his arguments about the determinants of the will, and a consistent attempt to explicate common sense.

One of the important functions of the discussion of sympathy in Book II is to explain the relationship of thought to action, of reason to passion. The actual connection is missed by those who fail even to read Book II of the *Treatise*. The relationship was brought out by Hume when he discussed sympathy as an *inferential process*.

There are three major points we want to stress about this form of inference. First, Hume insisted on the "exact correspondence" of sympathetic inference to inference as discussed in the theory of the understanding. Specifically, Hume compared sympathetic inference to causal inference and the employment of general rules. Even the transmission of vivacity is common to sympathy and believed causal inferences. Second, sympathy requires the presence of the relation of resemblance as well as the relation of cause and effect. Sympathetic inference functions only because human beings resemble each other. Third, it should be clearly noted that sympathy does not require any idiosyncratic logical principles, that is, it is not a special and unique form of inference limited to moral ideas.

Hume emphasized the fact that inference in sympathy is analogous to inference in causal judgments. Both inferences give rise to judgments of matter of fact. This should reinforce our discussion in Chapter Four of the factual nature of moral judgments in Hume's moral theory.

> What is principally remarkable in this whole affair is the strong confirmation these phaenomena give to the foregoing system concerning the understanding, and consequently to the present one concerning the passions; since these are analogous to each other. 'Tis indeed evident, that when we sympathize with the passions and sentiments of others, these movements appear at first in *our* mind as mere ideas, and are conceiv'd to belong to another person, as we conceive any other matter of fact...sympathy is exactly correspondent to the operations of our understanding... (*Treatise*, pp. 319-20)

The causal inference involved in sympathy is an inference about the emotions of another person, an observer's inference about a subject or the situation of the subject. We do not, and cannot, directly observe or inspect the emotions of a subject. The emotion is inferred from the appearance and language of the subject. "When any affection is infus'd by sympathy, it is at first known only by its effects, and by those external signs in the countenance and conversation, which convey an idea of it" (*Treatise*, p. 317).

Since causal inferences depend upon a history of frequent conjunction, and since we never directly observe someone else's emotion, how can the foregoing inference be a causal one? Further, as Passmore has urged, "causal inference from 'external signs' supplies us with evidence that other people have affections; but it provides us with no more than an idea of these affections (one must simply forget Hume's general theory of causality)."[50] Hume's answer is that we know about the frequent conjunction of our own emotions and our appearance and language, and we extend this conjunction to other persons. The extension is permissible because human beings resemble each other.

> Now 'tis obvious, that nature has preserv'd a great resemblance among all human creatures, and that we never remark any passion or principle in others, of which, in some degree or other, we may not find a parallel in ourselves. The case is the same with the fabric of the mind, as with that of the body...this resemblance must very much contribute to make us enter into the sentiments of others, and embrace them with facility and pleasure. (*Treatise*, p. 318)[51]

Passmore's objection can be side stepped by noting the analogy between sympathy and belief with respect to causal inference. What Passmore has overlooked is the role of vivacity transfer and belief. Operating from an *I Think* perspective, Passmore can only see the epistemological issue. Hume, on the contrary approaches the situation from a *We Do* perspective in which agency or action, and therefore belief, are central. The operation of the understanding in judgments of matter of fact involves a causal inference which begins with one impression and moves to the idea which customarily attends that impression. We believe in this inference because vivacity is transferred from the impression to the idea. We should recall that ideas differ from impressions in the degree of force and vivacity with which they strike upon the soul. In sympathy we transmit the vivacity of the impression or consciousness of our own person to the idea of the sentiments and passions of others.

> In sympathy there is an evident conversion of an idea into an impression. This conversion arises from the relation of objects to ourself. Ourself is always intimately present to us. Let us compare all these circumstances,

and we shall find, that sympathy is exactly correspondent to the operations of our understanding. (*Treatise*, p. 320)

The inference is also assisted by the presence of the relations of resemblance and contiguity.

> For besides the relation of cause and effect, by which we are convinc'd of the reality of the passion, with which we sympathize; besides this, I say, we must be assisted by the relations of resemblance and contiguity, in order to feel the sympathy in its full perfection. And since these relations can entirely convert an idea into an impression, and convey the vivacity of the latter into the former, so perfectly as to lose nothing of it in the transition, we may easily conceive how the relation of cause and effect alone, may serve to strengthen and inliven an idea. (*Treatise*, p. 320)

Sympathy not only helps to create similarity in human beings but is itself a product of pre-existing similarity. Hume spoke of the "force of sympathy" as the animating principle behind a host of passions which human beings have because we are gregarious and "can form no wish, which has not a reference to society" (*Treatise*, p. 363). Human beings desire things in society which cannot be explained by speculation about life in a pre-social state. Although resemblance reveals a capacity for being sociable in that "Every pleasure languishes when enjoy'd a-part from company, and every pain becomes more cruel and intolerable" (*Treatise*, p. 363), resemblance alone does not delineate the limits of such a community.

Hume gave a further explanation of sympathy by means of another phenomenon having an analogue to the understanding. In his discussion of the understanding, Hume noted our tendency to make generalizations from a small number of instances. This belies any narrow inductive interpretation of Hume's epistemology. Such generalizations take the form of a general rule or rules which provide our judgments with a certain degree of uniformity. Even when our present observation informs us differently, we have a tendency to trust the generalization or what Hume called 'general rules'. These general rules, as we should expect, owe their influence to vivacity.[52]

> By them [general rules] we learn to distinguish the accidental circum-
> stances from the efficacious causes....our general rules are in a manner set
> in opposition to each other. When an object appears, that resembles any
> cause in very considerable circumstances, the imagination naturally car-
> ries us to a lively conception of the usual effect....Here is the first influ-
> ence of general rules. But when we take a review of this act of the mind,
> and compare it with the more general and authentic operations of the
> understanding, we find it to be of an irregular nature, and destructive of
> all the most establish'd principles of reasonings; which is the cause of re-
> jecting it. This is the second influence of general rules, and implies the
> condemnation of the former. Sometimes the one, sometimes the other
> prevails, according to the disposition and character of the person....yet 'tis
> only by following them that we can correct this, and all other unphilo-
> sophical probabilities. (*Treatise*, pp. 149-50).

Nor is the operation of general rules limited to the understanding; it has its effects on the passions as well.

> ...*general rules* have a great influence upon pride and humility, as well as
> on all the other passions....Custom readily carries us beyond the just
> bounds in our passions, as well as in our reasonings. (*Treatise*, p. 293)

The most important point that Hume makes about general
rules concerns the naturalness of their growth. General rules
are not arbitrarily selected but are the product of customary experience. They grow out of experience in an experimental way
and are the result of a predominance of positive over negative
instances.

> ...in order to establish a general rule, and extend it beyond its proper
> bounds, there is requir'd a certain uniformity in our experience, and a
> great superiority of those instances, which are conformable to the rule,
> above the contrary. (*Treatise*, p. 362)

The influence of such general rules upon the imagination in the process of sympathy is most clearly seen in Hume's discussion of love and hatred. It should be remembered that *sympathy is an inferential process* involving two beings who resemble each other. Furthermore, such an inference involves an idea, heretofore gathered through the observation of countenance and conversation, and the enlivening of that idea by the vivacity transmitted from the impression of self. The employment of general rules facilitates this process by referring to the situation as well as to the person observed. This use of general rules is a noteworthy addition to the conception of sympathy.

Hume had already intimated the role of general rules when, in his discussion of compassion he had mentioned the possibility of sympathy with affections which did not exist (*Treatise*, p. 370). Hume had also pointed out that we do not directly observe the passions of others. It is even possible, claimed Hume, that an opposite passion can arise by sympathy to the one felt by the subject (*Treatise*, p. 375). We form a notion of the subject's condition rather than relying exclusively on countenance and conversation. This underscores, by the way, why Hume was not terribly concerned by our inability to intuit directly the emotions of someone else. This also underscores the thoroughly social and common sense perspective from which Hume proceeds. The imagination moves from the cause to the usual effect or passion in this case.

> ...and tho' there be an exception in the present case, yet the imagination is affected by the *general rule*, and makes us conceive a lively idea of the passion, or rather feel the passion itself, in the same manner, as if the person were really actuated by it. (*Treatise*, p. 371)

There are two factors involved: the present lively impression and a customary transition that is the result of a previous history of regularity.

> When an object is found by experience to be always accompany'd with another; whenever the first object appears, tho' chang'd in very material

circumstances; we naturally fly to the conception of the second, and form an idea of it in as lively and strong a manner, as if we had infer'd its existence by the justest and most authentic conclusion of our understanding. Nothing can undeceive us, not even our senses, which, instead of correcting this false judgment, are often perverted by it, and seem to authorize its errors. (*Treatise*, p. 374)

Consider the following example of how sympathy might thus function in a moral context. We know from past experience that honesty tends to the advantage of recipients in particular and to society in general. We ourselves have frequently been the beneficiaries of honest acts on the part of others, and therefore, we can recall the pleasure associated with such actions. As a consequence, we judge such acts to be good in a non-moral sense, that is, our judgment reports the fact that honest acts gave to us a pleasurable feeling. When, however, we come to judge that such actions give pleasure to members of society as a whole, and we participate in that pleasure through sympathy, our judgment becomes moral. The sympathetic inference involved is that acts of honesty usually have certain consequences. We infer the consequences even before they occur, or even if they do not occur. The inference is sanctioned by general rules. The mechanism of sympathy completes its operation when the idea arrived at through inference, namely, that a certain consequence will occur, is converted into an impression of pleasure. The impression is then a moral sentiment and productive of the indirect passion of love. To call the honest act virtuous is to report the presence of the moral sentiment and to ascribe to the act the production of the moral sentiment. From the *non-moral judgment* that an act will have certain consequences we may infer the *moral judgment* that people will feel a *moral sentiment* when they contemplate the act. In the next chapter we shall see that this example exemplifies why sympathy is the general principle of morals in the *Treatise*.

Sympathy is thus not merely an inference about a subject on the part of an observer, it is also an inference on the part of the observer that can be standardized in terms of general rules.[53]

The process of sympathy is not so much the placing of an observer in the subject's circumstances as it is an attempt to standardize the judgments of all observers including the subject. It should also be clear that the uniformity among human beings, their resemblance, has an important influence on our imagination because it is among human beings that general rules are established. Finally, the appeal to general rules underscores the ultimate non-moral basis of morality in that general rules are frequently generalizations based upon past non-moral experience.

CHAPTER SIX

SYMPATHY IN THE MORAL THEORY OF THE TREATISE

The Moral Function of Sympathy

In the previous chapters, we have arrived at the following conclusions concerning Hume's moral theory.

1. There is a clear distinction in Hume's moral theory between a moral sentiment and a moral judgment.

2. The moral judgment, when propositional, is a report about the existence of a moral sentiment under a specific set of circumstances. Moral judgments are intersubjective matter of fact judgments. We may therefore eliminate all purely subjectivist interpretations of Hume's theory of moral judgment.

3. Morality is not an autonomous subject matter. That is, moral sentiments are not different in kind from non-moral sentiments. Hence we may dismiss all "deontologized" moral sense interpretations of Hume.

4. If (3) is true, then moral sentiments may be described in non-moral terms.

5. If (4) is true, then we may infer moral judgments, which report the presence of moral sentiments, from other, non-

moral, judgments. Moral judgments are a sub-class of matter of fact judgments.

6. Moral sentiments are moral because they are felt under a
certain set of conditions. Therefore, Hume must provide
some explanation of how our ordinary sentiments may be
brought under those conditions.

7. Those conditions include reference to a general perspective, or general rules, and the ability to produce the indirect
passions.

8. The key condition for the production of a moral sentiment
is that such sentiments must be based upon certain beliefs
about the consequences of the actions performed by human beings. That is, as Hume so often stressed, our sentiments are produced in these cases by our beliefs, i.e. our inferences about what will follow from certain kinds of human action. Hume never confused the beliefs about the
consequences with the sentiment that is produced by such
beliefs.

9. Thus, there must be a process which:
    a. begins with an inference about the consequences of
       human action,
    b. and leads to a conclusion about the existence of a moral
       sentiment,
    c. as well as actually producing the moral sentiment.

10. (9a) is a matter of fact.

11. (9b) is an inference from one fact (which is non-moral) to a
    second fact (which is moral).

12. (9c) is analogous to believing the inference and at the same
    time confirms the truth of the inference by producing the
    sentiment referred to in the judgment.

13. *Sympathy is the psychological process that Hume introduced precisely in order to account for the conversion of non-moral characteristics into peculiarly moral sentiments. The importance of sympathy is that it involves, as part of the conversion, a form of inference from the presence of non-moral characteristics to the existence of moral sentiments.*

Moral Motivation

In order to understand Hume's discussion of moral motivation we must distinguish three issues. The first issue is logical, namely, what is the status of moral motivation? In order to answer this question we must recall that moral distinctions are not 'objective', i.e. moral distinctions do not refer to states of affairs totally independent of human beings. If moral distinctions are not 'objective' in the foregoing sense then moral motivation cannot be 'objective' in the same sense. This follows from Hume's contention that there must be a direct connection between the apprehension of moral distinctions and our moral motivation. Moral distinctions arise in part from human artifice. Hence, moral motivation must arise in part from human artifice. There are two other terminological ways of making this same point in Hume. To say that moral motivation is not 'objective' is to say that it is not 'natural' where 'natural' means to exist independent of human artifice. To say that moral motivation is not 'objective' is also to say that it is not 'original' where 'original' means having an origin totally independent of human artifice. When, therefore, Hume says that our original motives cannot be moral he is making the logical point that moral motivation, like moral distinctions, arise in part from human artifice.

The second issue is empirical, namely, what is the original non-moral basis of moral motivation and what is the process by which the original non-moral motive or basis of motivation is turned by human artifice into moral motivation? Recall that in the previous paragraph we pointed out that there is no original moral motive in the ontological sense that there is no foundation totally independent of human artifice for moral distinctions and motives, and keep in mind the fact that from the time we are children we must be taught to make moral distinctions and encouraged to act on the basis of our moral motives. Hume proposed to answer the empirical question by asking what in human nature makes possible the development of moral motivation. His answer in the *Treatise* is that sympathy is the process which makes this possible. Sympathy is a 'natural' psychological process present in all human beings according to Hume, and it is present even in non-moral dimensions of our experience.

Since sympathy is a 'natural' psychological process, by Hume's own account we are bound to ask if this does not contradict Hume's contention that moral motivation is not original or natural. Hume was the first to complain and admit that the natural vs. artificial distinction was misleading. "We readily forget, that the designs, and projects, and views of men are principles as necessary in their operation as heat and cold, moist and dry" (*Treatise*, p. 474). Clearly there is a moral dimension to human experience. Clearly in one sense there is a natural origin to moral motivation. It is important to recall Hume's critique of Hobbes and those who reduced everything to artifice. On the other hand, Hume went out of his way to stress not only the natural origin but the role of artifice. It is the presence of human artifice in the form of general rules and the human social perspective which rules out a totally 'objective' account. *Hume made clear that he accepted the 'naturalness' of human social convention, although he did not confuse this with an ontological structure independent of human beings.* We must keep in mind that Hume was arguing against those who tried to construe moral apprehension and motivation as a totally 'objective' affair. It would be highly misleading to confuse this with contemporary efforts on the part of some moral theorists to divorce totally the moral realm from the natural realm of fact.

The third issue is practical, namely, how does human artifice enter into the natural psychological process of sympathy? Put very crudely, how do we teach or inculcate moral motivation? The wrong answer to this question according to Hume and the wrong answer therefore to attribute to Hume is that private self-interest finds it convenient to accept the public or social interest. This wrong answer, the Hobbesian answer so to speak, fails to grasp the moral dimension to human experience. In writing the *Treatise*, Hume thought that the sympathy mechanism not only made possible the adoption of the social perspective, something we stressed in the last chapter, but that sympathy made possible our desire to adopt that perspective. As we shall see in this chapter, when Hume worked through his account of sympathy he came to realize that sympathy is a necessary but not a sufficient condition for the adoption of a social perspective. When he wrote *An Enquiry Concerning Human Understanding*, Hume came to admit that sympathy could only make possible the adoption of the social perspective of human artifice but that some kind of benevolence is necessary to explain our desire to adopt that perspective. These later emendations in no way alter Hume's contention that the 'original' motive is not moral nor is anything in his theory of moral judgment undermined. On the contrary, we shall show that these emendations strengthen the claims we have already made on behalf of Hume's theory.

The Non-moral Basis of Morality

We have just summarized the argument of this chapter and the last two chapters. Let us return now to the presentation of Hume's views in the *Treatise*. If there are no original moral sentiments and if moral sentiments motivate us by producing the indirect passions, then there are no original moral motives. This is the point behind Hume's remark that "the first virtuous motive, which bestows a merit on any action, can never be a regard to the virtue of that action, but must be some other natural motive or principle" (*Treatise*, p. 478). As a consequence, "*no action can be virtuous, or morally good, unless there be in human nature some motive to produce it, distinct from the sense of its morality"* (*Treatise*, p. 479).

Although Hume insisted that original motives are non-moral, he also insisted that the sense of duty may be a motive.

> But may not the sense of morality or duty produce an action, without any other motive? I answer, It may...But tho', on some occasions, a person may perform an action merely out of regard to its moral obligation, yet still this supposes in human nature some distinct principles, which are capable of producing the action... (*Treatise*, p. 479)

Hume's own theory of morals is guided by the belief that morality has a great "influence on human passions and action" (*Treatise*, p. 457).

> ...common experience...informs us, that men are often govern'd by their duties, and are deter'd from some actions by the opinion of injustice, and impell'd to others by that of obligation. (*Ibid.*)

Since the sense of duty is the motive for virtuous conduct in the case of the artificial virtues[1] in a mature individual, and as we have no original motives impelling us to duty, *Hume must account for two things: the original motive for virtuous conduct and the conversion of that original motive into the sense of duty.* The original motive for virtuous conduct will turn out to be the natural functioning of the passions. The conversion of the original motive into the sense of duty is accomplished by means of sympathy.

Hume had earlier raised the question, "whether these moral distinctions be founded on natural and original principles, or arise from interest and education" (*Treatise*, p. 295). He immediately showed a preference for the former possibility.

> The most probable hypothesis, which has been advanc'd to explain the distinction betwixt vice and virtue...is, that from a primary constitution of nature certain characters and passions, by the very view and contemplation, produce a pain, and others in like manner excite a pleasure. (*Treatise*, p. 296)

Although admitting that education and public praise and blame bestowed by politicians and others can increase our sense of virtue, Hume denied that such artifice by itself was sufficient.

> Nothing can be more evident, than that the matter has been carry'd too far by certain writers on morals, who seem to have employ'd their utmost effort to extirpate all sense of virtue from among mankind. Any artifice of politicians may assist nature in the producing of those sentiments, which she suggests to us, and may even on some occasions, produce alone an approbation or esteem for any particular action; but 'tis impossible it should be the sole cause of the distinction we make betwixt vice and virtue. For if nature did not aid us in this particular, 'twou'd be in vain for politicians to talk of *honourable* or *dishonourable, praiseworthy* or *blame-able*. These words wou'd be perfectly unintelligible, and wou'd no more have any idea annex'd to them, than if they were of a tongue perfectly unknown to us. The utmost politicians can perform, is, to extend the natural sentiments beyond their original bounds; but still nature must furnish the materials, and give us some notion of moral distinctions. (*Treatise*, p. 500)

Exactly the same point is repeated in the discussion of justice in Part III (*Treatise*, pp. 578-79). In the conclusion to Book III, Hume reminded us that no artifice or artificial system by itself can produce a moral sentiment.

> 'Tis the combination of men, in a system of conduct, which renders any act of justice beneficial to society. But when once it has that tendency we *naturally* approve of it; and if we did not so, 'tis impossible any combination or convention cou'd ever produce that sentiment. (*Treatise*, pp. 619-20)

In his analysis "Of the obligation of promises," Hume repeated what he said about the other artificial virtues. Although the first obligation to perform promises is interest, a moral obligation is attached to the performance in the same way, that is, through sympathy. "This sentiment of morality, in the performance of promises, arises from the same principles as that of the abstinence from the property of others" (*Treatise*, p. 523). Again,

Hume pointed out that when moral words in general, or the concept of a promise in particular, are viewed as referring to a special mental act in abstraction from our sentiments, the words can have no meaning. "We cannot readily conceive how the making use of a certain form of words shou'd be able to cause any material difference" (*Treatise*, p. 523). We cannot change our sentiments at will.

> But 'tis certain we can naturally no more change our own sentiments, than the motions of the heavens; nor by a single act of our will, that is, by a promise, render any action agreeable or disagreeable, moral or immoral; which, without that act, wou'd have produc'd contrary impressions, or have been endow'd with different qualities. (*Treatise*, p. 517)

One misunderstanding must be avoided. Hume's admission of a "natural sentiment of approbation and blame" (*Treatise*, p. 579) is not an admission of basic moral instincts, nor does it contradict his belief that morality has a non-moral basis. We have a natural inclination to approve and to disapprove, that is, to feel satisfaction and uneasiness. Our natural sentiments do not become moral until felt under a certain set of conditions, namely the socially objective perspective. That perspective is accounted for through sympathy, but sympathy is itself a natural and non-moral process.

Given that there are no original moral motives, we must find the original non-moral motives which serve as the foundation for the important artificial virtues. Hume considers three candidates: self-interest, private benevolence, and public benevolence. Hume rejected the notion that self-interest could always be the original non-moral motive, although this does not mean that self-interest cannot sometimes be such a motive. Self-interest when it acts at its liberty, instead of engaging us to honest actions, is the source of all injustice. At the same time, following Butler's lead, Hume stressed the extent to which selfishness in human beings had been exaggerated and misrepresented.

I am sensible, that, generally speaking, the representations of this quality have been carried too far; and that the descriptions, which certain philosophers delight so much to form of mankind in this particular, are as wide of nature as any accounts of monsters, which we meet in fables and romances. So far from thinking, that men have no affection for any thing beyond themselves, I am of opinion, that tho' it be rare to meet with one, who loves any single person better than himself; yet 'tis as rare to meet with one, in whom all the kind affections, taken together, do not over-balance all the selfish. (*Treatise*, pp. 486-87).

Since Hume recognized the important role of limited or private benevolence, i.e. benevolence to one's friends and family, it is natural to suppose that private benevolence might be the original non-moral motive. Hume, however, rejected as well the notion that private benevolence could always be the original non-moral motive, but again we must caution the reader that this does not exclude private benevolence from sometimes being the original non-moral motive. He gave two reasons for why "*private benevolence, or a regard to the interests of the party concern'd*" "cannot be the original motive to justice" (*Treatise*, p. 482). First, just acts do not always serve the interest of those who are the objects of private benevolence. For example, repaying a loan to a "profligate debauchee" because of private benevolence is self-defeating if the repayment causes more harm than benefit. Second, private benevolence often conflicts with the requirements of justice.

This we may observe in our common judgments concerning actions, where we blame a person, who either centers all his affections in his family, or is so regardless of them, as, in any opposition of interest, to give the preference to a stranger, or mere chance acquaintance. From all which it follows, that our natural uncultivated ideas of morality, instead of providing a remedy for the partiality of our affections, do rather conform themselves to that partiality, and give it an additional force and influence. (*Treatise*, pp. 488-89)

Since our intuitive conception of morality presupposes some sort of concern for others, and since private benevolence has been eliminated, it seems as if public benevolence may be the original non-moral motive to justice. Nevertheless, Hume found public or extended benevolence to fail for three reasons to be the sought after motive. First, honest or just action is expected in cases where public benevolence is not directly involved (*Treatise*, pp. 480-81). Second, public benevolence is "a motive too remote and too sublime to affect the generality of mankind" (*Treatise*, p. 481).

The third reason for eliminating public benevolence is that "there is no such passion in human minds, as the love of mankind, merely as such, independent of personal qualities, of services, or of relation to ourself" (*Treatise*, p. 481). The point behind Hume's qualifications about personal qualities and relationship to ourself is that love and hatred are indirect passions which require "a double relation of impressions and ideas" in order to be exerted (*Treatise*, p. 482). To be sure, we are concerned with human welfare, we are even concerned with beings who are not members of our own species, but that concern says Hume results from sympathy (*Treatise*, p. 481). Human beings in general are the objects of love and hatred but not the causes of these passions (*Treatise*, pp. 481-82). *Hume's argument is that public benevolence is the effect of the artificial establishment of justice but not its cause.* The foregoing objection to public benevolence, by referring to the double association of ideas and impressions and by noting the indirect passions, is paving the way for sympathy.

The difference between extended or public benevolence, which is benevolence to those who are neither family members nor friends, and disinterestedness which is the perspective of concern for institutional or social interest and therefore the criterion of what is moral, is an important difference. Public benevolence is not necessarily moral because we might be concerned for the interests of strangers in a way which conflicts with either private obligations or which conflicts with social interest. Extended benevolence could be the original non-moral motive if it existed naturally, something which Hume denies, and if it were corrected through general rules to reflect the social interest. In fact, if extended benevolence existed and if the "bounty of nature" permitted the satisfaction of all our desires, we would not need the rules of justice. Hume concluded "*that 'tis only from the selfishness and confin'd generosity of men, along with the scanty provision nature has made for his wants, that justice derives its origin*" (*Treatise*, p. 495).

The original non-moral motive for the artificial virtue of justice is both self-interest *and* limited benevolence. As Hume's analysis unfolds, we shall see that sometimes self-interest is the original non-moral motive, sometimes limited benevolence is the original non-moral motive, and sometimes a combination of the two serve as the original non-moral motive. It would be highly misleading to select only those contexts in which Hume says that self-interest is the original non-moral motive and then to argue that Hume tried to generate morality out of self-interest.[2] Hume's conception of the self in the *Treatise* is not egoistic. On the contrary, the self is frequently benevolent, though benevolence is restricted to family and friends. Thus, the problem for Hume is not how to make the self benevolent, but to explain how a self of limited benevolence is made into a socially-oriented self. Hume must show how men come to accept social responsibility, aims, obligations and the social perspective on moral grounds, that is, with a motive of public-mindedness. In one sense, Hume's problem could be formulated entirely in terms of the conflict between confined benevolence and the disinterested perspective. The formulation need not be, and in Hume is not, made in terms of egoism versus benevolence: "...we may easily remove any contradiction, which may appear to be betwixt the *extensive sympathy*, on which our sentiments of virtue depend, and that *limited generosity* which I have frequently observ'd to be natural to men" (*Treatise*, p. 586).

Having shown why there can be no original moral motives, and having shown that self-interest and limited benevolence are the original non-moral motives for the artificial virtues, Hume then showed how sympathy could account for the transition from the non-moral motives to a moral one. In order to show that transition, we must recall what Hume means by a moral motive as well as his distinction between a natural and a moral obligation.

We are motivated in one of two ways, either when a course of action is pleasing or when the omission of an action would displease us. In the former case we are directly motivated by a passion which seeks to be satisfied. In the latter case we have no direct inclination, but we perform the action because if we do not we shall be displeased. In this case the motivation is said to involve a natural obligation. Moral motivation follows the same general pattern. Actions which please us, the virtues, may motivate us without considerations of obligation. On the other hand, we may be motivated by the anticipated displeasure of non-performance, that is, by moral obligation.

> All morality depends upon our sentiments; and when any action, or quality of the mind, pleases us *after a certain manner*, we say it is virtuous; and when the neglect, or non-performance of it, displeases us *after a like manner*, we say that we lie under an obligation to perform it. (*Treatise*, p. 517)

The manner which makes the sentiment moral is disinterested. Moral motivation cannot be self-interested, or interested in terms of limited benevolence. Moral motivation must be disinterested. To be disinterested does not mean to be uninterested, rather it means that our perspective is that of the social or public interest.

Since Hume found moral motivation to be disinterested, he faced two problems. The first problem is that if the artificial virtues are not themselves original passions or basic inclinations, then we can be motivated by them only if they are indirectly pleasing. The artificial virtues depend upon basic non-moral inclinations or the "designs, and projects, and views of men" along with causal judgments as to the best means of satisfying those inclinations. it is quite possible for someone to construe the pleasure of "artificial virtue" as only the pleasure of self-interest or limited benevolence. Hume must show that the pleasure of virtue can be disinterested if it is to be moral.

The second problem is that since there are no sufficient natural passions of extended benevolence, there is no naturally disinterested passion. Therefore, there can be no original moral obligation, no original moral feeling of displeasure at omission. Hume must show that we can feel disinterested displeasure if we are to have a sense of duty or of moral obligation. This problem is best seen in the example of a promise.

> No action can be requir'd of us as our duty, unless there be implanted in human nature some actuating passion or motive, capable of producing the action. This motive cannot be the sense of duty. A sense of duty supposes an antecedent obligation; And where an action is not requir'd by any natural passion, it cannot be requir'd by any natural obligation; since it may be omitted without proving any defect or imperfection in the mind and temper, and consequently without any vice. Now 'tis evident we have no motive leading us to the performance of promises, distinct from a sense of duty. If we thought, that promises had no moral obligation, we never shou'd feel any inclination to observe them. This is not the case with the natural virtues. Tho' there was no obligation to relieve the miserable, our humanity wou'd lead us to it; and when we omit that duty the immorality of the omission arises from its being a proof, that we want the natural sentiments of humanity....there is naturally no inclination to observe promises, distinct from a sense of their obligation...
> (*Treatise*, pp. 518-19)

The second problem may also be stated in terms of the question, why should we inconvenience ourselves where we have no natural inclination to perform an act? Hume faced this problem because he had excluded the sense of duty, as it concerns the artificial virtues, from the realm of the naturally virtuous inclinations or motives. Even if we can show that there are interests to be served by the artificial virtues the interest need not be moral. Neither can the obligation be moral without disinterestedness. Why should we be displeased with the omission of an artificial virtue, especially our own omission?

Hume's answer was that sympathy not only motivated us to perform the artificial virtues in a disinterested manner, but sympathy also made us feel displeasure with omission. Moral obligation in the case of the artificial virtues depends upon sympathy.

Our concern for performing disinterested actions for which we have no direct inclination is supposed to be effected through sympathy. Sympathy is to provide us with the moral obligation for the artificial virtues. In the course of time we come to reflect upon the consequences of such actions, originally motivated by self interest and limited benevolence, and the sentiment we feel is the sense of duty. "Afterwards a sentiment of morals concurs with interest, and becomes a new obligation upon mankind" (*Treatise*, p. 523). It is sympathy, therefore, that accounts for the transition from non-moral to moral motivation.

Sympathy and the Artificial Virtues and Vices

For Hume, the general problem of moral theory is to answer the question "*why any action or sentiment upon the general view or survey, gives a certain satisfaction or uneasiness*" (*Treatise*, p. 475). Is it possible that actions which produce feelings of satisfaction or uneasiness have nothing in common? Hume, in the Newtonian spirit of *simplicity*, rejected this possibility.

> ...'tis absurd to imagine, that in every particular instance, these sentiments are produc'd by an *original* quality and *primary* constitution. For as the number of our duties is, in a manner, infinite, 'tis impossible that our original instincts should extend to each of them, and from our very first infancy impress on the human mind all that multitude of precepts, which are contain'd in the compleatest system of ethics. Such a method of proceeding is not conformable to the usual maxims, by which nature is conducted, where a few principles produce all that variety we observe in the universe, and every thing is carry'd on in the easiest and most simple manner. 'Tis necessary, therefore, to abridge these primary impulses, and find some more general principles, upon which all our notions of morals are founded. (*Treatise*, p. 473)

The specific problem posed for Hume's moral theory is the nature of the general principle or principles which makes us feel moral satisfaction and uneasiness.

If there is a general principle of morals, it must account for two distinguishing properties of moral sentiments: disinterestedness and the production of the indirect passions. A clue to the general principle of morals has already been found in the fact that sympathy is a cause of the indirect passions. Hence, sympathy qualifies as a candidate for the general principle of morals.

In sympathy, the pleasures and the pains of others are communicated to us. It is through sympathy that we become aware of interests which are not our own. Thus, sympathy satisfies the second required property of the general principle of morals, disinterestedness or public-mindedness. The determination of good and evil follows the production of a feeling either of satisfaction or uneasiness, but the feeling cannot be personal.

> We are quickly oblig'd to forget our own interests in our judgments of this kind, by reason of the perpetual contradictions, we meet with in society and conversation, from persons that are not plac'd in the same situation, and have not the same interest with ourselves. The only point of view, in which our sentiments concur with those of others, is, when we consider the tendency of any passion to the advantage or harm of those, who have any immediate connexion or intercourse with the person possess'd of it. And tho' this advantage or harm be often very remote from ourselves, yet sometimes 'tis very near us, and interests us strongly by sympathy. (*Treatise* pp. 602-03)

Sympathy is the general principle of morals precisely because it can account for both disinterestedness and the indirect passions.

Hume defended a middle position between those, on the one hand, like Hobbes and Mandeville, who had argued for a totally artificial basis for morality in interest and education and those, on the other hand, like the sentimentalists such as Shaftesbury, Butler, and Hutcheson, who had argued for natural and original principles. Hume believed that there was something correct about both of these positions, although he insisted that natural and original principles had to be basic in order for education to be grafted upon it. Where those who advocate natural principles go wrong is in ignoring that even natural principles must be corrected to bring them into line with the social perspective, and hence the ever present need for artifice. The value of sympathy is that it is at once a natural, but non-moral, process that accounts for the adoption of the social perspective. Hume's theory of sympathy thus neatly solves one of the major controversies of moral theory in his day. Hume's way of bringing out this point is to divide the virtues into the artificial, which clearly require reference to interest and education, and the natural, which do not. Hume then goes on to show that both kinds of virtue require sympathy in order to give a complete and comprehensive account. This is the point of the division in the *Treatise* between Parts II and III of Book III.[3]

The artificial virtues include justice, allegiance, the laws of nations, modesty, and good manners. They are artificial virtues because they "produce pleasure and approbation by means of an artifice or contrivance, which arises from the circumstances and necessities of mankind" (*Treatise*, p. 477). Justice is the artificial virtue Hume examined in greatest detail. He established three important points about justice. First, "a regard to public interest, or a strong extensive benevolence, is not our first and original motive for the observation of the rules of justice" (*Treatise*, pp. 495-96). Second, Hume reaffirmed his conviction that "the sense of justice, therefore, is not founded on our ideas, but on our impressions" (*Treatise*, p. 496). Third, "*those impressions, which give rise to this sense of justice, are not natural to the mind of man, but arise from artifice and human conventions*" (*Ibid.*). The natural obligation to justice is self-interest and limited benevolence, that is, the natural obligation is non-moral.

In the course of time, a moral obligation, a sentiment of right and wrong, is attached to the observance of the rules of justice. We are especially sensitive to the infractions of the rules of justice that are committed by others and that are prejudicial to our personal interests.

> But tho' in our own actions we may frequently lose sight of that interest, which we have in maintaining order, and may follow a lesser and more present interest, we never fail to observe the prejudice we receive, either mediately or immediately, from the injustice of others... (*Treatise*, p. 499)

Later we begin to feel the unjust consequences of actions that influence others. It is through sympathy that we come to feel the pleasure and pain of others.

> Nay when the injustice is so distant from us, as no way to affect our interest, it still displeases us; because we consider it as prejudicial to human society, and pernicious to every one that approaches the person guilty of it. We partake of their uneasiness by *sympathy*...this is the reason why the sense of moral good and evil follows upon justice and injustice. (*Ibid.*)

Finally, we extend the moral sense of justice or injustice to our own actions by means of general rules.

After the establishment of justice as a virtue attended by moral approbation, it is possible for politicians and educators to reinforce the observance of the rules of justice.

> Tho' this progress of the sentiments be *natural*, and even necessary, 'tis certain, that it is here forwarded by the artifice of politicians, who, in order to govern men more easily, and preserve peace in human society, have endeavour'd to produce an esteem for justice, and an abhorrence of injustice....As publick praise and blame increases our esteem for justice; so private education and instruction contribute to the same effect. (*Treatise*, p. 500)

An additional motive is also provided by "the interest of our reputation" (*Treatise*, p. 501). It should be recalled that sympathy was first invoked by Hume to explain how "our reputation, our character, our name" caused the passions of pride and humility (*Treatise*, p. 316).

Sympathy is the general principle that accounts for the approbation of all of the artificial virtues. The artificial virtues have a "tendency" to the social good. They are means to an end, the end being the social welfare.

> Now as the means to an end can only be agreeable, where the end is agreeable; and as the good of society, where our own interest is not concern'd, or that of our friends, pleases only by sympathy: It follows, that sympathy is the source of the esteem, which we pay to all the artificial virtues. (*Treatise*, p. 577)

Sympathy thus accounts for disinterestedness and for the production of the indirect passions so essential to virtue and vice.

Prior to his entering into a discussion of the other virtues and vices, Hume recalled his discussion of the sympathy mechanism.

> We may begin with considering a-new the nature and force of sympathy. The minds of all men are similar in their feelings and operations, nor can any one be actuated by any affection, of which all others are not, in some degree, susceptible. As in strings wound up, the motion of one communicates itself to the rest; so all the affections readily pass from one person to another, and beget correspondent movements in every human creature. When I see the *effects* of passion in the voice and gesture of any person, my mind immediately passes from these effects to their causes, and forms such a lively idea of the passion, as is presently converted into the passion itself. In like manner, when I perceive the *causes* of any emotion, my mind is convey'd to the effects, and is actuated with a like emotion....No passion of another discovers itself immediately to the mind. We are only sensible of its causes or effects. From *these* we infer the passion: And consequently *these* give rise to our sympathy. (*Treatise*, pp. 575-76)

Nor must we forget the systematic importance of sympathy, its role in explaining a wide variety of phenomena. "Thus it appears, *that* sympathy is a very powerful principle in human nature, *that* it has a great influence on our taste of beauty, and *that* it produces our sentiment of morals in all the artificial virtues" (*Ibid.*).

Sympathy and the Natural Virtues and Vices

If sympathy is to serve as the general principle of morals, it must explain the natural virtues as well as the artificial ones. Hume asserted that the approbation of the natural virtues, and the disapprobation of the natural vices, was explicable in terms of the mechanism of sympathy without appeal to any other principle (*Treatise*, p. 578). In discussing the natural social virtues such as "meekness, beneficence, charity, generosity, clemency, moderation, equity" (*Ibid.*), the only difference which Hume notes between these virtues and the artificial virtues is that the former are immediately advantageous to some part of society, "whereas a single act of justice, consider'd in itself, may often be contrary to the public good; and 'tis only the concurrence of mankind, in a general scheme or system of action, which is advantageous" (*Treatise*, p. 579). Even though the imagination is more affected by the particular than by the general (*Treatise*, p. 580), the explanation of both sets of virtues remains the same, namely, sympathy with anything having a tendency to a larger social good.

Hume considered a third group of virtues that are valuable only to the possessor, "prudence, temperance, frugality, industry, assiduity, enterprize, dexterity" (*Treatise*, p. 587), and he concluded that sympathy is the general principle which explains even their approbation.

In this case, the qualities that please me are all consider'd as useful to the person, and as having a tendency to promote his interest and satisfaction. They are only regarded as means to an end, and please me in proportion to their fitness for that end. The end, therefore, must be agreeable to me. But what makes the end agreeable? The person is a stranger: I am no way interested in him, nor lie under any obligation to him: His happiness concerns not me, farther than the happiness of every human, and indeed of every sensible creature: That is, it affects me only by sympathy. From that principle, whenever I discover his happiness and good, whether in its causes or effects, I enter so deeply into it, that it gives me a sensible emotion. The appearance of qualities, that have a *tendency* to promote it, have an agreeable effect upon my imagination, and command my love and esteem. (*Treatise*, p. 588-89)

There is one group of natural virtues, or mental qualities, that is not explicable in terms of sympathy alone. This group has two subcategories: those virtues which are immediately agreeable to their possessor; and those virtues which are immediately agreeable to someone other than the possessor and without consideration of their effect on the public good. Among the former is love (*Treatise*, p. 604). Among the latter is wit (*Treatise*, p. 590). Hume maintains, however, that in both cases we still find considerable dependence upon the principle of sympathy (*Ibid.*).

In summation, we may say that sympathy is the general principle of morals because it is the chief source of moral distinctions or sentiments (*Treatise*, p. 618). Sympathy explains the approbation of justice and the other artificial virtues. The approbation of the natural virtues is also explained through sympathy but with more qualifications.

> Every quality of the mind is denominated virtuous, which gives pleasure by the mere survey; as every quality, which produces pain, is call'd vicious. This pleasure and this pain may arise from four different sources. For we reap a pleasure from the view of a character, which is naturally fitted to be useful to others, or to the person himself, or which is agreeable to others, or to the person himself. (*Treatise*, p. 591)

Nevertheless, our approval of anything having a "tendency" to the good of other people and society is due to the mechanism of sympathy. "We may presume the like with regard to all the other virtues, which have a like tendency to the public good. They must derive all their merit from our sympathy with those, who reap any advantage from them..." (*Treatise*, p. 618).

Sympathy in the Moral Theory of the Treatise
Judgment and Sentiment in Hume's Theory of Sympathy

Hume's conception of moral judgment is that such judgments describe actions or characters by attributing moral qualities to those actions or characters. Such judgments are empirically confirmable in that other observers or agents who regard the action or character likewise feel a moral sentiment. The moral sentiment generally is felt under two different sets of circumstances: either when the action or character produces an immediate feeling of pleasure or pain, or when the action or character has a tendency to produce a feeling of pleasure or pain. The moral sentiment also produces the indirect passions of pride or humility, love or hatred. Moral judgments must be made under standard conditions if they are to be verifiable, where the standard conditions involve a social perspective in the case of the artificial virtues and vices and an impersonal or social perspective in the case of the natural virtues and vices. The principle that accounts for all of these factors, according to Hume, is sympathy. Thus Hume's account of moral judgment as descriptive and his view of moral sentiments as productive of the indirect passions necessitates a general principle of morals which can account both for intersubjective verifiability and the production of the indirect passions. Hume found that general principle in the mechanism of sympathy.

> One may, perhaps, be surpriz'd, that amidst all these interests and pleasures, we shou'd forget our own....'tis impossible men cou'd ever agree in their sentiments and judgments, unless they chose some common point of view, from which they might survey their object, and which might cause it to appear the same to all of them. Now, in judging of characters, the only interest or pleasure, which appears the same to every spectator, is that of the person himself, whose character is examin'd; or that of persons, who have a connexion with him. And tho' such interests and pleasures touch us more faintly than our own, yet being more constant and universal, they counter-balance the latter even in practice, and are alone admitted in speculation as the standard of virtue and morality. They

215

alone produce that particular feeling or sentiment, on which moral distinctions depend. (*Treatise*, p. 591)

In his endeavor to give a complete and comprehensive analysis adequate to explain all of the factors involved, especially the intersubjectivity of a moral judgment and the capacity of a moral sentiment to produce an indirect passion, Hume was led to give three different accounts of judgment and sentiment in the theory of sympathy, accounts which are sometimes at variance. Before discussing these three variant accounts of sympathy, I want to reiterate my contention that Hume's problems in the various accounts of sympathy arose precisely because he viewed moral judgments as descriptive and as involving an objective (intersubjective) perspective.

The *first variant view of sympathy* is the one we have stressed. The role of sympathy in this variant is twofold: it accounts for both social objectivity and the capacity of moral sentiments to produce the indirect passions. This theory is exemplified by, and is wholly confined to, Hume's discussion of the artificial virtues in general and of justice in particular.

The approval of justice is a function of "sympathy with public interest" (*Treatise*, pp. 499-500). What did Hume mean by the 'public interest'? When he summarized his view of justice at the beginning of Part III of Book III of the *Treatise* he went on to speak of the "good of society" (*Treatise*, pp. 577-78) and the "good of mankind" (*Treatise*, p. 578). Sympathy with the public interest is a sympathy with other persons, "with those, who reap any advantage from them" (*Treatise*, p. 618), not a sympathy with some hypostatized abstraction.

...moral distinctions arise, in a great measure, from the tendency of qualities and characters to the interest of society, and that 'tis our concern for that interest, which makes us approve or disapprove of them. Now we have no such extensive concern for society but from sympathy; and consequently 'tis that principle, which takes us far out of ourselves, as to give us the same pleasure or uneasiness in the characters of others, as if they had a tendency to our own advantage or loss. (*Treatise*, p. 579)

216

Sympathy with the "public good" is the same as sympathy with any person who profits from a virtue having a tendency to his own good, as "the virtues, which have a tendency to the good of the person possess'd of them, derive their merit from our sympathy with him" (*Treatise*, p. 618).

Besides accounting for social objectivity in the foregoing sense, sympathy is productive of the indirect passions of pride and humility or love and hatred. In addition, in the first variant account of sympathy general rules allow us to make moral judgments about our own personal action.

> And tho' this sense, in the present case, be deriv'd only from contemplating the actions of others, yet we fail not to extend it even to our own actions. The *general rule* reaches beyond those instances, from which it arose. (*Treatise*, p. 499)

The foregoing application of general rules seems perfectly plausible. We may recall the original description of the sympathy mechanism in which a quality of a situation often accompanies an emotion. In the present case, the quality of the situation is our own behavior that has a tendency to produce pleasure or pain in others. We partake of that pleasure or pain by means of sympathy. That is, we easily sympathize with those affected and adjust our action accordingly.

There is no moral judgment without a moral distinction or sentiment. The creation of a moral sentiment in the case of the artificial virtues is the product of time and social acculturation. "*Thus Self-interest is the original motive to the* establishment *of justice: but a* sympathy *with public interest is the source of the* moral approbation, *which attends that virtue*" (*Treatise*, pp. 499-500). Hume thus distinguished the 'natural obligation' or interest from the "*moral* obligation, or sentiment of right and wrong" (*Treatise*, p. 498). Sympathy accounted for the moral obligation.

In response to an objection to his theory of approbation, Hume introduced a *second variant account of sympathy*. The objection in question occurs in the discussion of the natural virtues and vices. It is generally acknowledged that a man may be considered virtuous even though he is prevented by circumstances from performing virtuous acts. "Virtue in rags is still virtue" (*Treatise*, p. 584). Sympathy permits us to feel the satisfaction or uneasiness of those affected by the virtue or vice of any action. If the virtue or vice does not take place, so the objection goes, and therefore produces no satisfaction or uneasiness, we cannot sympathize. Consequently, it would appear that we cannot call virtuous the person who is prevented from acting.

> Now this may be esteem'd an objection to the present system. Sympathy interests us in the good of mankind; and if sympathy were the source of our esteem for virtue, that sentiment of approbation cou'd only take place, where the virtue actually attain'd its end, and was beneficial to mankind. There it fails of its end, 'tis only an imperfect means; and therefore can never acquire any merit from that end. The goodness of an end can bestow a merit on such means alone as are compleat, and actually produce the end. (*Treatise*, p. 584)

Hume met this objection by invoking a legitimate use of general rules, that is, by appealing to the uniformity of experience and to a superiority of positive over negative instances.

> Where a character is, in every respect, fitted to be beneficial to society, the imagination passes easily from the cause to the effect, without considering that there are still some circumstances wanting to render the cause a compleat one. *General rules* create a species of probability, which sometimes influences the judgment, and always the imagination. (*Treatise*, p. 585)

Hume's answer is completely in keeping with the original description of the sympathy mechanism. In the original description general rules were said to produce a form of sympathy in cases where there is a quality of a situation that normally causes an emotion. Our idea of virtue will be produced when the observer contemplates that quality, even in the absence of the emotion, as long as the quality is the normal accompaniment or cause of the emotion. Finally, since Hume stated that we never directly inspect the emotion but simply infer it from the context of countenance or conversation or from the presence of a special set of circumstances, it is not necessary for the emotion actually to exist. Therefore, general rules permit us to be sympathetic even when a person is prevented "from being serviceable to his friends and country" (*Treatise*, p. 584).

What is most interesting in Hume's reply is the reference to the way in which he discusses the relation of imagination to the general view or to general rules. "The imagination adheres to the *general* views of things, and distinguishes betwixt the feelings they produce, from those which arise from our particular and momentary situation" (*Treatise*, p. 587). General rules, in this second variant account of sympathy, seem to create a weaker and somewhat different kind of sentiment. It is more an imagining of what the feeling would be like than an actual feeling. In the original description of the sympathy mechanism the general rules created a real and identical impression as if the emotion were there.

In the second variant account of sympathy, the general perspective is created by general rules. A moral judgment depends upon how general rules influence the imagination.

> Upon these principles we may easily remove any contradiction, which may appear to be betwixt the *extensive sympathy*, on which our sentiments of virtue depend, and that *limited generosity* which I have frequently observ'd to be natural to men....My sympathy with another may give me the sentiment of pain and disapprobation, when any object is presented, that has a tendency to give him uneasiness; tho' I may not be willing to sacrifice any thing of my own interest....Sentiments must touch the heart, to make them control our passions: But they need not extend beyond the imagination, to make them influence our taste. (*Treatise*, p. 586)

In this second variant, sympathy is still responsible for the creation of a moral sentiment.

The *seeming tendencies* of objects affect the mind: And the emotions they excite are of a like species with those, which proceed from the *real consequences* of objects, but their feeling is different. (*Ibid.*)

Although we are not impelled to action, there is still a sense in which our imagination can be said to feel a passion as well as a special sentiment.

The imagination has a set of passions belonging to it, upon which our sentiments of beauty much depend. These passions are mov'd by degrees of liveliness and strength, which are inferior to *belief*, and independent of the real existence of their objects. (*Treatise*, p. 585)

The example which Hume gives will clarify his point. If we stand next to the wall of a building which we believe to be tottering and insecure, then we are apt to feel an emotion because of the consequences that we expect to ensue. Not only will we feel an emotion, but we shall be impelled by a passion to move away or flee. The foregoing case is analogous to a moral judgment made where we have an immediate interest at stake. We not only feel the full force of the sentiment, but we are impelled to action. Now, consider a less extreme case. If we stand next to the wall of a building which seems clumsy and tottering to the eye "tho' we be fully assur'd of the solidity of the workmanship" (*Treatise*, p. 586) we feel a sentiment of some kind, *but* we are not impelled to move away. Generalizing from past experience, we know that we would flee if we really were next to a dangerous wall, but we are not really in that position at the present time. The appearance of a tottering quality may produce a sentiment, but the sentiment remains a weak one.[4]

In response to yet another objection, Hume offers a *third variant account of sympathy*. Because sympathy is an admittedly variable process, our moral sentiments receive a subsequent variation. Nevertheless, our moral judgments remain constant.[5] As a result, "we give the same approbation to the same moral qualities in *China* as in *England*" (*Treatise*, p. 581). Since, the objection goes, esteem is constant but sympathy is not, sympathy cannot be the general principle of morals. "The sympathy varies without a variation in our esteem. Our esteem, therefore, proceeds not from sympathy" (*Ibid.*).

Hume responded to this objection by once more employing a legitimate use of general rules. A moral judgment is made from a general perspective, thereby insuring a uniformity of response. "We fix on some *steady* and *general* points of view; and always, in our thoughts, place ourselves in them, whatever may be our present position" (*Treatise*, pp. 581-82). The general point of view specified by Hume is the influence of character and qualities upon those who have an intercourse with any person praised or blamed (*Treatise*, p. 582).

So far, Hume's answer to this objection is similar to his answer to the previous objection, namely, an appeal to general rules. General rules are so effective that, just as in the first or original account of sympathy, we extend them to our own behavior.

> We consider not whether the persons, affected by the qualities, be our acquaintance or strangers, countrymen or foreigners. Nay, we overlook our own interest in those general judgments; and blame not a man for opposing us in any of our pretensions, when his own interest is particularly concern'd. We make allowances for a certain degree of selfishness in men... (*Treatise*, pp. 582-83)

We do not become aware of any difference in this third variant account of sympathy until Hume announces that in the present case the general rules or principles may have no effect on our passions.

> But however the general principle of our blame or praise may be corrected by those other principles, 'tis certain, they are not altogether efficacious, nor do our passions often correspond entirely to the present theory...reason requires such an impartial conduct, but that 'tis seldom we can bring ourselves to it, and that our passions do not readily follow the determination of our judgment. (*Treatise*, p. 583)

In this third variant account of sympathy, the role of creating disinterestedness has been assigned to general rules, but more important is the absence of a sentiment and a passion. "Nor has it such an influence on our love and hatred" (*Treatise*, pp. 583-84). It is difficult to see how this process can be called sympathy[6]. The difference between the second and third variant accounts of sympathy is important. In the second variant account we have a combination of general rules and weak sentiments. In the third variant account we have no sentiment, only general rules insuring uniformity of judgment. We now have no double association, no conversion, and no impression. We have only an idea. This process corresponds to nothing in the original description of the sympathy mechanism. The admission of such a conception of moral judgment would seem to contradict some of the basic conclusions of Hume's moral theory. It is difficult to accept a moral judgment which refers to no sentiment.

The presence of three different accounts of sympathy leads to an ambivalence in the closing sections of Book III of the *Treatise*. On several occasions in the section on the origin of the natural virtues and vices, Hume claimed that moral sentiments are both present and necessary for moral judgments. For the remainder of Book III, Hume seemed resigned to the possibility of there being no sentiments and no passion.

> The intercourse of sentiments, therefore, in society and conversation, makes us form some general inalterable standard, by which we may approve or disapprove of characters and manners. And tho' the *heart* does not always take part with those general notions, or regulate its love and hatred by them, yet are they sufficient for discourse, and serve all our purposes in company, in the pulpit, on the theatre, and in the schools. (*Treatise*, p. 603)

We should note how different this is from the Hume who denied that obligations could be explained without reference to actual sentiments. There is no reason to believe that the same ambiguity noted here in Hume's treatment of the natural virtues and vices could not be extended to the artificial virtues and vices.

222

When Hume initially raised the objection to what we are here calling the third variant account of sympathy his immediate answer was that the objection "must have equal force against every other system, as against that of sympathy" (*Treatise*, p. 581).[7] Nevertheless, Hume nonchalantly passed over his immediate reply and went on to introduce his reference to general rules, as we have already seen. When he came to the conclusion of Book III, where he once more referred to artificial virtues, he once again found himself forced to defend his view by falling back on the immediate answer. "If we compare all these circumstances, we shall not doubt, that sympathy is the chief source of moral distinctions; especially when we reflect, that no objection can be rais'd against this hypothesis in one case, which will not extend to all cases" (*Treatise*, p. 618). All of this seems to indicate that Hume was aware of a difficulty or some difficulty in his accounts of sympathy.

One of the ways in which Hume tried to avoid this difficulty was to assimilate the third variant account of sympathy to the second variant account. That is, Hume frequently speaks of the lack of a moral sentiment as if it were no more than a weak sentiment. "Our sympathy is proportionably weaker, and our praise or blame fainter and more doubtful" (*Treatise*, p. 603). Sometimes he spoke as if we were simply correcting our present myopia on the basis of past regularity. This latter way of speaking can be seen in the attempt at assimilation to the analogies of beauty and distance perception. The first analogy is with the sense of beauty.[8]

> ...'tis evident, a beautiful countenance cannot give so much pleasure, when seen at a distance of twenty paces, as when it is brought nearer us. We say not, however, that it appears to us less beautiful: Because we know what effect it will have in such a position, and by that reflexion we correct its momentary appearance. (*Treatise*, p. 582)

The second analogy is with distance perception.

All objects seem to diminish by their distance: But tho' the appearance of objects to our senses be the original standard, by which we judge of them, yet we do not say, that they actually diminish by the distance; but correcting the appearance by reflexion, arrive at a more constant and established judgment concerning them. (*Treatise*, p. 603)

Neither analogy can facilitate the assimilation of the third variant account of sympathy to the second variant account. Hume would have to show us past instances where we overcame our own personal interests in a relevant context or contexts in order to prove that we could have a general rule by which to correct our present judgment. It is not enough to say that there are past instances where we sympathized with the interests of others while our own interests were not at stake. The crucial test occurs when interests conflict. Furthermore, each of the two foregoing analogies implicitly assumes the maximization of pleasure through correction. We know, for example, in the case of distance perception of the inconveniences which follow uncorrected perception. Can Hume, or should Hume, guarantee the same maximizing of pleasure in the case of sympathy? Within the present framework of sympathy, I do not think that Hume can. Finally, both analogies still preserve some reference to a present perception, however distorted, whereas in the case of the third variant account of sympathy we actually face the possibility of no sentiment or perception at all.

If Hume had some way of guaranteeing that in the long run interests do not really conflict and/or that correction leads to a greater satisfaction, or if we had a past history where such correction produced more pleasure or where lack of correction produced more pain, then he could assimilate the third variant account of sympathy to the second variant account. There are, however, difficulties in the mechanism of sympathy, difficulties which Hume honestly recognized, that prevent him from making any assumption or giving any proofs in the *Treatise* about the prospects of conflicting interests. What these difficulties are and what changes they foreshadow in *An Enquiry Concerning the Principles of Morals* will be discussed in the next section. In any case, it should be stressed that *Hume is forced to surrender his insistence on the presence of moral sentiments and the production of the indirect passions in order to preserve the objectivity of moral judgments.*

Although the three variant accounts of sympathy expose some of the difficulties within Hume's moral theory in the *Treatise*, those very same difficulties reinforce the points which we have previously made about Hume's moral theory. There could be no problem with sympathy if Hume believed that moral judgments were expressions of feelings. If moral judgments expressed feelings, then Hume would never have considered the necessity for the disinterested perspective and general rules. There could be no problem with sympathy, furthermore, if Hume had believed in a double theory, where some moral judgments were objective and others were expressions of feelings. He would simply have dismissed the objections raised on the ground that two classes of judgment were necessary. It was precisely because Hume wished to avoid both a double theory and a theory where moral judgments express feelings that he appealed to general rules to answer objections. Moral judgments are influenced by general rules. Moral judgments have predicates which refer to moral sentiments. It is precisely because Hume tried to account for both of these properties of moral judgments that he faced a problem with the sympathy mechanism. The problem of the sympathy mechanism forces us to recognize the distinction between a moral judgment and a moral sentiment.

Difficulties in the Sympathy Mechanism[9]

By distinguishing the possibility of disinterestedness from the production of a moral sentiment, and by noting the variability of the sympathy mechanism, Hume raised the problem of accounting for the existence of a moral sentiment in his third variant account of sympathy. It is not apparent how a sympathy with the public interest, especially in cases where that interest conflicts with a personal one, can always generate a moral sentiment. *The major defect of the sympathy mechanism is that it is unable to account in every case for the production of a moral sentiment which is necessary for the confirmation of a moral judgment.* The irony is that sympathy was inaugurated precisely to account for the moral sentiment.

We have already seen how Hume attempted to avoid this conclusion in his third variant account of sympathy by attempting to assimilate the third variant account to the second variant account of sympathy. That is, Hume attempted to buttress sympathy by an appeal to general rules. Although there can be no objection to the use of general rules in order to stabilize judgments, it is our contention that the sympathy mechanism does not provide sufficient materials upon which the general rules can be formulated. In short, general rules alone cannot generate a disinterested sentiment.[10]

In denying that Hume can solve the difficulty raised by the third variant account of sympathy, lack of a moral sentiment, by appealing to general rules, we must answer two questions. First, what determines the use of general rules? Second, in view of the fact that the general perspective is generated from our experience of self-interest and limited benevolence, how can sympathy interest us in the affairs of others where our own interests are not involved or where our interests conflict?

General rules are the result of customary experience and the predominance of positive over negative instances. We have no original experiences of disinterestedness and no original experiences of a sufficient extended benevolence. Our past original experience is one of self-interest and limited benevolence. Quite obviously, general rules cannot produce disinterestedness from self-interest and limited benevolence. Nor can we simply appeal to sympathy in view of the fact that it is precisely the ability of sympathy to produce disinterested sentiments that is in doubt.

Within sympathy, general rules operate as inferences from a present idea whose association with a particular sentiment or passion is insured by means of a previous history of regularity. In the case at hand, we have a conflict between self-interest and a present idea which has been previously associated with social interest. The question is, can general rules produce at least a faint impression or sentiment of the social interest? In view of Hume's earlier admission in his discussion of the passions that "when self is the object of a passion, 'tis not natural to quit the consideration of it, till the passion be exhausted; in which case the double relations of impressions and ideas can no longer operate" (*Treatise*, p. 341), it seems impossible for general rules to facilitate the production of a moral sentiment. To this we might add that the entire mechanism of sympathy depends upon the transmission of vivacity and the fact that the self is the source of vivacity. It is inconceivable that any transmission can occur in the case of personal interest.

General rules also aid us in distinguishing accidents from efficacious causes. For example, general rules inform us that a particular man is not two inches tall but six feet tall. We can confirm this judgment by reference to a standard perspective. It seemed likely that we would experience different moral perceptions by instituting a standard perspective. On the contrary, Hume was forced to admit that in some cases we did not receive a new perception or feel a sentiment at all. This was why Hume's analogies with esthetics and distance perception were not helpful. It is one thing to hold that we can judge past or future situations on the basis of sympathetically conceived general rules and to predict how we would feel and act even though we are not feeling the sentiments as strongly at the present time. This use of general rules is unobjectionable, although still necessitating a present impression.

> But however we may look forward to the future in sympathizing with any person, the extending of our sympathy depends in a great measure upon our sense of his present condition. 'Tis a great effort of imagination,

227

to form such lively ideas even of the present sentiments of others as to feel these very sentiments; but 'tis impossible we cou'd extend this sympathy to the future, without being aided by some circumstance in the present, which strikes upon us in a lively manner....and gives me a lively notion of all the circumstances of that person, whether past, present, or future; possible, probable, or certain. By means of this lively notion I am interested in them; take part with them; and feel a sympathetic motion in my breast, conformable to whatever I imagine in his. (*Treatise*, p. 386).

But it is quite another thing to expect a general rule to give us a feeling of disinterestedness if the present impression is one of self-interest. All judgments, including moral judgments, rely upon a present impression, and we cannot have a confirmable judgment without an impression or with a contrary impression.

The role of sympathy as the general principle of morals was both to make the self socially oriented and to account for the production of moral sentiments. Where there is no conflict between self-interest, limited benevolence, and social interests where the members of the community are not family members and friends, sympathy is an acceptable explanation. Where such a conflict does exist, sympathy apparently cannot begin to operate. If we assume that all such conflicts are merely apparent and that as a *matter of fact* all interests coincide in the long run, then it is not clear why we would need sympathy at all. It would seem in the latter case that all we need are general rules about the coincidence of individual and group interest. Under such circumstances we leave open the question whether there is even a moral domain to human existence, a domain marked off by the presence of moral sentiments.

The answer to the second question we raised earlier, namely, how can sympathy function to generate moral sentiments in the presence of a conflict of interest, is that it is not apparent how general rules alone can create a moral sentiment. No one will deny that we can change our perspective, but a change in perspective is supposed to produce a sentiment of some sort. Hume is forced to argue, in the third variant account of sympathy, for a perspective in which we have no impression at all. Furthermore, we cannot appeal to artificial social procedures such as education, social recognition, the artifices of politicians, etc, for Hume has insisted that they alone are not responsible for the production of a moral sentiment (*Treatise*, p. 500). This brings to a head the conflict between the two requirements of a moral judgment, namely, objectivity and a present moral sentiment.

Let us for a moment forget the foregoing arguments and see what would happen if we could acquire a general perspective without reference to our past non-moral experience. Like Hume, let us postulate a judicious spectator whose position we adopt through sympathy. The stable position that Hume recommends is "that of the person himself, whose character is examin'd; or that of persons, who have a connexion with him" (*Treatise*, p. 591). The assumption of this position involves the sympathetic process. It is obvious, once more, that this alternative will not help us because there is no rule for determining whether the person himself or those affected are basic, without involving more general rules and so on *ad infinitum*. Moreover, there seems to be no reason, either moral or non-moral, for choosing this perspective in the first place. In short, to postulate another spectator as a prop for sympathy is to argue in a circle, since we can only assume the spectator's position through sympathy itself.

What Hume has done in the third variant account of sympathy is to reduce sympathy to the status where it is no longer involved in the production of a moral sentiment and where there is no influence upon action. Hume has done all of this, we should remind ourselves, in order to preserve the objectivity of moral judgments. It is, however, difficult to conceive of the importance of sympathy if it merely involves the making of a judgment about someone else's interests in terms of a specific context, especially if it produces no effect upon the observer. Hume admitted this very point.

> The sentiments of others can never affect us, but by becoming, in some measure, our own; in which case they operate upon us, by opposing and

229

increasing our passions, in the very same manner, as if they had been originally deriv'd from our own temper and disposition. While they remain conceal'd in the minds of others, they can never have any influence upon us: And even when they are known, if they went no further than the imagination, or conception; that faculty is so accustom'd to objects of every different kind, that a mere idea, tho' contrary to our sentiments and inclinations, wou'd never alone be able to affect us. (*Treatise*, p. 593)

Under the foregoing conditions moral predicates would sometimes refer to no moral sentiment but to an idea. Even then the idea would only be of someone else's interests and not necessarily moral ones at that. Under these conditions objectivity would mean no more than mere conformity to arbitrary linguistic conventions.

Hume's attempt to institute a standard perspective is dictated by a major property of moral judgments, their uniformity, their objectivity, their appeal to social concurrence. The other major property of moral judgments, the presence of a moral sentiment that confirms the judgment and that influences action, can only be accounted for by reference to the indirect passions. "Moral good and evil are certainly distinguish'd by our *sentiments*, not by *reason*" (*Treatise*, p. 589). The mechanism of sympathy seemed a likely candidate to do both jobs, because it produced the indirect passions and because it permitted us to adopt a different perspective. In any case, sympathy allowed us to be concerned with the interests of every member of the moral community, including those who were not family members and friends. Although the third variant account of sympathy allowed us to make objective judgments about the interests of others, it could not explain how we overcome our own interests. This is in large part a reflection of the important role of the self in the sympathy mechanism. The third variant account is sympathy in name only because it does not necessarily refer to how we feel or can feel. It does not refer to a moral sentiment. The result is a universal moral judgment, *with no explanation of what makes the judgment moral*, with no potential effect on action, with no reference to a moral sentiment, with no account or justification for its intrinsically objective perspective, and whose only value seems to lie in the social lip-service which is paid to it: "And tho' the *heart* does not always take part with those general notions, or regulate its love and hatred by them, yet are they sufficient for discourse, and serve all our purposes in company, in the pulpit, on the theatre, and in the schools" (*Treatise*, p. 603).

In order to maintain the objectivity of moral judgments, Hume has not only compromised his earlier views, but he is in danger of making his position morally vacuous. Sympathy is no longer the conversion of an idea into an impression, it is merely concerned with ideas. We have shown that while general rules do provide for a stable viewpoint they do not account for a moral sentiment which produces the indirect passions, and they do not account for the influence of these passions upon action. General rules depend upon a history of regularity. Without a stronger role for something like benevolence we cannot form a general rule which is sufficiently broad with regard to the interests of others. Nor can we guarantee that people will adopt the proposed perspective, and, even if they do adopt it, we cannot guarantee that they will feel differently or feel at all. Finally, we should recall that objectivity or disinterestedness is a necessary but not a sufficient condition for distinguishing what is moral. That the sympathy mechanism is incapable of accounting for the presence of a moral sentiment is, by far, the most serious shortcoming in Hume's moral theory. A moral judgment that cannot be confirmed by a moral sentiment is *prima facie* no moral judgment.

Hume, quite clearly, was trying to do all of the things which we have emphasized. He was trying to show how moral judgments could be disinterested and how moral judgments could be confirmed by moral sentiments that produce the indirect passions. His problem is that the sympathy mechanism is an inadequate tool for the analysis and explication of the nature of moral judgments and moral sentiments. We have presented his three variant accounts of sympathy as a gradual development in order to emphasize the disparity between and the complementary nature of the doctrines which Hume was led to embrace and then to surrender. We have criticized the sympathy mechanism not because general rules are to be suspect but because they alone cannot remedy the defects of the sympathy mechanism. The only alternative would seem to be the postulation of a broader kind of benevolence. Hume did not accept this alternative in the *Treatise*, but he seems bound to accept it if we are to retain our ability to make a judgment of taste which can elicit social concurrence based upon an appeal or reference to a common sentiment. It will be a covert admission of failure on Hume's part, but such an admission is not forthcoming until we arrive at the *Enquiry*. As we shall argue in the next two chapters, such an admission will deepen and strengthen Hume's own position.

The reader should have noticed by now the important change in the tenor of our discussion. At the beginning, the major obstacle to the understanding of Hume's moral theory was the failure on the part of readers to see that Hume differentiated the moral judgment from the moral sentiment. The entire discussion of sympathy reinforces the importance of making that distinction. The major problem now seems to be to find some conception of moral sentiment which can fit the stringent demands of Hume's conception of a moral judgment.

The other dimension to the problem with the sympathy mechanism has to do with the transition from non-moral to moral motives. To evaluate the effectiveness of sympathy in performing this task of transition, we must remind ourselves why Hume insisted upon the non-moral basis of morality and what constitutes the source of the moral motive.

Hume's moral theory is based upon the supposition that morals influence human conduct. "Morals excite passions, and produce or prevent actions" (*Treatise*, p. 457). Our action depends upon pleasure and pain, for pleasure or pain is the "chief spring or actuating principle of the human mind" (*Treatise*, p. 574). Consequently, moral sentiments arising from the observation of the actions of ourselves and others must be pleasurable or painful and produce the indirect passions.

...moral distinctions depend entirely on certain peculiar sentiments of pain and pleasure....Now since every quality in ourselves or others, which gives pleasure, always causes pride or love; as every one, that produces uneasiness, excites humility or hatred: It follows, that these two particulars are to be consider'd as equivalent with regard to our mental qualities, *virtue* and the power of producing love or pride, *vice* and the power of producing humility or hatred. (*Treatise*, pp. 574-75)

The original description of the sympathy mechanism seemed admirably fitted to account for the characteristics of a moral sentiment.

At the same time, Hume insisted that we have no basic or innate moral motives. The non-moral basis of morality, by the way, reinforces our earlier contention that Hume could not have been maintaining that morality is *sui generis* and hence could not have been maintaining that moral judgments are not derivable from non-moral judgments. A moral motive is grafted upon a non-moral one. No cohesion of motives can occur as long as there is the possibility of conflict. In the conclusion to the third book of the *Treatise* Hume offered an argument designed to show that there was a natural non-moral foundation for the moral dimension created through sympathy. That is, Hume attempted to show that there was a sort of *natural approval of the moral!*

Those who resolve the sense of morals into original instincts of the mind, may defend the cause of virtue with sufficient authority; but want the advantage, which those possess, who account for that sense by an extensive sympathy with mankind. According to their [the latter] system, not only virtue must be approv'd of, but also the sense of virtue: And not only that sense, but also the principles, from whence it is deriv'd. So that nothing is presented on any side, but what is laudable and good. (*Treatise*, p. 619)

Our approval of sympathy is analogous to the approval of acts of limited benevolence. That is, once sympathy has created the benefits of communal interest, we naturally approve of it upon reflection.

> 'Tis the combination of men, in a system of conduct, which renders any act of justice beneficial to society. But when once it has that tendency we *naturally* approve of it; and if we did not so, 'tis impossible any combination or convention cou'd ever produce that sentiment. (*Treatise*, pp. 619-20)

The point of Hume's remark is that unless human beings were favorably predisposed to each other's interests, there could be no morality, much less a society.

Since the approval of sympathy is so much like the approval of limited benevolence, we may well ask why limited benevolence is not the source of the moral motive. Hume ruled out limited benevolence because he claimed that it was not effective enough to serve communal interest. Nor can the source of the moral motive be any form of extended benevolence. Extended benevolence is not, according to Hume, strong enough to influence human conduct (*Treatise*, pp. 481-82). This leaves only sympathy as the source of the moral motive or the motive capable of making us pursue communal interest. Unfortunately, we have already seen that sympathy is incapable of motivating us in crucial cases. We cannot reflect upon the benefits of communal living and approve of it if sympathy prevents us from creating the communal interest or is impotent to do so. If sympathy is unable to motivate, then it is subject to the very same criticisms which Hume had used against its rivals, limited benevolence and extended benevolence. Finally, by Hume's own admission, artificial measures alone cannot create a moral sentiment nor move us to action.

Sympathy thus failed to achieve its second objective, the transition from non-moral motives to moral motives. Hume must maintain the non-moral basis of morality, for all of his arguments about morality presuppose that morality influences conduct. Therefore, Hume must find a non-moral motive which can create a moral sentiment and move us to action. Such a motive must be capable of creating a sense of communal interest or operate within a context where ultimate conflicts of interest are precluded. If Hume could find such a motive he would resolve the conflict created by the sympathy mechanism with regard to moral judgment. Every moral predicate would then refer to an objectively confirmable sentiment precisely because everyone would in principle share the same moral sentiment. Finally, it would be part of the confirmation of a moral judgment that it move us to action.

The public nature of moral judgment and the non-moral basis of morality, where the non-moral basis is linked to the ultimate springs of human conduct, presuppose the existence of a community with no *ultimate* conflicts of interest. Without that assurance, there can be no moral theory as Hume conceived of it. *The difficulties in the sympathy mechanism thus not only confirm what we have maintained all along about Hume's moral theory and his theory of moral judgment but those very same difficulties reveal the foregoing presupposition as crucial to morality.*

CHAPTER SEVEN

THE MORAL PHILOSOPHY OF THE ENQUIRY

The Treatise and An Enquiry Concerning the Principles of Morals

The three main issues we have explored in Hume's moral philosophy in the *Treatise* are: (a) the source of moral insight or apprehension, (b) the source of moral motivation, and (c) the relationship between insight and motivation. In comparing the *Treatise* with the *Enquiry*[1] with respect to these three issues, we shall find the following. Hume's position with regard to moral insight remains unchanged. Hume's position with regard to the source of moral motivation is altered so as to allow what Hume calls the sentiment of humanity to emerge as a source of moral motivation. Hume's position with regard to the third issue, the relationship between insight and motivation is altered as a consequence of the alteration with regard to motivation, and the final result is that the sentiment of humanity replaces sympathy as the general principle of morals. In what follows we shall document these changes, explain the reasons behind them, point out the implications of these changes for the rest of Hume's moral philosophy in particular and his philosophy in general, and assess the overall significance of these alterations.

A brief comparison of the *Treatise* with the *Enquiry* (i.e., the *EPM*) reveals some interesting surface changes. First, Hume has jettisoned his idea-impression terminology and speaks almost exclusively about moral distinctions and moral sentiments. Of course the latter expressions appeared in the *Treatise*, but what we are calling attention to is the virtual disappearance of the idea-impression framework. One plausible explanation of the disappearance of the idea-impression terminology is that it was in response to critics like Reid, who had charged that Hume's views on morality were the result of the use of the Lockean theory of ideas.[2] If the same or similar conclusions can be presented without the idea-impression terminology and framework, then those conclusions will have to be examined on their own merit and not dismissed on misguided terminological and genetic grounds. A second reason is that the substitution of humanity for sympathy as the general principle of morals radically alters the need and role of the underlying Newtonian order of association and vivacity transfer as we discussed them in earlier chapters. Newton is still invoked but only as a methodological guide, and even here we shall find a significant qualification.

Second, Hume restated his views on the relationship between reason and moral sentiment, presenting not only the same arguments but also stronger and clearer statements of those arguments. What is noteworthy is that he places those arguments in the first appendix rather than at the beginning of his analysis. Tactically speaking, Hume claims that this is a more effective way of making his case. "If we can be so happy, in the course of this enquiry, as to discover the true origin of morals, it will then easily appear how far either sentiment or reason enters into all determinations of this nature" (*EPM*, p. 173). Since the sentiment of humanity is the newly designated origin of morals or the general principle of morals, it follows that moral apprehension is fundamentally affective. It would seem as if the focus of Hume's analysis of morals has shifted even if the substance of his position has not.

Third, Hume has added to the *Enquiry* a second appendix entitled "Of Self-love". In this appendix, Hume restates the position which Bishop Butler had asserted quite effectively in the *Analogy of Religion*. The substance of Hume's agreement with Butler is that the distinction between the selfish and the benevolent motives is usually misrepresented. To argue that men are benevolent because benevolence gives them a selfish pleasure is to misconstrue both the concepts of benevolence and of selfishness. To be selfish is to be indifferent, or even hostile, to the interests of others. To be benevolent is to be vitally concerned for, and sensitive to, the interests of others without reduction to personal interest. It may be, and in fact is, true that we have benevolent impulses whose satisfaction gives us a pleasure, but the pleasure is not the motive or the explanation of the impulse. This position had been Hume's view in the *Treatise* as well, but, for reasons we shall discuss shortly, Hume thought it important to discuss the issue at greater length and to call special attention to it. The assertion of the Butler distinctions is not new, but it underscores a heightened awareness on Hume's part of the relationship between individual interest and the public interest, a heightened awareness necessitated by the fourth and most important difference between the *Treatise* and the *Enquiry*, namely, the revision of the role of sympathy.

The most significant change in the Enquiry is the revision of the role of sympathy. Although continuing to use the concept of sympathy as a vital factor in stabilizing perspective for moral judgments, Hume now assigns to the sentiment of humanity the role of being the general principle of morals, and he rejects that part of the sympathy mechanism that was supposed to be responsible for the transition from self-interest to public interest. The new general principle of morals reflects dissatisfaction with the capacity of the sympathy mechanism to perform all of the functions previously assigned to it. Moreover, the assigning of such an important function to the sentiment of humanity calls for a more pointed reaffirmation of the relation between self-interest and public interest, as the appendix on self-love indicates. Finally, we shall mention again that an important shift of focus has taken place in Hume's approach to moral philosophy, but one which we shall argue makes his position more consistent.

In making humanity the general principle of morals, Hume said the following: "everything which contributes to the happiness of society, recommends itself directly to our approbation and good will. Here is a principle which accounts in great part for the origin of morality: And what need we seek for abstruse and remote systems, when there occurs one so obvious and natural" (*EPM*, p. 219). What Hume means is explained in a footnote: "It is needless to push our researches so far as to ask why we have humanity or a fellow feeling with others" (*Ibid.*). In short, there will be no attempt to explain our humanity by generating it from the sympathy mechanism, and Hume leaves us in no doubt about this.

> It is but a weak subterfuge, when pressed by these facts and arguments, to say that we transport ourselves, by the force of imagination, into distant ages and countries and consider the advantage, which we should have reaped from these characters, had we been contemporaries; and had any commerce with the persons. It is not conceivable, how a real sentiment or passion can ever arise from a known imaginary interest; especially when our real interest is still kept in view, and is often acknowledged to be entirely distinct from the imaginary, and even sometimes opposite to it. (*EPM*, p. 217)

The foregoing, of course, is a perfect description of the sympathy mechanism in the *Treatise*. In speaking of the "force of imagination" Hume is reminding us of his earlier description of the sympathy mechanism in the *Treatise*.

> When I see the *effects* of passion in the voice and gesture of any person, my mind immediately passes from these effects to their causes, and forms such a lively idea of the passion, as is presently converted into the passion itself....No passion of another discovers itself immediately to the mind. We are only sensible of its causes or effects. From *these* we infer the passion: And consequently *these* give rise to our sympathy. (*Treatise*, p. 576)

In speaking of "the advantage, which we should have reaped from these characters, had we been contemporaries, and had any commerce with the persons," Hume reminds us that general rules were supposed to create an objective perspective which he had described as "a sympathy with those, who have any commerce with the person we consider" (*Treatise*, p. 583).

There are several reasons why Hume revised his position. As we argued in the previous chapter, the difficulties mentioned became apparent to Hume when he wrote the last part of the *Treatise*.

Revising the Role of the Sympathy Mechanism

What is behind Hume's revision of the role of the sympathy mechanism? Recall that in the *Treatise* Hume insisted that there was no original moral motive. There is a natural motive which is non-moral, the so-called natural obligation. The moral obligation only develops later and is grafted onto the natural obligation allegedly through the process of sympathy.

> Now we have no such extensive concern for society but from sympathy; and consequently 'tis that principle, which takes us so far out of ourselves, as to give us the same pleasure or uneasiness in the characters of others, as if they had a tendency to our own advantage or loss. (*Treatise*, p. 579)

In the *Enquiry*, Hume still insists that there must be an original non-moral motive, but he no longer invokes the sympathy mechanism for the purpose of transforming natural obligations into moral obligations.

With some plausibility we can see the revision of the role of sympathy as reflecting Hume's more sophisticated understanding of the relationship between self-interest and benevolence. But there appears to be a more immediately important but related answer. Hume's theory of moral judgment required that all such judgments be socially objective and correctable by general rules. This is a requirement that he carefully repeated in the *Enquiry*.

General language, therefore, being formed for general use, must be moulded on some more general views, and must affix the epithets of praise or blame, in conformity to sentiments, which arise from the general interests of the community. (*EPM*, p. 228)

At the same time, Hume insists that the predicate of moral judgments must refer to a sentiment, a moral sentiment. The importance of the sympathy mechanism in the *Treatise* is that it permitted the inferred moral idea to be converted into the very impression or sentiment it represented. That is why sympathy could be the general principle of morals in the *Treatise*. However, toward the end of the *Treatise*, in considering objections to his theory, Hume recognized the possibility of moral judgments that did not refer to a real sentiment. He concluded:

"The intercourse of sentiments, therefore, in society and conversation, makes us form some general inalterable standard by which we may approve or disapprove of characters and manners. And tho' the heart does not always take part with those general notions, or regulate its love and hatred by them, yet are they sufficient for discourse, and serve all our purposes in company, in the pulpit, on the theatre, and in the schools" (*Treatise*, p. 603).

I cannot resist the temptation to point out that Hume, the moral philosopher often represented as a subjectivist, the man who argued for the lack of objectivity in moral judgments, and the man who reduced moral judgments allegedly to the expression of personal feelings, is here faced with a choice between objectivity and the existence of the sentiment. His choice is to affirm objectivity.

If we return to Book II of the *Treatise*, to the original discussion of the sympathy mechanism as it appeared in the treatment of the passions, we can locate the source of Hume's difficulty. *Sympathy cannot operate to produce the double relation of impressions and ideas when the self is involved.* In short, where a conflict of interest exists, the sympathy mechanism cannot function.

In sympathy our own person is not the object of any passion, nor is there any thing, that fixes our attention on ourselves; as in the present case, where we are supposed to be actuated with pride and humility. Ourself, independent of the perception of every other object, is in reality nothing: For which reason we must turn our view to external objects; and 'tis natural for us to consider with most attention such as lie contiguous to us, or resemble us. But when self is the object of a passion, it is not natural to quit the consideration of it, till the passion be exhausted; in which case the double relations of impressions and ideas can no longer operate. (*Treatise*, pp. 340-41)

Such is the reason for the revision of the role of sympathy. Although it is not necessary in Hume's theory that every moral judgment we make commit us to action, it is necessary that every moral judgment refer to a sentiment that is capable on the appropriate occasion of committing us to action. The crucial element is the presence of a sentiment under standard conditions. It is no use appealing to the disinterested spectator, since we can only assume that position by sympathy, and if the sympathy mechanism is rendered inoperative we cannot assume the designated perspective. When Hume returned to this theme in the *Enquiry*, he argued that the sentiment of humanity allowed for correction by general rules and provided us with a moral sentiment even if only a weak one.

In the previous chapter I criticized Hume's attempt to support sympathy by reference to the analogies of aesthetic perception and distance perception where it is important to make corrections. Correction in the case of aesthetic perception and distance perception implies a new and more vivid sentiment. I have shown that in some of Hume's accounts of sympathy in the *Treatise* we had no sentiment at all or, worse, a contrary sentiment. In the *Enquiry*, Hume recognized this disparity.

A man, brought to the brink of a precipice, cannot look down without trembling; and the sentiment of *imaginary* danger actuates him, in opposition to the opinion and belief of *real* safety. But the imagination is here assisted by the presence of a striking object; and yet prevails not, except it be also aided by novelty, and the unusual appearance of the object. Custom soon reconciles us to heights and precipices, and wears off these false and delusive terrors. The reverse is observable in the estimates which we form of characters and manners; and the more we habituate ourselves to an accurate scrutiny of morals, the more delicate feeling do we acquire of the most minute distinction between vice and virtue. Such frequent occasion, indeed, have we, in common life, to pronounce all kinds of moral determinations, that no object of this kind can be new or unusual to us; nor could any false views or prepossessions maintain their ground against an experience, so common and familiar. Experience being chiefly what forms the association could not establish and support itself, in direct opposition to that principle. (*EPM*, pp. 217-18)

What Hume is insisting upon in the *Enquiry* is that moral perception involves a real sentiment and finer discrimination, not the absence of a sentiment or an imaginary sentiment which is really an idea and no sentiment at all. It is also useful in this context to remember that general rules based upon the association of ideas and impressions can only extend past experience and never controvert it. Hume is thus striving to make his position more consistent.

Since Hume recognized all of the criticisms which we directed against his sympathy mechanism in Chapter Six, and since he consequently revised the role of sympathy, we may investigate the fate in the *Enquiry* of some of the paradoxical statements made in the *Treatise* in order to salvage the third account of sympathy. The paradoxical statements concerned *six issues*: the presence of a moral sentiment in cases of conflict, the presence of the indirect passions, the influence of moral sentiment upon behavior, the operation of general rules, the effectiveness of general rules in correcting our sentiments, and the possibility of purely verbal moral judgments.

To begin with, Hume not only insisted upon the presence of finer moral sentiments but also affirmed that we feel a moral sentiment even where circumstances or more limited interests prevent us from acting. "And if these sentiments, in most men, be not so strong as those, which have a reference to private good; yet still they must make some distinction, even in persons

244

the most depraved and selfish..." (*EPM*, pp. 228-29). Hume specifically recognized in the *Enquiry Concerning the Principles of Morals* the possibility of conflicting sentiments, whereas the sympathy mechanism in the *Treatise* had made it impossible for the moral sentiment to exist in certain cases.

> ...there is no human creature, to whom the appearance of happiness (where envy or revenge has no place) does not give pleasure, that of misery, uneasiness. This seems inseparable from our make and constitution. But they are only the more generous minds, that are thence prompted to seek zealously the good of others, and to have a real passion for their welfare. With men of narrow and ungenerous spirits, this sympathy goes not beyond a slight feeling of the imagination, which serves only to excite sentiments of complacency or censure, and makes them apply to the object either honourable or dishonourable appellations. (*EPM*, p. 234)

Second, Hume asserts that the presence of indirect passions is necessary in order to distinguish moral sentiments from other sentiments.

> We ought not to imagine, because an inanimate object may be useful as well as a man, that therefore it ought also, according to this system, to merit the appellation of *virtuous*. The sentiments, excited by utility, are, in the two cases, very different; and the one is mixed with affection, esteem, approbation, etc. and not the other. In like manner, an inanimate object may have good colour and proportions as well as a human figure. But can we ever be in love with the former? There are a numerous set of passions and sentiments, of which thinking rational beings are, by the original constitution of nature, the only proper objects... (*EPM*, p. 213)

Third, Hume confirms the fact that moral sentiments do influence our conduct.

> Taste...[which] gives the sentiment of...vice and virtue...as it gives pleasure or pain, and thereby constitutes happiness or misery, becomes a motive to action, and is the first spring or impulse to desire and volition. (*EPM*, p. 294)

Fourth, general rules continue to operate in the *Enquiry* in the exact manner in which they operated in the *Treatise*. That is, general rules correct our perceptions as well as our descriptions. Fifth, the correction extends to our sentiments so that the analogy with distance perception is now acceptable.

> A statesman or patriot, who serves our own country in our own time, has always a more passionate regard paid to him, than one whose beneficial influence operated on distant ages or remote nations; where the good, resulting from his generous humanity, being less connected with us, seems more obscure, and affects us with a less lively sympathy. We may own the merit to be equally great, though our sentiments are not raised to an equal height, in both cases. The judgment here corrects the inequalities of our internal emotions and perceptions; in like manner, as it preserves us from error, in the several variations of images, presented to our external senses. The same object, at a double distance, really throws on the eye a picture of but half the bulk; yet we imagine that it appears the same size in both situations; because we know that on our approach to it, its image would expand on the eye, and that the difference consists not in the object itself, but in our position with regard to it. And, indeed, without such a correction of appearances, both in internal and external sentiment, men could never think or talk on any object; while their fluctuating situations produce a continual variation on objects, and throw them into such different and contrary lights and positions.
>
> For a like reason, the tendencies of actions and characters, not their real accidental consequences, are alone regarded in our moral determinations or general judgments... (*EPM*, p. 227-28)

Sixth, the conception of a purely verbal moral judgment is absent from the *Enquiry*. The statement of the *Treatise* where such a conception was expressed has been radically transformed so that the statement now simply denies that general rules can overrule all of our interests, while affirming that where no ultimate conflict exists there is an influence of general rules upon conduct.

> And though the heart takes not part entirely with those general notions, nor regulates all its love and hatred by the universal abstract differences

of vice and virtue, without regard to self, or the person with whom we are more intimately connected; *yet have these moral differences a considerable influence,* and being sufficient, at least for discourse, serve all our purposes in company, in the pulpit, on the theatre, and in the schools. (*EPM*, p. 229) [*italics mine*].

Hume is not foolish enough to maintain that general rules can make us completely forget our own non-moral interests, nor can such rules make the moral sentiment feel more vivid than it really is. Nevertheless, we feel something, and we do know how we would act in such cases.

In his revision of the role of sympathy, Hume has not only recognized and accounted for all of the difficulties in his earlier accounts of sympathy but has also maintained the same position in his general moral theory in the *Enquiry* that he had held in the *Treatise.* For example, he reiterated his belief in the natural origin of moral distinctions founded on the "original constitution", and he reiterated his denial that purely external sanctions can on their own artificially create moral distinctions.

From the apparent usefulness of the social virtues, it has readily been inferred by sceptics, both ancient and modern, that all moral distinctions arise from education, and were, at first, invented, and afterwards encouraged, by the art of politicians, in order to render men tractable, and subdue their natural ferocity and selfishness, which incapacitated them for society. This principle, indeed, of precept and education, must so far be owned to have a powerful influence, that it may frequently increase or diminish, beyond their natural standard, the sentiments of approbation or dislike; and may even, in particular instances, create, without any natural principle, a new sentiment of this kind; as is evident in all superstitious practices and observances: But that all *moral* affection or dislike arises from this origin, will never surely be allowed by any judicious enquirer. Had nature made no such distinction, founded on the original constitution of the mind, the words honourable, and shameful, lovely and odious, noble and despicable, had never had place in any language; nor could politicians, had they invented these terms, ever have been able to render them intelligible, or make them convey any idea to the audience. (*EPM*, 214)

Since Hume has revised the role of the sympathy mechanism, and yet maintained the same general theory of morals, and now shown even greater confidence about the effectiveness and presence of moral sentiments, we may well ask what substitute is provided to account for moral sentiments.

Moral Philosophy in the Enquiry

The explanation of Hume's change of heart is that he now has a new general principle of morals. Hume calls this new general principle the *'sentiment of humanity'* and describes it as a "concern for others" not limited to family and friends but extending to the whole of society. Hume also describes the sentiment of humanity as "benevolence" and "sympathy". The reasons for the overlap in terminology should be noted. Sympathy still has an important role in Hume's moral philosophy with regard to perspective and general rules, but sympathy no longer performs the same function of generating the moral sentiment. The sentiment of humanity in conjunction with sympathy now performs that function. The sentiment of humanity is not to be confused with limited benevolence, it is not to be confused with that extensive benevolence which would render justice superfluous, yet clearly it is a kind of benevolence.

In what follows we shall briefly summarize the general moral theory of the *Enquiry* in order to show that the sentiment of humanity accounts for everything formerly explained by means of sympathy. In Section II of the *Enquiry*, Hume discussed (limited) benevolence and concluded that since benevolence contributed to the happiness of the community, that is, to the happiness of other people not just the benevolent person, benevolence is useful. Therefore, we approve of benevolence on account of its utility. As we shall see, the approval of utility is derived from the sentiment of humanity. So humanity is more fundamental than limited benevolence. This is why we should not be misled by terminology.

248

In the *Treatise*, Hume had explained the approval of acts of limited benevolence and the approval of sympathy as the result of a reflection on the favorable tendencies of these sentiments. Hume also explained the approval of limited benevolence as being reinforced by the fear of disapproval or the fear of being suspected of lacking "the natural sentiments of humanity" (*Treatise*, p. 518). In the *Enquiry*, Hume now claims that, in time, we reflect on our own moral behavior and receive *reinforcement from our natural social inclinations*.

> Another spring of our constitution, that brings a great addition of force to moral sentiments, is the love of fame; which rules, with such uncontrolled authority, in all generous minds, and is often the grand object of all their designs and undertakings. By our continual and earnest pursuit of a character, a name, a reputation in the world, we bring our own deportment and conduct frequently in review, and consider, how they appear in the eyes of those who approach and regard us. This constant habit of surveying ourselves, as it were, in reflection, keeps alive all the sentiments of right and wrong, and begets, in noble natures, a certain reverence for themselves as well as others... (*EPM*, p. 276)

In Section III, we find that justice is approved of because of its utility. " Public utility is the *sole* origin of justice, and that reflections on the beneficial consequences of this virtue are the sole foundation of its merit" (*EPM*, p. 183). Since two important virtues, benevolence and justice, are approved of because of their utility, utility becomes "an opening by which the others [other virtues] may be accounted for" (*EPM*, p. 175).

In addition to the virtues which are approved because of their utility to the possessor, such as prudence and industry, Hume pointed out that we approve of qualities which are immediately agreeable to ourselves, or to the possessor, such as cheerfulness; qualities which are immediately agreeable to others, i.e. persons other than the possessor, such as wit and modesty. Just as in the *Treatise*, Hume concluded that there are four classes of qualities which elicit our approval, "mental qualities, useful or agreeable to the person himself or to others" (*EPM*, p. 268).

Since we approve of what is publicly and socially useful, and since our approval extends to actions where our personal interest could not possibly be involved, our morality must involve two things. First, we need a moral sentiment which prefers the socially useful, and second, we need an original non-moral motive which is not limited in its approval to ourselves and our family and friends.

> Usefulness is agreeable, and engages our approbation. This is a matter of fact, confirmed by daily observation. But, *useful?* For what? For Somebody's interest, surely. Whose interest then? Not our own only: For our approbation frequently extends farther. It must, therefore, be the interest of those, who are served by the character or action approved of; and these we may conclude, however remote, are not totally indifferent to us. By opening up this principle, we shall discover one great source of moral distinction. (*EPM*, p. 218)

The sentiment of humanity is an original non-moral motive which performs all of these functions, and it is for these reasons that the sentiment of humanity is the general principle of morals.

Hume offers several reasons why the sentiment of humanity can give rise to the sentiment of morals. Both sentiments are aroused by the same objects; both sentiments show a similar variation under the same conditions; both sentiments are found in the same temperament. "By all the rules of philosophy, therefore, we must conclude, that these sentiments are originally the same; since, in each particular, even the most minute, they are governed by the same laws, and are moved by the same objects" (*EPM*, p. 236). It is important to emphasize the word "original". The sentiment of morals and the sentiment of humanity are not identical. Under certain circumstances, the sentiment of humanity becomes the sentiment of morals, and this conversion or development is possible because of the similarity of their natures.

The circumstances under which the sentiment of humanity is converted into the sentiment of morals is the presence of an object with public utility and the assurance of no ultimate conflict with our non-moral interests.

> Let these generous sentiments be supposed ever so weak; let them be insufficient to move even a hand or finger of our body, they must still direct the determinations of our mind, and where everything else is equal, produce a cool performance of what is useful and serviceable to mankind, above what is pernicious and dangerous. A moral distinction, therefore, immediately arises; a general sentiment of blame and approbation; a tendency, however faint, to the objects of the one, and a proportionable aversion to those of the other. (*EPM*, p. 271)

The sentiment is then encouraged and fostered by social intercourse.

It makes no difference that the moral sentiment springs from our sentiment of humanity, "principles, which may appear, at first sight, somewhat small and delicate" (*EPM*, p. 275). We become aware not only of the benefits of the public interest but also of the advantages contributed by the sense of morals. "Other passions, though perhaps originally stronger, yet being selfish and private, are often overpowered by its force, and yield the dominion of our breast to those social and public principles" (*EPM*, pp. 275-76). Thus is the sentiment of morals reinforced.

Aside from the revision of the role of sympathy and the substitution of the sentiment of humanity, the theory of moral judgment in the *Enquiry* is the same as the theory of moral judgment in the *Treatise*. The universality of moral judgments is still accounted for in terms of a general perspective. Although Hume spoke in the *Enquiry* of a "general sentiment of blame and approbation" (*EPM*, p. 271), the context makes clear that the sentiment is only "general" in the sense that the sentiment is felt when the perspective is general (i.e. disinterested or reflecting the public interest as opposed to private interest). This corresponds exactly to the position of the *Treatise* where a moral sentiment is described as one which is felt disinterestedly. "'Tis only when a character is considered in general, without reference to our particular interest, that it causes such a feeling or sentiment, as denominates it morally good or evil" (*Treatise*, p. 472). Again, when Hume spoke of "general approbation" in the *Enquiry*, he was referring to the fact that "every man, or most men, agree in the same opinion or decision" (*EPM*, p. 272). As in the *Treatise*, the "general" perspective preserves a "stable judgment of things," in our "general decisions" (*Treatise*, p. 582). Hence it is not the sentiment *per se* which is general but the perspective from which it is felt. To attribute logical generality to the sentiment is once more to confuse what Hume said about moral judgment with what he said about moral sentiment. Hence there is still a need in the *Enquiry* for some form of the sympathy mechanism to aid us in adopting the proper perspective.

What the sentiment of humanity replaces is one part of the former role of sympathy. The sentiment of humanity provides for a moral sentiment and not for the whole of the moral judgment, although each moral judgment is confirmed by the presence of a moral sentiment. What Hume needed in the *Enquiry* was a sentiment which is "common to all mankind" and whose presence is to "extend to all mankind" (*EPM*, p. 272). The properties of commonness and temporality that belong to the sentiment of humanity correspond to "resemblance" in the mechanism of sympathy. When Hume contrasted the sentiment of humanity in the *Enquiry* to other sentiments, he found that the other sentiments were not common in the required sense, for my enemy is not necessarily your enemy. We may both have enemies but not the same ones. Nor are these other sentiments "comprehensive" because it is difficult to feel strong sentiments otherwise about past ages. What Hume is talking about is a moral sentiment felt with respect to social or public interest and not just a special kind of sentiment.

The continuity between the *Treatise* and the *Enquiry* on the issue of moral judgment is also seen in the way that a moral predicate functions. Moral predicates refer to moral sentiments, that is, to sentiments felt under the general perspective. Moral predicates do not, in any way, refer to one's personal feelings.

> The distinction, therefore, between these species of sentiment being so great and evident, language must soon be moulded upon it, and must invent a peculiar set of terms, in order to express those universal sentiments of censure and approbation, which arise from humanity, or from views of general usefulness and its contrary. (*EPM*, p. 274)

Moreover, since moral predicates refer to moral sentiments and since moral sentiments imply a special perspective, moral judgments are verifiable by testing to see if the sentiment is felt under the indicated perspective.

> But when he bestows on any man the epithets of *vicious* or odious or depraved, he then speaks another language, and expresses sentiments, in which he expects all his audience are to concur with him....If he mean, therefore, to express that this man possesses qualities, whose tendency is pernicious to society, he has chosen this common point of view, and has touched the principle of humanity, in which every man, in some degree, concurs. (*EPM*, p. 272).

Hume no more confused judgment and sentiment in the *Enquiry* than he did in the *Treatise*.

The objective nature of Hume's theory of moral judgment is in no way affected by the revision of the role of sympathy. The revision of the role of sympathy and the substitution of the sentiment of humanity not only guarantee that every moral judgment may be confirmed by a moral sentiment but also insure a measure of uniformity. If human conduct displays such regularity, then our moral judgments will not only reflect such predictability but also will permit those very judgments to guide human conduct in a predictable way. That influence is based upon the information supplied by the judgment and the motivational power of the sentiments involved. The moral sentiment has that motivational power because it is not only derived from non-moral sentiments but is also consistent with our basic non-moral interests. In short, the nature of a moral judgment is integrally tied to the sentiment of humanity,[3] the revised role of sympathy, and to the non-moral basis of morality.

> Virtue and Vice become then known; morals are recognized; certain general ideas are framed of human conduct and behavior; such measures are expected from men in such situations. This action is determined to be conformable to our abstract rule; that other, contrary. And by such universal principles are the particular sentiments of self-love frequently controlled and limited. (*EPM*, p. 274)

The Non-Moral Basis of Morality (Egoism vs. Humanity)

Most of the recent literature on Hume's moral philosophy has either ignored or down played the differences between the *Treatise* and the *Enquiry*.[4] The older literature was more sensitive to this problem. The consensus of the older literature, however, was to interpret the revised role of sympathy as the result of Hume's concern with the relation of egoism to benevolence, or the problem of self-love. T.H. Green attributed an egoistic theory to Hume.[5] Kemp Smith and F.C. Sharp claimed that Hume's theory was altruistic.[6] E.V. McGilvary claimed that the *Treatise* was more egoistic and the *Enquiry* more altruistic.[7] Hedenius claimed that the *Treatise* and *Enquiry* were both intended as altruistic but came out sounding egoistic.

There is an element of truth in each of the above positions, but the issue is much more complicated. To begin with, Hume was neither a psychological egoist nor a moral egoist. Hume recognized benevolence in both the *Treatise* and the *Enquiry*. It is also true that despite his intention and protestations, the *Treatise* at times sounds as if Hume is advocating a kind of sophisticated egoism. Why the *Treatise* sounded that way is something to which we shall have to address ourselves.

There are in fact two issues involved in the revision of the role of sympathy and the substitution of the sentiment of humanity as the general principle of morals. Neither of these issues involves a direct problem with the relationship between egoism and benevolence, although one of these issues indirectly touches upon it. The first issue, on which we have already dwelt at length above, is the issue of moral judgment. The second issue, which will be our primary concern in this section, is the issue of the relationship between self-interest and the public interest.

Before entering into the second issue, let us briefly remind ourselves why the revision of the role of sympathy and the substitution of the sentiment of humanity reflect earlier problems in Hume's theory of moral judgment. If anything, this serves to confirm our previous lengthy analysis of what has been said about moral judgment in Hume's moral philosophy. Moral judgments are disinterested, that is, they are intersubjective and involve social concurrence. Moral judgments have a descriptive meaning such that they are applicable to all specified actions regardless of temporal or spatial considerations. Moral judgments must be confirmed by reference to a moral sentiment. Finally, the moral sentiment under appropriate circumstances must move us to action. The sentiment of humanity fills all of these functions by providing every moral judgment with a moral sentiment with which to confirm the judgment, and it also meets the conditions of social concurrence and applicability to all times and places. Moreover, as we shall see once again the sentiment of humanity can motivate us.

> The notion of morals implies some sentiment common to all mankind, which recommends the same object to general approbation, and makes every man, or most men, agree in the same opinion or decision concerning it. It also implies some sentiment, so universal and comprehensive as to extend to all mankind and render the actions and conduct, even of persons the most remote, an object of applause or censure, according as they agree or disagree with that rule of right which is established. *These two requisite circumstances belong alone to the sentiment of humanity here insisted on.* (EPM, p. 272) [*italics mine*]

One of the reasons that readers fail to see this important revision in the *Enquiry* is that those readers have misperceived the whole nature of Hume's account of moral judgment on which we have insisted in this book.

In Chapter Six, we have seen that the third account of sympathy was problematic because it necessitated a moral judgment which could not be confirmed by any moral sentiment. The substitution of the sentiment of humanity for one of the functions of sympathy solves that problem. Every moral judgment is now confirmable by a moral sentiment. In Chapter Six, we also saw that sympathy was unable to account for moral judgments which were directed to past ages and events. The substitution of the sentiment of humanity for one of sympathy's roles solves this problem as well. Our approval and disapproval of past acts now seems much more plausible. In short, the revision of the role of sympathy seems much more consistent with Hume's theory of moral judgment.

We come now to the second issue involved in the revisions of the *Enquiry*, namely, the relationship of self-interest to the public interest. The long and the short of it is that any account of morality presupposes the consistency of self-interest and the public interest, i.e., that there is no necessary and ineliminable conflict between these interests. To put it more accurately, these respective interests are not so ontologically fixed that there can be ultimate irresolvable conflicts.[8] In the *Treatise*, Hume had tried to use the mechanism of sympathy to show how this coincidence or non-conflict comes about. In the *Enquiry*, Hume admits that the lack of conflict is a basic assumption of moral philosophizing. The way in which Hume explains the assumption in the *Enquiry* does not require any change in the degree of human benevolence.

One of the roles of sympathy was the conversion of nonmoral motives into moral motives, and this was necessitated by Hume's contention that there must be a non-moral basis of morality. Does Hume still maintain the non-moral basis of morality in the *Enquiry*? The answer is that he does. In the first place, moral sentiments are still pleasures and pains and are still described in non-moral terms.

> The hypothesis which we embrace is plain. It maintains that morality is determined by sentiment. It defines virtue to be *whatever mental action or quality gives to a spectator the pleasing sentiment of approbation*; and vice the contrary. We then proceed to examine a plain matter of fact, to wit, what actions have this influence. (*EPM*, p. 289)

Moreover, we see that Hume can infer a moral judgment, an assertion which ascribes a moral quality to an action, from the non-moral judgment that the action has social utility.

> It appears to be matter of fact, that the circumstances of *utility*, in all subjects, is a source of praise and approbation: That is constantly appealed to in all moral decisions concerning the merit or demerit of actions. (*EPM*, p. 231)

We should remind ourselves of Hume's reason for insisting upon the non-moral basis of morality. Moral sentiments influence human conduct. On the other hand, we have no innately moral motives. Moral motives, as they arise, must be consistent with more basic non-moral motives.

> And indeed, to drop all figurative expression, what hopes can we ever have of engaging mankind to a practice which we confess full of austerity and rigour? Or what theory of morals can ever serve any useful purpose, unless it can show, by a particular detail, that all the duties which it recommends, are also the true interest of each individual? The peculiar advantage of the foregoing system seem to be, that it furnishes proper mediums for that purpose. (*EPM*, p. 280)

Given that morality must have a non-moral basis, and given that we may infer moral judgments from factual judgments of public utility, we may ask if public utility is consistent with our non-moral motives. Here we have arrived inescapably at the question of the consistency of private interest with public interest. In the *Treatise*, the mechanism of sympathy was supposed to generate the consistency, and this was precisely why sympathy could theoretically effect the conversion of non-moral sentiments and motives into moral ones. As we saw in Chapter Six, sympathy could only be salvaged at the cost of assuming the very consistency that it supposedly guaranteed. *In the Enquiry, Hume separates the question of guaranteeing the consistency of public and private interest from the question of deriving moral sentiments from non-moral sentiments.*

Having separated the question of the consistency of private and public interest, we may now see how Hume resolves it in the *Enquiry*. To begin with, he considers and then *rejects* the view that the public interest is simply an extension of self-love.

> ...whatever affection one may feel, or imagine he feels for others, no passion is, or can be disinterested; that the most generous friendship, however sincere, is a modification of self-love; and that, even unknown to ourselves, we seek only our own gratification, while we appear the most deeply engaged in schemes for the liberty and happiness of mankind. By a turn of imagination, by a refinement of reflection, by an enthusiasm of passion, we seem to take part in the interests of others, and imagine ourselves divested of all selfish considerations...(*EPM*, p. 296)

What is interesting about the foregoing description is that it is not too far from Hume's own theory as expressed in the *Treatise*. What is important to see here is that Hume is really considering and rejecting two different but similar theories. First, Hume is rejecting the selfish system of Hobbes and Locke which denied outright that we had or could have true moral sentiments or motives. The assertion of the reality of benevolence remains the same in both the *Treatise* and the *Enquiry*, but whereas Hume sought to generate real moral motives through sympathy in the *Treatise*, he now generates those real moral motives in the *Enquiry* through the natural sentiment of humanity. Second, Hume is rejecting his own earlier *Treatise* attempt to generate the real moral sentiment and motive from self-love through sympathy. The difference between the Hobbesian-selfish system and the Humean-*Treatise*-sympathy-mechanism system is

that the latter always recognized the existence of moral motivation. What is at issue for Hume is how we account for the origin
of the moral motive, and not its existence.

Notice the manner in which Hume responds to the notion
that public interest is an extension of self-love. Hume begins by
insisting that benevolence and unselfish acts are obviously real
and a part of common experience. "Experience seems plainly to
oppose the selfish theory" (*EPM*, p. 215). Moreover, we approve
of qualities agreeable to others, we approve of past actions, and
sometimes we even approve of actions which are contrary to our
private interest. "But as qualities, which tend only to the utility
of their possessor, without any reference to us, or to the community, are yet esteemed and valued; by what theory or system
can we account for this sentiment from self-love or deduce it
from that favorite origin?" (*EPM*, p. 243). In addition, Hume
condemns those (like Hume himself in the *Treatise*) who admit
the reality of benevolence and moral motives but then "attempt,
by a philosophical chemistry, to resolve the elements of this passion, if I may so speak, into those of another, and explain every
affection to be self-love, twisted and moulded, by a particular
turn of imagination, into a variety of appearances" (*EPM*, p. 297).

Instead of attempting a refutation of the foregoing position
(his own *Treatise* position), Hume says that "the question concerning the universal or partial selfishness of man ...[is] not so
material as is usually imagined to morality and practice" (*Ibid*.).
The attempted reduction to self-love is called "more curious than
important" (*EPM*, p. 298). What Hume is suggesting is that the
attempted reduction is a misconception about the correct
starting point in moral philosophy. Finally, the attempted
reduction, claims Hume, is due to a desire for a false simplicity.
"All attempts of this kind have hitherto proved fruitless, and
seem to have proceeded entirely from that love of simplicity
which has been the source of much false reasoning in
philosophy" (*EPM*, p. 298).

The question we must now raise is why did Hume think that
the reduction of the public interest to self-interest was the

wrong kind of approach to moral philosophy. The reason is that the consistency of self-interest and public interest, or the lack of any ultimate conflict between the two, is a presupposition or necessary condition of both moral practice and moral theory.[9] Hume does not try to prove its existence, nor does he try to guarantee it. This presupposition is the basic starting point of moral philosophy.

> It is needless to push our researches so far as to ask, why we have humanity or a fellow-feeling with others. It is sufficient, that this is experienced to be a principle in human nature. We must stop somewhere in our examination of causes; and there are in every science, some general principles, beyond which we cannot hope to find any principle more general. No man is absolutely indifferent to the happiness and misery of others. The first has a natural tendency to give pleasure; the second pain. This every one may find in himself. It is not probable that these principles can be resolved into principles more simple and universal, whatever attempts may have been made to that purpose. But if it were possible, *it belongs not to the present subject*; and we may here safely consider these principles as original: happy, if we can render all the consequences sufficiently plain and perspicuous. (*EPM*, pp. 219-20n) [*italics mine*]

The Cultural Perspective of the Enquiry

At the beginning of this chapter we noted the three basic issues in moral philosophy to which Hume addressed himself, namely, the source of moral insight, the source of moral motivation, and the relationship between the two. With regard to these issues, we asserted that the major difference between Hume's earlier and later treatments lies in the new source of moral motivation, the sentiment of humanity. We pointed out how this change required an alteration in Hume's conception of the relation between motivation and insight, and we showed how Hume handled this in his revision of the role of the sym-pathy mechanism. This change in Hume's view about the source of moral motivation has an importance far beyond what we have indicated. It has clarified an important presupposition of moral philosophy, namely the assumed consistency of public and private interest. By showing us the basic presupposition which has emerged in his moral philosophizing, Hume has exhibited something crucial about moral philosophy in particular and philosophy in general.

What Hume has exhibited is that the Copernican Revolution in moral philosophy, the revolution which begins with the *We Do* perspective, must understand itself and its perspective as a cultural form of order and not a mechanical form of order. What *We Do* cannot itself be understood by searching for the hidden causes or secret structure behind it.

> The case is not the same in this species of philosophy [i.e. moral philosophy] as in physics. Many an hypothesis in nature, contrary to first appearances, has been found, on more accurate scrutiny, solid and satisfactory. Instances of this kind are so frequent that a judicious, as well as witty philosopher [Fontenelle], has ventured to affirm, if there be more than one way in which any phenomenon may be produced, that there is general presumption for its arising from the causes which are the least obvious and familiar. But the presumption always lies on the other side, in all enquiries concerning the origin of our passions, and of the internal operations of the human mind. The simplest and most obvious cause which can there be assigned for any phenomenon, is probably the true one. When a philosopher, in the *explication* of his system, is obliged to have recourse to some very intricate and refined reflections, and to suppose them essential to the production of any passion or emotion, we have reason to be extremely on our guard against so fallacious an hypothesis....Our predominant motive or intention is, indeed, frequently concealed from ourselves...but there is no instance that a concealment of this nature has ever arisen from the abstruseness and intricacy of the motive. (*EPM*, p. 299) [*italics mine*]

If moral philosophy is not the search for a secret structure, then there is *no need to supply an account for how conventions arise* or how we get from the parts to the whole. Moral philosophy begins and ends with the cultural whole. What Hume provides us with is a *deeper understanding of the historical context of interest, and not an appeal to a wholly abstract and timeless notion of ultimate or long-range self-interest.* Given Hume's metaphysics, the latter notion is unintelligible.

Perhaps the most startling suggestion to come out of Hume's account is that the attempt to supply a hidden structure explanation (as in the social contract theory) is not only inadequate but dangerous to the very practices it tries to explain. To see this point in context, let us quickly run through the fundamental shift in perspective in the *Enquiry.* Having reaffirmed his conviction that morality must have a non-moral basis, and having derived the moral sentiment from the original non-moral motive of the sentiment of humanity, Hume has completed the revision of the role of sympathy. Sympathy had been required to convert non-moral motives and sentiments into moral ones. The sentiment of humanity now performs that function. The only possible objection to such a substitution would be the potential conflict between humanity and private interest. Hume faced this issue squarely. "Having explained the moral *approbation* attending merit or virtue, there remains nothing but briefly to consider our interested *obligation* to it, and to inquire whether every man, who has any regard to his own happiness and welfare, will not best find his account in the practice of every moral duty" (*EPM*, p. 278). Hume realized that the presupposition of the consistency of private and public interest must be made regardless of our moral theory. Hume believed that most of us would grant this presupposition, and, if not, argument would be pointless. Finally the very distinction between public and private interest presupposes a social and historical framework. In considering "a public wrong" and a "private harm", Hume is led to remark that "the second consideration could have no place, were not the former previously established: for otherwise the distinction of *mine* and *thine* would be unknown in society" (*EPM*, pp. 310-11).

I must confess that, if a man think that this reasoning much requires an answer, it would be a little difficult to find any which will to him appear satisfactory and convincing. If his heart rebel not against such pernicious maxims, if he feel no reluctance to the thought of villainy or baseness, he

has indeed lost a considerable motive to virtue; and we may expect that
this practice will be answerable to his speculation." (*EPM*, p. 283)

The only viable perspective for the explication of the norms of
social practice, what *We Do*, is from within those practices, i.e.,
from the cultural perspective. Only an engaged socially responsible agent will understand and feel the norms. The external observer is engaged in a dangerous flirtation with amorality to say
nothing of the inadequacy of his explanation.[10]

The other dramatic suggestion made by Hume is that moral
communities can dissolve, and the dissolution is not because of
hidden private interests but because the historical conditions
which gave rise to and sustained the community have radically
altered.

> Suppose a society to fall into such want of all common necessaries, that
> the utmost frugality and industry cannot preserve the greater number
> from perishing, and the whole from extreme misery; it will readily, I be-
> lieve, be admitted, that the strict laws of justice are suspended, in such a
> pressing emergence, and give place to the stronger motives of necessity
> and self-preservation. Is it any crime after a shipwreck to seize whatever
> means or instrument of safety one can lay hold of, without regard to for-
> mer limitations of property?....
>
> Thus, the rules of equity or justice depend entirely on the particular state
> and condition in which men are placed, and owe their origin and exis-
> tence to that utility, which results to the public from their strict and reg-
> ular observance. Reverse, in any considerable circumstance, the condi-
> tion of men: Produce extreme abundance or extreme necessity: Implant
> in the human breast perfect rapaciousness and malice: By rendering jus-
> tice totally useless, you thereby totally destroy its essence, and suspend
> its obligation upon mankind. (*EPM*, pp. 186-88)

All of this reinforces the claim that a viable moral community
has to be understood in terms of its historical evolution. That is
one reason why Hume's response to the controversy between
Tories and Whigs was to write the *History of England*. This does
not mean that we cannot search for general principles within

the historical evolution. On the contrary, it is only within that historical development that we both can and must search for the general principles.

> What wide difference, therefore, in the sentiments of morals, must be found between civilized nations and Barbarians, or between nations whose characters have little in common? How shall we pretend to fix a standard for judgments of this nature?

> By tracing matters, replied I, a little higher, and examining the first principles, which each nation establishes, of blame or censure. The Rhine flows north, the Rhone south; yet both spring from the same mountain, and are also actuated, in their opposite directions, by the same principle of gravity. The different inclinations of the ground on which they run, cause all the difference of their courses.[11]

In the light of the kind of generality Hume thought was available to us, we can see the importance of the assumption of the consistency of private and public interest. It is the kind of general principle which can only be explicated from the *We Do* perspective now understood culturally, that is socially and historically. What this assumption literally does is to delimit moral issues from non-moral ones. When we add to this the prospect of changing circumstances, we begin to realize that moral positions cannot be specified timelessly but require constant adjustment. We have not only seen Hume's flexibility but we have also seen how his moral theory makes this prospect intelligible and capable of rational treatment.

Gone from Hume's work is the hope of an explanation of the *We Do* perspective as a kind of mechanical order. In the first section of the *Enquiry*, Hume reasserted the rules of the experimental method. However, he mentioned only the rules of finding "universal principles" the rejection of "Hypotheses", and the appeal to "experience" (*EPM*, pp. 174-75). He did not mention the rule of simplicity, something he had done in the *Treatise* almost every time the rule of universality was mentioned. These other rules are referred to throughout the *Enquiry*. The reason for not mentioning 'simplicity' is that Hume by now had concluded that his own first theory of the *Treatise* was unduly simplistic. The rejection of a false simplicity is stated in his discussion of humanity. "It is not probable, that these principles can be resolved into principles more simple and universal, whatever attempts may have been made to that purpose. But if it were possible, *it belongs not to the present subject; and we may safely consider these principles as original*" (EPM, p. 220)[*italics mine*].

Just how significant and far-reaching is the substitution of a cultural form of order for a mechanical form of order? The answer to that question can be seen by noting the consequences of the revision of the role of sympathy. The revision of the role of sympathy is also a revision of the importance of the communication of vivacity as the connecting link of the three books of the *Treatise*. Without denying the importance of association or the belief in the communication of vivacity, it remains the case that a major reason for presenting all of Hume's views as part of a single work has been lost. More specifically, the revision of the role of sympathy severs one important connection between Books II and III of the *Treatise*, between Hume's theory of the passions and Hume's moral theory. Aside from the sympathy mechanism, the major connecting link between the passions and moral theory was the account of motivation and the subordination of reason to sentiment. Hume has retained the account of motivation, but it now fits into his moral theory as part of the discussion of the relationship between reason and sentiment. The double association theory of the passions is no longer needed for the exposition of Hume's moral theory. That is why the theory of the passions can be consigned to a separate work, as one of the *Dissertations*. Finally, the present uselessness of vivacity to Hume's moral theory explains why it is no longer necessary to employ the idea-impression distinction for the exposition of that theory.[12]

If my interpretation is correct, then Hume was perhaps aware of these difficulties by the time he completed the *Treatise*. Certainly he must have been aware of them before he wrote An En-

quiry Concerning Human Understanding. In his 1742 essay "The Sceptic" Hume made the following admission in the opening paragraph: "When a philosopher has once laid hold of a favourite principle, which perhaps accounts for many natural effects, he extends the same principle over the whole of creation, and reduces to it every phaenomenon, though by the most violent and absurd reasoning." In the introductory section of *An Enquiry Concerning Human Understanding* (1748) there is a passage in which Hume appears to recognize the overly simplistic system he had developed in the *Treatise*. The passage is as follows:

> Moralists have hitherto been accustomed, when they considered the vast multitude and diversity of those actions that excite our approbation or dislike, to search for some common principle, on which this variety of sentiments might depend. And though they have sometimes carried the matter too far, by their passion for some one general principle; it must, however, be confessed, that they are excusabe in expecting to find some general principles, into which all the vices and virtues were justly to be resolved....Nor have their attempts been wholly unsuccessful; though perhaps longer time, greater accuracy, and more ardent application may bring these sciences still nearer their perfection. (*EHU*, p. 15)[13]

Summary

The revision of the role of sympathy has done little to alter what is crucial in the details of Hume's moral theory from the *Treatise* to the *Enquiry*.[14] What it has allowed Hume to achieve is a greater consistency and clarity about the fundamental perspective from which moral philosophizing becomes an intelligible activity. Hume has reiterated the importance of a non-moral basis of morality if morality is to have relevance to human conduct. And it is the relationship of human conduct to interpersonal interests that forms the concern of moral philosophy. Finally, it is this social dimension of moral theory which ultimately determines any theory of moral judgment.

Hume's moral theory is a progressive attempt to clarify the personal and public nature of moral judgments and moral sentiments. The revision of the role of sympathy and the acceptance of the sentiment of humanity testify to Hume's commitment to the objective (i.e. intersubjective) nature of moral judgment. The relationship of moral sentiment to moral judgment is one of confirmation. Yet Hume continues to emphasize that a moral judgment must enlist the motivation of individuals who identify their interests with those of the moral community. The moral community is, in fact, just such a consistency of private and public interests. Moral judgments are not the expressions of anyone's personal feelings, but neither are such judgments simple translations of the naked will of any group. The attempt to represent moral judgments as anything but descriptions of human conduct in relation to the historically evolving public interest is to ignore the relevance of moral judgments to life.

CHAPTER EIGHT

HUME'S PLACE IN MORAL PHILOSOPHY

Hume's Copernican Revolution in Moral Philosophy

In Chapter One, we argued for the existence of a Copernican revolution in Hume's general conception of philosophy. We identified that Copernican revolution as:

(1) a rejection of the *I Think* perspective in which human beings appear as subjects set over against an objective world and in which human beings face a primarily theoretical task;

(2) the substitution of the *We Do* perspective in which human beings are construed as agents interacting with and shaping the world as well as themselves and in which our fundamental task is practical.[1]

How important is it to stress the Copernican revolution in Hume's philosophy in general and in his moral philosophy? One way of answering this question is to examine briefly Alasdair MacIntyre's recent treatment of Hume.[2] MacIntyre begins by attributing to Hume what MacIntyre calls a first person starting point and attributes that starting point to the use of the way of ideas.[3] Having attributed that starting point to Hume [what we have called the *I Think* perspective], MacIntyre defines Hume's problem as the problem of getting to the social structure required by moral and social philosophizing.[4] The transition is attempted by Hume, according to MacIntyre, by way of the passions. In his treatment of Hume's account of the passions,

MacIntyre finds that the image of the self which enables us to identify with the social perspective is a product of pride and that pride comes largely from the ownership of property. The social world can thus be conceptualized as a refined form of self interest.[5] In his account of the passions Hume thought he was discussing universal traits of human nature, claims MacIntyre,[6] but in reality Hume was actually reflecting the values of eighteenth century Britain.[7] As a consequence, MacIntyre concludes that "Hume's philosophical psychology does not provide foundations for Hume's political philosophy, independent of that political philosophy."[8]

We have already rejected and argued against the notion that Hume's starting point is egocentric. We have also rejected and argued against the notion that Hume's starting point assumes that it is possible or even meaningful to begin with speculation about universal human nature independent of culture and history. Moreover, we have rejected and argued against the contention that the social world for Hume can be conceptualized as a refined form of self-interest. Instead of repeating all of those arguments, let me indicate two errors of MacIntyre's interpretation into which he is forced by the need to defend his thesis coherently. First, according to MacIntyre, love and hate are derivative from pride and humility.[9] Given our extensive investigation into Hume's account of the passions, it should be obvious that love and hate are not derivative and that benevolent impulses can be primary. Love and hate are as basic as pride and humility, and love and hate have other selves as their object. There would be no way of explaining this without presupposing a social context. Second, MacIntyre's explanation of why Hume criticized the Jacobites is that the latter challenged the status quo of property.[10] On the contrary, what the Jacobites refused to see was the importance of custom. Property is a form of custom, and it is custom which is primary for Hume. The Jacobites appealed to a timeless metaphysical principle like dynastic right instead of to custom. By anchoring his social world in custom, Hume was presupposing a social and historical starting point.[11] MacIntyre is forced to attribute to Hume the view that a social consensus is future oriented from the point of view of the individual.[12] We have argued that the consensus is anchored in the past.

In the body of this book, Chapters Two through Seven, we have interpreted Hume's moral philosophy not only by a close analysis of the text and by reference to his historical, cultural, and intellectual milieu but also in the light of the Copernican revolution. What emerged was a treatment of basic issues in modern moral philosophy which was revolutionary in this Copernican sense despite what it shared and owed to its predecessors. It is now time to spell out in greater detail what is unique and challenging in Hume's Copernican revolution in moral philosophy.

Ironically it was the problems generated in Hume's *Treatise* which led to the gradual transformation and growing consistency in his views so that his endorsement of *An Enquiry Concerning the Principles of Morals* as his greatest work is now intelligible precisely because it embodies in a deeper way the manifest Copernican revolution in moral philosophy.[13] This is why the differences between the *Treatise* and the *Enquiry* must be attended to with care. Both of the major difficulties in Hume's *Treatise*, the conception of the self and the sympathy mechanism, were problems which reflected Hume's attempt to understand the *We Do* perspective itself as a mechanical form of order. In *An Enquiry Concerning Human Understanding*, Hume started to replace the mechanical (Newtonian) form of order with an organic conception of order, i.e., seeing the agent as an organism within an environment. But it is in *An Enquiry Concerning the Principles of Morals* that the *We Do* perspective is finally treated exclusively as a form of cultural order. By culture, we understand the conjunction of the social and the historical. It is not enough to see mankind as a collection of agents interacting with the world, rather we must also see ourselves as beings whose interactions with the world and with each other are mediated by culture. We must see ourselves as immersed in the world by way of a community of responsible persons.

The differences between the two *Enquiries* are enlightening. In *An Enquiry Concerning Human Understanding*, Hume describes our epistemological and metaphysical concerns from the action viewpoint, but his discussion of these topics, now separated from the larger context of the *Treatise*, is lacking an account of social exchanges. In *An Enquiry Concerning the Principles of Morals*, the cultural order is first and foremost. Instead of treating moral philosophy as a kind of empirical research, Hume launches into an explication of the ordinary social and historical understanding of the moral concepts we already have and use. That is, Hume is now primarily concerned to explain what we *mean* by what we say.

> ...we shall endeavour to follow a very simple method: we shall analyze that complication of mental qualities which form what, in common life, we call Personal Merit....The very nature of language guides us almost infallibly in forming a judgment of this nature; and as every tongue possesses one set of words which are taken in a good sense, and another in the opposite, the least acquaintance with the idiom suffices....Men are now cured of their passion for hypotheses and systems in natural philosophy, and will hearken to no arguments but those which are derived from experience. It is full time they should attempt a like reformation in all moral disquisitions; and reject every system of ethics, however subtle or ingenious, which is not founded on fact and observation. (*EPM*, pp. 173-75)

Nowhere do we find human beings living in a state of nature. Everywhere we find human beings in a social system. Moreover, there is little, if anything, we do that was not already conceived by our predecessors. Hence there is an historical dimension that is critical to what we do as well as a social dimension.

Man is a social being.[14] The very first state is a social state, and the reason for this is obviously biological, namely, that human beings cannot survive unless cared for by others. The fact that the first state is a social state and that the reason behind this is biological does not mean that Hume deduced the nature of man from biology. Knowing the biological facts allows us to make certain assumptions about human beings, but all further insights into human beings hinge on the social contexts within which human beings operate. Hume's science of man consists of generalizations abstracted from particular social and historical contexts, and where like circumstances hold the generalizations will hold. That is, we are trying to discern analogies rather than underlying laws. But Hume would be the first to admit that the circumstances could change.[15]

Part of Hume's critique of the social contract is that the social contract theory presupposes that it is possible to speak meaningfully about human beings in a pre-social state and to draw normative conclusions from speculation about that state. From Hume's point of view it does not make sense to talk about human nature in a pre-social state, hence no normative conclusions or policy decisions can be drawn meaningfully from such speculation. A large part of Hume's opposition to the social contract theory is that there is no empirical evidence for the existence or the possible existence of such a condition.[16] Note that the experience Hume appealed to here is not the introspection of ideas and impressions but the social experience of the historical and anthropological record.

If mankind cannot be understood apart from a social state, the obvious question which has to be raised is how are we to understand the social state. Clearly the social state cannot be understood in terms of its origins in a pre-social state. This further reinforces the importance of the denial of the social contract theories of the seventeenth and eighteenth centuries. If the social state cannot be understood in terms of or deduced from a pre-social state, then no abstract theory of human nature or psychological theory can be the basis for understanding the social state. That is why a reductive Newtonian explanation is ultimately not wholly adequate. In a very important sense, the social state is *sui generis*. What can be asked is, and this is the kind of question Hume did ask, what must human beings be like in

273

order for the social state to be possible. Here it makes sense to say, as Hume did, that human beings must be inherently social beings capable of sympathetic identification with others and with the social perspective.

The process of sympathy even in the *Treatise* is best understood as a social-psychological process which is instrumental in creating uniformities. Sympathy is originally defined by Hume as the process in which our idea of someone else's mental state is enlivened so as to become the very same mental state in ourselves (*Treatise*, p. 319). But Hume does not actually argue that there is a mental state and that we can check its existence independently in sympathy. Rather, he argues that the sympathy process creates in us the mental state that we normally expect to find in a given social situation. Sympathy as a social process creates the mental state in the observer and often even in the original actor. To us, this is an awkward eighteenth century faculty psychology way of saying what is now a commonplace, namely, that our understanding of our own mental states is socially structured linguistically from the very beginning. (*Ibid.*, pp. 317, 589).

Sympathy allows us to monitor our own behavior because we can imagine how others will perceive us. The element of monitoring also makes intelligible how values are consciously incorporated into our action, how these values change, and how they develop without recourse either to crude reductionism or to naively rationalistic accounts. Values arise as follows:

economic needs → division of labor → new social and political arrangements

↓

self-conscious rules

↓

we act according to the rules

Rules are not simple descriptions, they do not simply predict, but are norms with both a history and the conscious participation of human agents.

It should also be clear that the social condition cannot be understood by reference to some utopian scheme. That is, the social state as we find it anywhere is not an imperfect copy of some ideal state, nor can the social state be understood as aspiring to some utopia. In his essay, "Idea of a Perfect Commonwealth," Hume does consider a utopia, but he warns us in the essay not to take this notion literally. "Of all mankind, there are none so pernicious as political projectors, if they have power, nor so ridiculous, if they want it."[17] Any recommendation must be implemented "by such gentle alterations and innovations as may not give too great disturbance to society."[18] No wise magistrate should ever "try experiments merely upon the credit of supposed argument and philosophy."[19]

This would seem to suggest that Hume would be closer to the Aristotelian tradition, with its emphasis on the close scrutiny of how institutions actually work in our experience. But Hume is more cognizant of the purely historical dimension rather than the supposed teleology of social institutions. An interesting contrast can be made with the original Aristotelian claim that the unity of action in poetry brings us closer to the truth than history. As opposed to this doctrine, ultimately based upon a teleological view of explanation, Hume maintained that there is no difference in kind between the unity of action in poetry and in history, rather, there is only a difference of degree. Moreover, that unity according to Hume is not the revelation of some ultimate end but the chain of causes and effects.[20] Hume's anti-Aristotelian (i.e. anti-teleological) bias is nowhere brought out better than in his critique of the concept of the "natural," a good instance of which is Hume's letter to Hutcheson where he declared "I cannot agree to your [Hutcheson's] sense of *Natural*. 'Tis founded on final Causes; which is a Consideration, that appears to me pretty uncertain & unphilosophical."[21]

Hume did not have a Hegelian theory of the social dimension of human experience. There is no notion in Hume of a grand synthesis of social institutions and no notion of a necessary progression of social institutions in either past history or in the future.[22] Hume did not share the general Enlightenment feeling about inevitable progress. We should remind ourselves as well that Hume, despite the influence of Cicero, did not subscribe to any cyclical view of history and human institutions. Human beings are "to a certain degree, inconstant and irregular," so that institutions reveal "a diversity of characters, prejudices, and opinions," and therefore no social theorist should ever "prophesy concerning any event, or foretell the remote consequences of things."[23]

We have already indicated that there is something *sui generis* about our understanding of the social dimension of human experience. This dimension was brought out in Hume's *Treatise* when he maintained that we have in moral philosophy a privileged way of explaining past actions which is not available to purely natural philosophy. We can understand the social world better because we can sympathetically identify with the agents involved.

> We must certainly allow, that the cohesion of the parts of matter arises from natural and necessary principles, whatever difficulty we may find in explaining them: And for a like reason we must allow, that human society is founded on like principles; and *our reason in the latter case, is better than even that in the former*; because we not only observe, that men always seek society, but can also explain the principles, on which the universal propensity is founded. (*Treatise*, pp. 401-02)[*italics mine*]

Moreover, the kind of explanations we find in moral philosophy are not such as establish any symmetry between explanation and prediction.

> ...we can better account for [moral phenomena] after they happen, from springs and principles, of which everyone has within himself, or from observation, the strongest assurance and conviction; but it is often fully as

impossible for human prudence beforehand to foresee and foretell them.[24]

In his essay "Of Some Remarkable Customs", Hume analyzed the Athenian law of indictment of illegality, in which a guardian may be punished for measures embraced because of his persuasion. What appears to us as an irrational law is explained by showing that, relative to their intentions and their conception of their situation, the Athenians had a good reason to enact the law. Thus, social action is explained by reference to the good reasons agents had for acting. Instead of an appeal to a hidden structure, human action is explained in terms of the agents' understanding of their situation. Whatever hidden structures we may discover, physiological, psychological, etc., the knowledge of the hidden structures is valuable only insofar as it may be used to achieve ends which must themselves be both consciously held and socially acceptable. Hence, *the cultural frame of reference is conceptually and normatively prior to all other frames of reference.*[25]

It is important to see that Hume is not an historical reductionist. That is, Hume does not maintain that history is a process which we merely observe and which justifies itself. What history reveals is the evolution of practices, each of which embodies some norms that we can recognize and identify in our own actions. The dictionary, for example, is both descriptive of past practice, the evolution of that practice, and it prescribes rules for future practice.

There are two elements in Hume's cultural frame of reference which must be carefully separated: the historical and the normative. An essential part of any explanation of what we do is to determine the *origin* of the practice and how the practice has *evolved*. No practice is an objectively timeless structure. No practice or hardly any originates in a self-conscious plan. The English language, for example, has a grammatical structure but it was not consciously planned. Once we become self-conscious of a practice and our role within it, we are capable of engaging in critical reflection upon the practice. The critical reflection does not consist in judging the practice or practices by reference to any standard external to the practices themselves. Reflection on the evolution of the practices leads to some notion of a norm embodied within the practice itself. Once we are conscious of this norm we are in a position to employ the norm self-consciously and extend the norm to new situations. When we discover conflicts within our practices, the conflicts are resolved by reconsideration of the conflicts within the norms the practices exemplify.

An examination of two examples of Hume's developmental accounts will perhaps clarify the extent to which Hume tried to understand what we do by reference to a cultural form of order. In his examination of justice, Hume distinguished between the origin of the rules of justice which he explained developmentally and the moral value of these rules. When he turned to the problem of justifying what had evolved he proceeded as follows. First, justice ratifies *de facto* practice. That is why, for example, present possession is so important in the case of property. When we have to apply these precedent practices to new circumstances, we do so by *analogical* extension. When promising, originally motivated by self-interest, becomes a regular part of our behavior, and when sympathy with the beneficial tendencies of promise keeping causes us to approve of this behavior, and when we note the tendency in ourselves to interpret all action as an expression of a motive and motives as the expression of character, we are led to imagine that there is a natural motive called willing an obligation behind the promise. We approve of this motive, imagined though it is, through sympathy and we detest ourselves on occasion for not having the motive. This sense of detestation creates the sense of duty. The self-conscious act of sympathy becomes a reason, not a cause, and it is an act consistent with our past experience but not entailed by our past.

Sometimes we give retrospective utilitarian rationales for our practices, but this was not and could not have been the original motive. In so doing, what we are giving is a reason for continuing a form of

278

action which in the past grew piecemeal and unintentionally. This retrospective glance is accomplished through sympathy, but a sympathy aided by self-conscious general rules.

Hume's refusal to embrace a totally utilitarian account of justice is made more intelligible in view of his interpretationism, that is, his recognition that human beings act because of their reasons, not just from causes.[26] Hume did not maintain that we accepted justice because it is consistent with our long range interests. This could only happen if we could define our long range interests in some clearly objective fashion. But if human beings do not have built-in-natures or interests independent of culture, then it is not intelligible to specify such an interest. "Justice establishes itself by a kind of convention or agreement; that is, by a sense of interest, suppos'd to be common to all..."(*Treatise*, p. 498).

The explanation of the development of science follows the same pattern. Society develops on two distinguishable but interrelated levels. On the material level, we have commercial and economic developments, including the specialization of the division of labor. Posterior to this, there is a corresponding intellectual development in ideas and theory which criticizes and modifies the economic process. The intellectual component is not, at first, an object of distinct consciousness on its own account, but it emerges as such when further developments in the arts, the sciences, and law cannot proceed without the critical appraisal of old institutions.

Hume argued that law, for example, must necessarily precede developments in science. In addition, the growth of the division of labor in commerce and manufacture creates the conditions for the rise of justice and laws as a public institution. When the application of the laws necessitates criticism and argument, i.e. critical reappraisal, this prepares the way for other intellectual developments. Even the exact sciences begin on an informal, trial and error basis but become institutionalized as we know them only after society appreciates their relevance. Science thus arose among artists and craftsmen whose objectives were not to satisfy curiosity or to establish a particular state of natural or social affairs but to increase our ability to control the environment. Failure to understand this historical and evolutionary element in science is as destructive of future progress in science as the failure to understand the evolution of political institutions. One may employ critical scientific thinking in the reappraisal of institutions only as long as one recognizes the social norms constitutive of scientific thinking itself. And these norms can only be gleaned by reference to origins and developments.[27]

The evolutionary account of the rise of science is not just irrelevant historical background but leads to a deeper insight into the nature of the human thinking process. The verification process, which is inseparable from that growth of science and law which fosters their continual progress, involves a necessarily social dimension. This social dimension had gone unnoticed in epistemology or was rejected by the Platonic-Cartesian individualism, just as the Aristotelian humanistic tradition in ethics had stressed that moral restraint was rational self-restraint, instead of considering the possibility of social restraint through sympathy. Both were guilty of an *I Think* perspective. The further importance of critical self-detachment is that, by showing the social foundations of science, it stimulates the continuing dialogue between intellectuals and the practical artisan. It rescues science from the potential evil of being mere theory and aids in material progress.

The Copernican Revolution as Explication

The attempt to understand our cultural values, that is to grasp the normative dimension and not just the historical development, may take one of three different forms: elimination, exploration, or explication.

Elimination: When we theorize from an elimination point of view, there is an explicit substitution of new ideas for old ideas. Elimination is a form of radical innovation. All forms of reductionism are forms of elimination. Elimination is most character-istic of revolutionary thinking in physical science and technol-ogy. One example would be the elimination of Ptolemy's geo-centric theory of the universe in favor of Copernicus' heliocen-tric theory. Another example would be the elimination of earlier theories of disease by the discovery of microbes.

Exploration: In this mode of understanding we attempt to fol-low the implications of some hypothetical model in order to re-alize its possibilities. We begin with our ordinary understanding of how things work and speculate on what might be behind it. In time, we come to change our ordinary understanding. The new understanding does not evolve from or elaborate the old understanding, rather it replaces it by appeal to underlying structure.

Exploration is also a mode of thinking found in physical sci-ence, but it is preeminently the mode of thought in much of so-cial science. By analogy with physical science, the social sciences have persistently sought to discover the hidden structure behind the everyday understanding of social activity. Among Hume's predecessors those who invoked the state of nature or those who advocated that behind our acts of benevolence is really a hidden structure of self-interest were offering exploratory hy-potheses about our cultural order. Later social scientists such as Durkheim, Marx, Freud, Chomsky, etc. have persistently sought to reveal a structural level of which we are not immediately aware and have attributed to factors on that level the origin of our action. What is at issue here is not the correctness or incor-rectness of particular theories but rather the general mode of theorizing by speculation about the underlying structure.

By further analogy with physical science, the objective of ex-ploration is in time to produce a social technology in which there can be scientific control of man and his environment al-legedly for their mutual enhancement. Exploration, then, stresses the search for structure rather than meaning, a search for the formal elements underlying the everyday world rather than believing that the everyday world can constitute its own level of understanding, and it is an attempt to stabilize the social order by constructing a science of man which will serve the purposes of social control.

Explication: Here we try to clarify that which is routinely taken for granted, namely, our ordinary understanding of our practices in the hope of extracting from our previous practice a set of norms which can reflectively be used to guide future practice. Explication presupposes that efficient practice precedes the theory of it. *Explication attempts to specify the sense we have of ourselves when we act and to clarify that which seems to guide us.* We do not replace our ordinary understanding but rather come to know it in a new and better way. Explication seeks to arrive at a kind of *practical knowledge* which takes as primary the notion that a human being is an agent.[28] It rejects the perspective of exploration because the latter adopts a theoretical perspective in which human beings are viewed as thinking subjects facing an objective world. Put another way, whereas exploration is an attempt to conceptualize the relation between theory and practice, explication seeks to mediate practice from within practice itself. From the point of view of explication, neither practice nor the relation of theory to practice can be coherently conceptualized. *Explication is what Hume's Copernican revolution in moral philosophy is all about.*

Critics of explication are apt to charge that it must pick and choose "key" practices but that the choice cannot be justified by an appeal to anything other than an intuition about our practice. The defenders of explication would respond by saying that there is no coherent alternative. Moreover, the defenders of explication would then turn around and charge the proponents of exploration with the following form of incoherence. In order to theorize, that is, in order to explore an hypothesis about the hidden structure behind our practice, one must first identify the object of analysis, i.e., one must first identify the practice. Therefore, one must already possess an intuitive common sense understanding of practice before it can be analyzed. The theoretical analysis is forever parasitic upon the intuitive understanding and can never get beyond it. In examining any social practice we are not really observing an independent object as the physical sciences presumably do, rather, we are examining what we *mean* by what we are doing. It is therefore logically impossible to explore the hidden structure of our practice. That is the crucial difference between practical knowledge and theoretical knowledge.

Norms do not form a neat deductive system but are embedded within practice. That is why they can never be definitively articulated. As Wittgenstein once put it, we can never definitively circumscribe the concepts we use. This does not reflect ignorance on our part but rather that there is no "real" definition of those concepts.[29] In addition to rules there have to be principles for the application of the rules; but there are no rules for understanding the principles. Moreover, the norms can conflict, but the conflict can only be discovered retrospectively. Even the resolution of the conflict can only be by reference to other implicit norms, not by appeal to anything outside of prior practice. Here the best analogy to what Hume has in mind is the English common law. The logic of explication is inherently conservative, for the explication of practice is supervenient upon practice itself.[30] In this context, David Miller has made the important point that in Hume there cannot be a "theory" of resistance because a theory presupposes an authoritative framework, and the only authoritative framework Hume recognizes is the previous practice within an established political order.[31]

The standard objection raised against explication within the moral sphere is: what does one do when one lives in an immoral tradition? The immediate answer is that no tradition can be declared immoral except from the point of view of another tradition whose explication is the presumed basis for making such evaluations. Hence there is no escaping explication. It is perfectly legitimate to condemn despotism from the point of view of non-despotic traditions. Perhaps a more refined version of the standard objection is: how are we to understand living in a tradition that has become immoral (e.g. Nazi Germany)? Here

283

part of the answer would have to be that what one means by a tradition becoming immoral is that the tradition has been undermined by a group which holds an exploratory theory which has been allowed to pervert explicatory thinking. We suggest that historical research will bear out this interpretation of when traditions become perverted.

Perhaps the most significant point to be made in the debate between exploration and explication is the charge by advocates of explication that *exploration is inherently incoherent*. This incoherence can be seen on two levels. First, before one can investigate the hidden structure of a social practice one must clearly identify the social practice itself. No analysis can proceed unless there is a clear conception of the fundamental entities which are the subject matter of analysis. A social practice is an *intersubjectively* shared framework of norms within which we interpret what we are doing. In order to identify the social practice, therefore, one must specify clearly the intersubjectively shared framework of norms. Since the framework is intersubjective no specification of the framework is legitimate which does not accord with the previous (historical) practice. In short, one must already have engaged in explication before one can engage in exploration.

It is precisely here that the incoherence arises. What would be the point of exploration in the light of a consensus on explication? In the presence of a consensus on explication, an exploration is redundant at best. If there is no consensus on the explication, what would be the function of an exploration (or hypothesis about hidden structure) of our social practice? An exploration in the absence of a consensus on the explication could only be both (a) a form of advocacy for one version of explication and (b) an attempt to discredit rival explications. But it is difficult to see on the one hand how we can judge between alternative explications of a social practice without appealing to a consensus explication on another (higher) level. The inherently conservative nature of explication once more asserts itself. On the other hand, it is difficult to see how we should tell the difference between an outright elimination (a form of radical innovation) and an exploration which operates in the absence of consensus on explication and which is at the same time an attempt to discredit rival explications.

If the foregoing argument is correct then those who engage in exploration are doing something that is intellectually incoherent, analogous to pulling themselves up by their own bootstraps, or they are doing something that is indistinguishable from attempting to introduce a radical revolution disguised as a contextual clarification. If we remain on this level, the advocates of exploration are guilty either of fuzzy thinking or of moral and political disingenuousness. To compound their difficulty, we note that there is a higher order resolution of the charge of incoherence by intellectual appeal to the theories of Hegel and Marx. Here one can argue that behind conflicting views is a hidden historical structure, a teleological process which reaches closure in favor of one of the contestants. This amounts to an exploration about exploration. To speculate on the hidden structure behind rival views amounts to construing rivals as incapable of properly conceptualizing either a social practice or their own practice. But this way of trying to escape the dilemma of exploration compounds the embarrassment of advocates of exploration. To embrace the methodological moves of Hegel and/or Marx is incontrovertibly to cross the boundary from exploration to elimination and to endorse radical revolution.

The entire argument about the incoherence of exploration can be articulated at an even higher level. No technical form of thinking (including mathematics and physical science) can itself be understood except by appeal to something which is pre-technical (i.e. common sense). This is, of course, Hume's Copernican revolution in philosophy in general and the starting point of the *Treatise*. Technical thinking, no matter how valuable within its limited and circumscribed sphere, can never replace pre-technical thinking. Hume's insistence on this point is always treated by his critics as Hume's "confusion" of logic and psychology. Rival hypotheses within technical discourse must ultimately be judged by appeal to pre-technical norms. Nor can one ever develop a technical account of pre-technical thinking, for, on pain of incoherence, there would be no possible way to judge the adequacy of the proffered technical account. Briefly stated, the implications of this argument are that (1) technical expertise is no substitute for common sense moral feelings about our intersubjectively held norms and that (2) quasi-physiological, psychological, or sociological explorations are not adequate substitutes for explicatory moral arguments.

Let us now turn to Hume's explicit answers to the major issues within moral philosophy in order to determine the extent to which he follows through on his Copernican Revolution in moral philosophy.

Moral Insight

The *first* issue concerns the nature and the source of moral insight or apprehension. How do we come to recognize that there is a moral dimension to the world in which we live? What are we doing and what are we saying when we make moral judgments either about our own action or the actions of others? How are we to understand our own moral conflicts and the way in which we resolve them? Such an issue would never occur to someone who either had no conception of morality or whose experience never led to conflicts.

The discussion of moral insight presupposes a positive answer to a previous question: "Is there a specifically moral realm or moral dimension to our experience or to our engagement with the world and each other?". It is because some thinkers believe that there is such a dimension that they go to great pains to understand it. Hume forthrightly identifies himself with those who believe that there is such a moral dimension. In the *Treatise,* he asked the question "Whether 'tis by means of our ideas or impressions we distinguish betwixt vice and virtue..."

(*Treatise*, p. 456). The question for Hume is not whether there is a moral dimension but how we apprehend it.

In *An Enquiry Concerning the Principles of Morals* Hume begins by stating in an unambiguous fashion that there is a moral dimension to our experience, and he does so with a scathing dismissal of those who think otherwise.

> Those who have denied the reality of moral distinctions, may be ranked among the disingenuous disputants; nor is it conceivable, that any human creature could ever seriously believe, that all characters and actions were alike entitled to the affection and regard of everyone....Let a man's insensibility be ever so great, he must often be touched with the images of Right and Wrong; and let his prejudices be ever so obstinate, he must observe, that others are susceptible of like impressions. The only way, therefore, of converting an antagonist of this kind, is to leave him to himself. (*EPM*, pp. 169-70).

There are two reasons why even well-intentioned individuals might subscribe to a kind of moral relativism in which the existence of a moral dimension is denied or radically relativized. First, the nature of the times may lead serious thinkers to believe that in order to combat dogmatism one must espouse some form of sceptical relativism. This is transparently ineffective because it presupposes some other normative position which will have to be defended. It is difficult to conceive of such a defense once the ground has been removed by denying the reality of our moral experience. It would be much more plausible to show that dogmatists have misconstrued our moral experience.

A second reason for subscribing to moral relativism is that many thinkers hold metaphysical and epistemological views that they cannot accept as an adequate intellectual account of morality. Rather than question the appropriateness of their metaphysical and epistemological preconceptions, these thinkers have opted for a radical dichotomy of fact and value which at least temporarily relieves them of the necessity of resolving why values do not fit into their overall philosophical scheme. What Hume would question here is the adequacy of the metaphysical and the epistemological views. It is no accident that Hume introduces his Copernican Revolution first in metaphysics and epistemology in the *Treatise* before discussing moral philosophy. Those thinkers who have alienated values from the task of rational reconstruction are, according to Hume, victims of the *I Think* perspective.

Having accepted the existence of a moral dimension in our interaction with the world and each other, and having dismissed those who deny it, Hume next turns his attention to those who have misconstrued the nature of the moral dimension.

The first group that has misconstrued the moral dimension of human experience consists of those who appeal to theology. Hume's objections to theologically based moral philosophy are well known and fall into two categories, internal and external. Internally Hume reiterated the question of how an all powerful God can create a universe with such seemingly evil components. From an external perspective he raises questions about whether there are plausible proofs of God's existence, but most especially he argues that all such proofs are unable to generate moral attributes in God. Hume reminded us as well of the socially destructive religious wars of the seventeenth century in which religious zeal undermined the moral fabric of communities. Finally, he repeated the claim that the whole notion of an external sanction is incompatible with the belief in intrinsically moral motivation. Religion, narrowly construed, typically fails to capture our sense of what morality is all about.[32]

The second group that has misconstrued the moral dimension of human experience consists of those who draw an analogy between moral apprehension and *a priori* reason. On the positive side, by recognizing the existence of a moral dimension to human experience, this position overcomes the disadvantages both of those who deny the existence altogether of such a dimension and those who try to reduce the moral dimension to something which is ultimately amoral. Ralph Cudworth puts the case as follows:

Moral good and evil...cannot possibly be arbitrary things, made by will without nature; because it is universally true, that things are what they are, not by will but by nature....omnipotent will cannot make things like or equal one to another, without the natures of likeness or equality. The reason whereof is plain, because all these things imply a manifest contradiction....Wherefore the natures of justice and injustice cannot be arbitrarious things...the right or authority of the commander, which is founded in natural justice and equity, and an antecedent obligation to obedience in the subjects; which things are not made by laws, but presupposed before all laws to make them valid.[33]

Hume offered three objections to this analogy between moral apprehension and *a priori* reason. First, Hume argued that no one could specify the existence of moral relations in a non-question-begging way. Second, Hume argued that this position both failed to account for how such alleged moral relations could relate to human action, and it obscured important differences. There is a tendency in this position to reduce all three moral issues, insight, motivation, and their relation to the first issue alone. For example, the conflict of action and principle is spoken of in terms of the conflict between reason and passion, and the latter problem is allegedly solved by saying that if one "really knew" the first principles then it would be impossible to act contrary to them. All wrongdoing is explained not as passion overcoming reason but as an inadequate use of reason. There is thus on this version no real difference between "right" and "ought". The identity of "right" and "ought" derives from the tendency to treat all of moral philosophy as being concerned with only one issue, namely the source of moral insight. This tendency to ignore questions of moral practice, to dismiss the question of relating practice to theory as a special case of recognizing the first principles, to subsume the third issue under the first issue, is precisely what both Hutcheson and Hume criticized. Finally, this approach has as a policy implication a rigid hierarchical structure to society wherein we separate those who "really know" from everyone else.

One way in which advocates of the analogy to *a priori* reason might try to defend themselves is to agree that moral principles even when known do not always influence conduct, but that such principles "ought" to influence conduct. This "ought" does not describe the moral principles themselves, nor does this "ought" describe human action or feeling. What this "ought" represents is another kind of alleged relation, this time between moral principles and human action. *The function of Hume's is-ought paragraph is to question the very intelligibility of such an alleged relation.* Failure to account adequately for the moral principles (i.e. moral apprehension) leads to the failure to explain the relation.

The third group that has misconstrued the moral dimension to human experience consists of those who liken moral apprehension to empirical reason about structures independent of human nature. Hume's critique of the view that there are moral first principles abstracted from experience which reflect independent objective structures is even clearer in *An Enquiry Concerning the Principles of Morals* than it was in the *Treatise*. Hume asked, first, what does it mean to say that an act is right? The answer given by advocates of this third group is that the act conforms to our moral precepts or rules. When Hume next asked for the origin of these rules, the advocates answered that the rules are abstracted from experience. Hume then asked from what kind of experience are they abstracted. The advocates must answer from experience concerning the relevant facts, namely moral situations. Hume then replied that in order to identify the relevant facts one must presuppose some criterion for identifying them, and thus one must presuppose already some moral principle. The argument of the advocates of the third group is circular.

Hume avoided their difficulty by asserting that moral experience and therefore moral principles are the result of an interaction of human beings with their environment, including other human beings. Hence there is no special difficulty for Hume in identifying moral experience, because we are in part responsible for bringing a criterion to our experience. This is an important rebuttal of those who attribute a simplistic empiricism to Hume.

> Reason judges either of *matter of fact* or of *relations*. Enquire then, *first*, where is that matter of fact which we here call crime....we may infer, that the crime of ingratitude is not any particular individual fact; but arises from a complication of circumstances, which, being presented to the spectator, excites the *sentiment* of blame, *by the particular structure and fabric of his mind* [*italics mine*]....This doctrine will become still more evident, if we compare moral beauty with natural, to which in many particulars it bears so near a resemblance.–...beauty is not a quality of the circle. It lies not in any part of the line, whose parts are equally distant from a common centre. It is only the effect which that figure produces upon the mind, whose peculiar fabric of structure renders it susceptible of such sentiments. In vain would you look for it in the circle, or seek it, either by your senses or by mathematical reasoning in all the properties of that figure. (*EPM*, pp. 287-292)

For Hume, moral knowledge is empirical matter of fact knowledge similar to our knowledge of all secondary qualities. It is not knowledge of an objective structure totally independent of mankind. Furthermore, like knowledge of secondary qualities, moral knowledge appeals to intersubjective rules about perspective, etc. Moral knowledge differs from other kinds of factual secondary quality knowledge in that the kinds of intersubjective rules that form the framework of our reaction have evolved culturally over a long period of time and are rooted in past practice or action.[34] Although factual secondary quality knowledge like judgments about the colors of things may be indirectly related to action, moral knowledge is directly related to action. The direct relation to action is not a matter of always and immediately leading to action, but rather that the context out of which this moral knowledge emerges is a context of action or past social practices, and not just linguistic practices. Having emerged from such a context, moral knowledge leads to action at the appropriate moment in a direct way without the interposition of additional passions or interests. Ordinary matters of fact do not have this direct connection with action, so one of Hume's arguments against those who construe moral experience as *a priori* is used as well against those who construe moral knowledge as empirical knowledge of structures totally independent of human beings. As Hume repeatedly insisted, ordinary matter of fact knowledge gets its motive power by association with practical concerns. That is, the theoretical is dependent upon the practical.

Failure to accept Hume's account of moral knowledge as a kind of practical knowledge leads to one of two extremes. One can deny the existence of moral knowledge altogether. This denial itself comprises a spectrum all the way from nihilism, to emotivism, to relativism at one end to those who reduce the moral dimension to social philosophy at the other end, including Hobbes as well as Hegel and Marx! The other possibility is to insist that moral knowledge is a unique kind of objective theoretical knowledge. The difficulty with the latter possibility is that to date it has not succeeded in capturing our moral intuitions, and it has obfuscated the relation between such alleged moral knowledge and action.

One other possibility remains for those committed to defending a totally objective account of moral knowledge. That possibility is to maintain that although moral knowledge seems to depend upon *custom*,[35] perhaps it is possible to give an exploratory account of custom itself. That is, we can speculate on the presence of a hidden structure behind custom itself, a structure which might be understood as a kind of theoretical knowledge and not a form of practical knowledge.

In order to search for the alleged hidden structure of custom, one must assume either that social practices or institutions have structures independent of the consciousness of participants or that there is some hidden reductive structure in the agents themselves. Hume has already rejected the notion of understanding institutions independent of the agents' conception of the institution. Recall the charge that exploration is ultimately incoherent. Moreover, we should not confuse the fact that practices have unintended consequences with the existence of hidden structures to institutions. Once we are conscious of unintended consequences we are free to modify them in a way that would not be true of objective but hidden social structures. This leaves only the possibility that there is a hidden reductive structure in the agents themselves.[36]

The major stumbling block in the attempt to conceptualize the alleged hidden structure behind custom by reference to the agents alone is that such an attempt fails totally to capture the normative dimension of custom. In order to see this point clearly, let us review Hume's critique of the social contract theory, an early version of the attempt to conceptualize custom.

That the rule of morality, which enjoins the performance of promises, is not *natural*, will sufficiently appear from these two propositions, which I proceed to prove, viz. *that a promise wou'd not be intelligible, before human conventions had establish'd it*; and *that even if it were intelligible, it wou'd not be attended with any moral obligation.* I say, *first*, that a promise is not intelligible naturally, nor antecedent to human conventions; and that a man, unacquainted with society, could never enter into any engagements with another, even tho' they could perceive each other's thoughts by intuition. If promises be natural and intelligible, there must be some act of the mind attending these words, *I promise*.... The act of the mind, exprest by a promise, is not a *resolution* to perform anything: For that alone never imposes any obligation. Nor is it a *desire* of such a performance: For we may bind ourselves without such a desire, or even with an aversion, declar'd and avow'd. Neither is it the *willing* of that action...– For a promise always regards some future time, and the will has an influence only on present actions. It follows, therefore, that since the act of the mind, which enters into a promise, and produces its obligation, is neither the resolving, desiring, nor willing any particular performance, it must necessarily be the *willing* of that *obligation*, which arises from the promise.

....But 'tis certain we can naturally no more change our own sentiments, than the motions of the heavens; nor by a single act of our will, that is, by a promise, render any action agreeable or disagreeable, moral or immoral; which without that act, wou'd have produc'd contrary impressions....It wou'd be absurd, therefore, to will any new obligation....A promise, therefore, is *naturally* something altogether unintelligible, nor is there any act of the mind belonging to it. (*Treatise*, pp. 516-17)

293

Looking at custom from the inside, that is, from the We Do perspective construed as a cultural form of order, we can account not only for its descriptive but also for its prescriptive dimension. Looking at custom from the outside, that is, from the I *Think* perspective, we fail to find any normative dimension. The practice can only be understood from within, and the understanding must capture our pre-conceptual practice. That is why in the middle of his foregoing discussion of promising, Hume stated that his position was not "only a conclusion of philosophy...but is entirely conformable to our common ways of thinking and expressing ourselves" (*Treatise*, pp. 517). Nor will it do to cite some particular custom which can be explained from the outside if that custom occurs within an already ongoing moral community.[37] This still fails to account for the fundamental customs which render intelligible the later accretions. Moreover, persistent adoption of the I *Think* perspective actually leads to undermining custom which it eventually finds unintelligible. As Hume put it, "there is no virtue or moral duty but what may, with facility, be refined away, if we indulge a false philosophy in sifting and scrutinizing it, by every captious rule of logic, in every light or position in which it may be placed."[38]

The search for a hidden structure which attempts to capture the normative dimension usually terminates, among utilitarians, in a theory which makes social utility the one supreme inherent moral principle. When pressed to explain the supreme principle itself, utilitarians offer a naturalistic explanation in terms of maximizing self-interest. That is, the utilitarian assumes that behind the concern for the public good is the hidden concern for maximizing self-interest. We have already noted Hume's objections to and rejection of this approach. What we should add is that the plausibility of utilitarianism relies partly on its appeal to customary norms of which we do approve like social utility. Where utilitarianism becomes implausible is in its reductive account of the customary norms. Invariably, utilitarianism has to assume teleological views of human beings, views which Hume both rejects as empirically false in the light of common experience and as incapable of empirical confirmation. Put another way, utilitarianism as a search for hidden structure is in the final analysis an elimination and not even an exploration.[39]

For Hume, one begins with moral sentiments or language and then proceeds to offer some sort of account or generalization to explain moral approbation. But the explaining generalization is not itself a first principle or set of first principles from which moral approbation is deduced. Hume's explanation is on another level entirely. Failure to see this leads sometimes to the exasperating charge that Hume is confusing psychology with logic. Such a charge is symptomatic of the dim awareness that Hume is doing something totally different. Like his utilitarian opponents, Hume does believe that you can infer value judgments from factual judgments, but the issue is which factual judgments. For Hume's opponents the factual judgments are atemporal judgments about maximizing self-interest. For Hume those factual judgments have to be about the norms already implicit in past historical practice. The practice of the world goes farther in teaching us the degrees of our duty than the most subtle philosophy which was ever yet invented.

What all of these attempts to construe the moral dimension of human experience as a form of objective theoretical knowledge have in common is the *I Think* perspective in which theoretical knowledge is taken as basic. What Hume's *We Do* perspective does is to maintain that practical knowledge is more fundamental.[40] That is why subscribers to the *I Think* perspective always fail to capture the normative dimension of our thinking, thought's relation to action. In their unease, the subscribers to the *I Think* perspective ignore the issue of motivation, disingenuously dismiss it as the concern of psychology, or attempt when honest to bridge the gap by invoking a metaphysical *deus ex machina*. In the case of Hume's contemporaries it was the appeal to a theological guarantee of the harmony of interests, whereas in the case of later utilitarians it is the assumption of the long range coincidence of self-interest and social interest. In both cases the appeal to a "hidden hand" is a metaphysical assumption without rational justification.[41]

In Hume's case what we find is the empirical claim that human beings have a capacity for benevolence or humanity which allows them to approve of what is beneficial to others even when their interest is not at stake. Moreover, Hume makes the claim that we do not have a self-interest apart from our membership within an on-going social whole with which we identify sympathetically. Hence the question can never arise in Hume's moral theory of whether I ought to be moral.[42] The question is, rather, what is the moral thing to be done. The conventional nature of moral insight within Hume's account not only captures the normative dimension of our moral insight but makes it much easier to understand how there can be an intersubjective consensus.

We might at this point briefly tie in this discussion with points we have made elsewhere about Hume's philosophy in general. Hume is an *ontological realist* in believing that there is a physical world which does exist independent of us. On the other hand, Hume is an *epistemological Copernican* in believing that our knowledge is always and necessarily a reflection of the structure of understanding we as agents bring to the world. Our contribution to the interaction with the world is not based upon permanent *a priori* principles but is rather experimental and cultural. It is therefore time bound and subject to change or evolution. The process of change in our structuring of our experience cannot be construed as progressive or teleological because that would imply a viewpoint that transcends that of the agent. There may, retrospectively, be "progress from" but not "progress to". The dynamics of this process leads the Copernican to recognize the extent to which our practical interests are intrinsic to the process. Hence, the Copernican is the first to stress the importance of practice and not relegate it to a limbo or treat it as a mysterious dependent upon theory. As a result, there can be no ultimate distinction between fact and value.

Again, as we indicated early on in this book, claiming that Hume explains everything by appeal to sentiment is inadequate because it fails to capture the thoroughly social dimension and the internally self-critical dimension of the *We Do* perspective in Copernicanism. There is both a secondary literature which faults Hume for not recognizing the broader use of reason as well as a secondary literature which points out the extent to which Hume does exactly that. However, neither one of those literatures recognizes that this specific use of reason never amounts to epistemological realism. Moreover, referring to Hume's Copernicanism as a naturalism is also misleading in that naturalism attempts to explain human agents from the point of view of other natural processes.[43] The whole point of Hume's Copernicanism is that human artifice must be explained by explication from within the practice and not by any kind of external exploratory hypothesis. Finally, the perennial claim that Hume is a sceptic can be seen at this point as the recognition that Hume denied that we can definitively state the rules internal to a practice. But in essence this amounts to the recognition that for Hume practical knowledge is more fundamental than theoretical knowledge. It can be said that for Hume the intelligibility of theoretical knowledge is threatened unless it is seen as derivative from practical knowledge. Once more we are reminded of how Hume leads us both into and out of scepticism. "We must submit to this fatigue, in order to live at ease ever after: And must cultivate true metaphysics with some care, in order to destroy the false and adulterate....to subvert that abstruse philosophy and metaphysical jargon, which, being mixed up with popular superstition, renders it in a manner impenetrable to careless reasoners, and gives it the air of science and wisdom." (*EHU*, pp. 12-13).[44]

Moral Motivation

The *second* issue concerns moral motivation. Are there specifically moral motives? If so, how do specifically moral motives relate to our non-moral motives? Here moral philosophy unavoidably touches on issues of human psychology or philosophical anthropology. Not all philosophers will see this as a peculiarly philosophical problem. Those who do consider the issue of moral motivation a problem will at some point have to explain just why some other philosophers take the former attitude.

The existence, the presence, and the invoking of moral motivation, or the internal sanction, is never problematic in Hume's moral philosophy. This is clearly the result of grounding moral philosophy in a *We Do* perspective. By the time we engage in moral philosophizing we are already part of an on-going moral community with a network of moral obligations. Any moral decision we make or any moral problem with which we wrestle already presupposes that we are immersed in a culture and that we are concerned to act as responsible agents. Very often such moral philosophizing reflects a conflict among presently felt obligations. Moral philosophy could never make sense to someone who was not familiar with what it meant to be an agent in a culture.

Just as the *I Think* perspective has difficulties both in recognizing and construing moral insight, so it has difficulties either recognizing or properly construing moral motivation. Hence the position one holds with regard to moral motivation is largely determined by the position one holds with respect to moral insight or apprehension. There are theorists who systematically deny the existence of moral motivation or the internal sanction, e.g., Hobbes, Mandeville, Bentham, and many subsequent utilitarians. This denial is a reflection of the denial of the existence of a moral dimension to human experience.

What we mean by difficulties in construing moral motivation is brought out by briefly considering those theorists who do recognize the existence of moral insight. Locke is an interesting and insightful case, for although he recognized a moral realm he denied a specifically moral motive or internal sanction. Locke felt more comfortable with a purely external sanction. Those who invoked God as an external sanction fit into the same category. Even those theorists such as Butler and Hutcheson who argued for the continuity between the moral motive and the ultimate self interest of the agent end by making it difficult to decide exactly when a moral motive or internal sanction is present. The appeal to a higher level of self-interest has two negative consequences. First, it confuses the issue of moral motivation with the issue of the relation of moral motivation to moral insight. As a result it tends to invoke the alleged conflict of passion and reason or more dubious metaphysical-moral entities such as the alleged "moral ought". Second, it has a tendency to construe all moral conflict as a conflict between the internal sanction and self-interest. As a result it fails to recognize the extent to which moral conflicts are often conflicts among obligations.

Even subsequent discussions of this issue in continental moral philosophy display the same pattern. Beginning with an I Think perspective, Kant proclaims the existence of moral insight and a moral motive, and he sought to formalize the conditions of moral insight in his famous categorical imperative. However, the consensus of scholarly opinion is that although Kant specified necessary conditions of moral insight and motivation his formulation does not provide sufficient conditions. Even Kant himself admitted that we could never be sure if we were really motivated by a moral motive. This is the difficulty of determining not the existence but the presence of moral motivation. Further, Hegel's objection to Kant is that Kant's analysis cannot deal with the conflict of obligations, again a reflection of the fact that beginning with an I Think perspective enmeshes one in labyrinthine distinctions between moral and non-moral motivation. Unfortunately, Hegel's resolution of this difficulty is to try to transcend the conflict by subsuming individual self-interest within the interest of an alleged social whole. In effect this is no different from utilitarianism's invocation of a hidden hand.

Looking at the situation from the point of view of the disengaged outside observer, that is from the *I Think* perspective, there is no clear way to identify moral motivation. Hence one settles either for insisting upon the presence of something that can never be positively identified, or one denies that it is ever present, or one compromises by maintaining that moral motivation is a special case of non-moral motivation properly construed. On the contrary, looking at the same situation as Hume does from the *We Do* perspective does not make the existence or the presence of moral motivation a mystery. In action, not in thought, we both discover who we are and add to what we are. That is why, as we have argued already, the self is discovered in action according to Hume's account of the passions. Both moral motivation and non-moral motivation are ultimately the result of human artifice in Hume's sense. There is nothing objectively primary about self-interest that allows it to be weighed precisely from the *I Think* perspective.[45]

From Hume's *We Do* perspective moral motivation can be carefully distinguished from non-moral motivation. Moral motivation is as transparently present to us as moral insight in those cases or situations where insight leads to action. The social conventionality of the standards or perspective from which we interpret a situation make clear whether we are involved morally or non-morally. Just as Hume found those who denied the reality of moral insight to be disingenuous so he would find those who deny the presence of moral motivation disingenuous. The fact that we sometimes perform morally approved actions for self-interested reasons hardly counts against this claim, for it is only because we can on many occasions distinguish moral from non-moral motivation that we can recognize this possibility. The same holds for situations where both kinds of motives are present. Moreover, just as it is possible to be mistaken about moral motivation or to be guilty of self-deception with regard to morality so the same kinds of mistakes are possible about self-interest. There is nothing intrinsically primary about non-moral motivation. This only appears to be the case to those who approach moral philosophy from an *I Think* perspective rather than a *We Do* perspective. Finally from the point of view of real life, engaged, and socially responsible agents the great moral conflicts are not conflicts between moral and non-moral motivation but the conflict among obligations. Even our interpersonal conflicts often reflect conflicting interpretations of our obligations rather than the failure to recognize the existence of any obligation.

By demystifying moral motivation without denying its existence, Hume accomplishes something very important. Moral motivation, i.e. the internal sanction, is as natural (and as artificial) as non-moral motivation. By exhibiting that moral motivation is natural as well as conventional, Hume avoided construing the problem of moral motivation as one of reason versus passion or as requiring supernatural sanctions or the threat of external sanctions. Those who appeal to external sanctions exclusively, including Hobbes, never really transcend the reason versus passion conceptualization of the problem of moral motivation. Invariably they are forced to appeal to some notion of the higher or highest self-interest and then have to wrestle with why this vision of the highest self-interest is vested only in a few of us. The idea that human beings can be made whole only from the outside was the intellectual justification for the oppressively hierarchical medieval social and political order Hume so vehemently criticized and still remains the intellectual justification for modern forms of totalitarianism.[46] In addition, Hume helped to liberate the human spirit intellectually by showing that natural impulses are not intrinsically bad. Moral motivation is not only the result of the disinterested perspective but also the product of a natural benevolence which often delights in the good fortune of others. It is the link between natural benevolence and moral motivation that will allow Hume to develop a unique understanding of social philosophy and modern commercial republics.

The Relationship of Moral Insight and Moral Motivation

The *third* issue concerns the relationship between moral insight and moral motivation. This is not exactly the same as the second issue, although it clearly addresses itself to the same phenomena. Even those philosophers who do not address themselves to the issue of moral motivation *per se* find it necessary to say something about the relationship of insight to motivation.

It has always seemed to philosophers that part of their problem is to arrive at some understanding as to why some individuals behave in a moral manner or in a manner consistent with moral principles or some set of norms and why some individuals do not. It becomes especially important to identify and to explain individuals who know the norms and who at least verbally subscribe to them but sometimes fail to conform in their action to those norms.

It is at this point that some clarification is to be found in history. It is only during the modern period, since the Renaissance, that the issue of relating theory to practice became an acutely critical one for philosophers. It is only during this period and thereafter that thinkers begin to demand that a theory or a point of view prove itself in practice. Bacon's famous aphorism that "knowledge is power" is symptomatic of this new attitude. I do not mean to raise the theory-practice issue in any philistine sense but in the serious sense in which we nowadays ask, for example, for the empirical confirmation of a theory in science. Prior to the modern period, philosophers would not have taken such an issue so seriously or have conceptualized it in the same way. More often than not in the classical and medieval period, philosophers were content to explain the issue away rather than see it as a problem with which to grapple. But after the modern period commences, it becomes impossible to ignore the issue. It should also be clear that the theory-practice relationship is problematic not only for moral philosophy but for the relationship between science and technology and between social theorizing and social engineering. Finally, I note that it is precisely the third issue that emerges so forcefully in Hume's moral philosophy, and it is when this point is seen that we can begin to realize the significance of Hume for moral philosophy.

Of all modern moral philosophies, Hume's is the only one which is able to discuss intelligibly the relationship between moral insight and moral motivation without denying the existence of either, without appeal to metaphysical mysteries. Given the *We Do* perspective of Hume's Copernican Revolution in moral philosophy, the relationship is natural and empirically confirmable in the experience of the socially responsible agent, but not the disengaged intellect. In attempting to understand that relationship from the *I Think* perspective, an inevitable gap is created between the insight, however construed, and the motivation, however construed. In an attempt to close that gap, philosophers and theologians have invoked a whole host of concepts from weakness of will to sin, predestination, elaborate appeals to the higher self-interest, the alleged "moral ought", metaphysically transcendent social wholes, and even question-begging legalistic analogies. There is no need to repeat all that has already been said about Hume's critique of this vast variety of what he would consider subterfuges.

What is important for us to note here is that the natural and obvious relationship between moral insight and moral motivation that emerges from Hume's *We Do* perspective allows Hume to conceptualize the relationship between moral philosophy and social philosophy in a unique and insightful way. *Moral philosophy* is the most general and fundamental axiological division in philosophy. It is concerned with the relationships among human beings. *Social philosophy* is concerned with the relationships between human beings and social institutions. *Political philosophy* is concerned with the relationships among institutions. Hume's social philosophy and political philosophy can be characterized broadly as utilitarian. What we mean by *utilitarian* in this context is that *we* can evaluate institutions or persons acting within the framework of institutions in terms of whether and to what extent certain functions or actions are useful in the achievement of certain ends. Within the framework of a pre-existing moral community with certain clearly defined goals, goals which are explained as what has evolved historically, the utilitarian evaluation, in general, can be made and is meaningful. What does not make sense is a proposed utilitarian evaluation of the moral community as a whole, for without the pre-existing moral framework there is nothing from which or to which to calculate. There must be something beyond or outside of utility for utilitarianism to be meaningful. Put another way, if we insist upon remaining utilitarian in our social and political philosophy then we must appeal to a more primary moral philosophy which is not itself utilitarian. That is precisely what one finds in Hume's moral philosophy.

To propose utilitarianism as an account for moral philosophy is to presume that utility is a criterion which individual "moral agents" may use in order to evaluate how to maximize their self-interest. Without making question-begging or implausible metaphysical assumptions, including hidden structure ones, about how individual self-interest relates to the social interest (however social is conceived), we run into all the well known dilemmas of utilitarianism. Sometimes theorists propose the distinction between rule utilitarianism and act utilitarianism as a way of overcoming these dilemmas, in which case they are likely to see Hume as a rule utilitarian. But Hume's distinction between moral philosophy and social philosophy cuts across the distinction between rule and act utilitarianism, for in order to subscribe to rule utilitarianism one still needs to presuppose another frame of reference in order to make the necessary calculations.

Let us point out the non-utilitarian foundation of moral philosophy for Hume. We certainly approve of what is useful but we also approve of things that are not utilitarian, that is things which are immediately agreeable to moral agents. The more important question is why we approve of what is useful. The Humean answer is that we are benevolently disposed to what is useful to others. If we were not so disposed then utility could never at a another level enter our evaluations. Notice as well that being benevolently disposed to what is useful to others does not amount to any metaphysical claim about the ultimate coincidence of my self-interest with the self-interest of others or the social interest. What Hume thought he had uncovered was a confirmable element of our moral phenomenology, not some hypothesis about hidden structure. Within the *Treatise* sympathy was identified as the general principle of morals because it performed three functions: (1) it was the basis of making moral judgments through the adoption of the correct perspective, and hence the basis of moral insight; (2) the sympathy process served as the basis of moral motivation; (3) sympathy was the connecting link behind the moral and the social. Although Hume revised his previous conception of the sympathy mechanism when he wrote *An Enquiry Concerning the Principles of Morals*, he nevertheless retained the concept of sympathy in the latter work and made more explicit the necessity for a fundamental benevolence or sense of humanity.

Let there be no mistake about Hume's position on benevolence. Hume did not maintain that our fundamental motive was a general benevolence, in fact he rejected such a claim as empirically false. Hume always maintained that benevolence was limited. Moreover, Hume also recognized that limited benevolence could on occasion be a destabilizing factor as when our loyalty to a friend or family member causes us to overlook their criminally social behavior. These qualifications, important as they are, should not obscure the fact that all human beings are capable of benevolence toward others (i.e., the sentiment of humanity), and it is this capability which provides for the possibility of morality when extended through sympathy.

What some readers might find disturbing about this benevolent basis is that it does not seem sufficient for establishing a society or a moral community. It does not seem so, for such readers imagine themselves in a putative state of nature wherein they try to speculate on how to create a community from similarly isolated atomic individuals who putatively have some conception of a personal self-interest. This is precisely where those readers are mistaken and where Hume's Copernican Revolution in moral philosophy enters. We do not enter the world of a state of nature but rather a world of pre-existing communities. In retrospect, we can understand what sustains these communities morally, namely benevolence and sympathy, but what sustains them was not what established them. Nor does it matter what established them according to Hume and contra Locke, for, by the time we can engage in meaningful moral critique we are already in possession of a social framework which is the only meaningful basis for internal criticism.

There are other important strengths to Hume's position. Although we are capable of limited benevolence and benevolence about the good fortune of others, and although we are incapable of general benevolence as a primordial motive, we have self-interested motives as well. It is logically necessary that we have such self-interested motives otherwise our limited benevolence could not come into play, there being no one else's self-interest toward which we could feel benevolent.[47] There is nothing immoral or improper about the pursuit of self-interest in general, for Hume has already dismissed moral positions based on alleged conflicts between reason and passion. This makes Hume sound at times like Hobbes, Mandeville, and later utilitarians such as Bentham. But whereas the latter denied a moral realm, Hume insists that there must be one. He insisted that there must be such a realm otherwise we shall be forced to appeal to indefensible metaphysical and hidden structure claims. Not only is self-interest a normal motive, but *we are also predisposed to approve of* the good fortune of others and what is useful to them, i.e. to *their pursuit of self-interest*. This gives moral approval to the pursuit of wealth and luxury without apology and without elaborate and implausible subterfuges or questionable egoistic interpretations about our hidden motives.

Another strength of Hume's position is its ability to make sense of modern secular, pluralistic societies, i.e. societies which

lack an all encompassing ideology and try to encompass numerous subcommunities with their individually different moral
commitments. Modern commercial republics cannot be understood on the model of Aristotle's *polis* wherein a homogeneous
population has attained a consensus on goals and obligations.
That is why modern moral philosophy and social philosophy
have a different relationship from the one they have in classical
discussions. There can be no canonical ranking of goods except
by totalitarian imposition. This has nothing to do with individual choices being incommensurate (another metaphysical hypothesis) but with the different traditions which have spawned
the subcommunities. Nor is there any way in which the state
can transcend concrete moral intuitions without delegitimating
moral philosophy , i.e. by the wholesale substitution of social
philosophy for moral philosophy (hence the similarity of doctrinaire liberalism and Marxism). There is no way within social
philosophy alone to account for normativity or the internal
sanction, and theorists forced to do without the internal sanction end only with the conception of a police state. From the
point of view of particular moral subcommunities, there may be
social institutions like a market economy that are amoral or
morally neutral. Hence, the assessment of those institutions
cannot be simplistically utilitarian since different subcommunities would assess them differently, and the assessment cannot be
in terms of the benevolence that functions within a family or
close religious community. Rather the assessment must be in
terms of general interests resulting from previous agreements
where those agreements have given rise to abstract legal rights.
All of this is made possible according to Hume because our
moral philosophy is compatible with our sympathetic identification of what is useful to others, not just to ourselves. In short,
Hume's theory allows us to understand institutions that cut
across particular moral communities.[48]

We must distinguish the assumption that individual self-interest coincides with the social interest (an implausible metaphysical assumption in Hume's view) with the logical require-

ment that there be no ultimate conflict between individual self-interest and the interest of others interpreted socially. The latter requirement is not a metaphysical assumption but something negotiated within a pre-existing moral community. It is only in the light of historically evolving traditions, in the light of not believing in a fundamental human nature with fixed goals, and in the light of the capacity for benevolence toward the good of others that the logical requirement makes sense. These three elements are precisely what one finds in Hume's theory.

Social Philosophy Within the Bounds of Moral Philosophy

So far we have stressed the importance of the *We Do* perspective understood culturally (social and historical) as the crucial element in Hume's Copernican Revolution in moral philosophy. This may still leave the lingering impression that in getting away from either the *I Think* or *I Do* perspectives we have thrown out the proverbial baby with the bath water and saddled Hume with some kind of collectivist notion about human beings. This suspicion has to be put to rest by explicating what is involved in the *We Do* perspective. By the *We Do* perspective we mean the "We" to be understood as "you and I". To begin with the ineliminable social context in which human beings operate does not obviate that it is individuals who perform actions. Even where those individuals understand themselves as responsible social agents, the final responsibility and the final decision is made within the minds of individuals. Moreover, the "we" is made up of individuals who see themselves as social, who can sympathize, and who are capable of limited benevolence. Refusal to interpret ourselves as isolated "I's" is not tantamount to refusing to see ourselves as responsible individuals. What is most important is that the "I's" do not have a fixed nature. Part of what makes an "I" is that the "I" has a self-image, hence the importance in Hume's discussion of the self about how we come to see ourselves through others. The nature of the "I" is not fixed but evolves through time and context, and that is why any discussion of our self-interest must take the historical context into account. Hume's moral and social philosophy is still a philosophy of individualism, but it is not a doctrinaire individualism.

A community is an historical entity not an ontological one. The public interest is not a monolithic whole, rather it comprises the projects of oneself and others. Independent of those projects and their historical evolution it is difficult to see what the public interest could be. The dangerous notions are those derived from alleged attempts to go outside the historically evolving projects by appeal to supra-rational principles. Hume would deny that individuals could totally define themselves in terms of an independent social and public interest. His warnings about fanatics are to the effect that fanatics disguise hidden personal agendas as items of public interest construed supra-rationally. Individuals still seek their ultimate goods, for Hume, in private or in limited communities, and when they do unite politically it is in accordance with pre-existing agreements on process. The private dimension has primacy over the public dimension precisely because the latter is made up of the former. There is no theory in Hume of a human nature in which we have contextless goals or positive rights.

Knowing Hume as we do now not just as the author of Book I of the *Treatise* and *An Enquiry Concerning Human Understanding* but as the author of Book II and Book III of the *Treatise*, as the author of *An Enquiry Concerning the Principles of Morals*, as the author of *A History of England* and numerous political and economic and social essays, what sort of social, political, and economic philosophy would we expect him to hold?[49] Man is a complex being with internal conflicts where self-destructive impulses vie with wholesome ones. The moral changes in an individual's self-image that emerge from the internal struggle are more important than any external circumstances in fostering improvement. The internal sanction, in short, is more important than the external sanction. This is not to deny the importance or relevance of external circumstances but only to qualify what is relatively more important. An individual's self-image, his or her sense of integrity, and that of the society of which he or she is a part is the product of a long historical process of struggle. Neither the individual nor the institution can be understood abstractly apart from the particular traditions through which they have emerged. Just as conflict within the individual is real and requires moral restraint and integrity, so there is always potential conflict among the institutions of a society which develops over time. These conflicts in no way lead to an automatic delegitimation of those institutions. The role of the state is to serve as a kind of "umpire" to help resolve these conflicts. If the "umpire" becomes a direct participant in the conflicts, and an all-powerful one at that, there will be no power to restrain the destructive impulses that it might unleash.

Hume may have been the first thinker to recognize what Adam Ferguson described as social phenomena which are "the result of human action but not of human design."[50] Liberty is, for example, a natural and unintended by-product of justice. Liberty cannot be established or introduced, rather it must emerge from justice. Although justice may be established, it has to be sustained over time in order to produce liberty. Thus the critical rational question is how to sustain justice and ultimately liberty. That is the question the *History of England*, in part, tried to answer.[51] Those who would seek to produce liberty by discovering its necessary and sufficient conditions miss the point. Hume's analogue to Ferguson's notion of spontaneous order is custom, and it is custom that bridges the theoretical gap between the original motive and the sustaining motive. Spontaneous order accounts for the origin of a system. The further elaboration of the order in the face of new circumstances demands explication of the implicit norms. The implicit norms are not objective structures but rather a sense of what we as agents have been trying to do. Without the spontaneous order, the further explication could not take place.

As an approximation, we can characterize Hume's view of social dynamics as conservative. That is, all norms are contextual and cannot be grasped from an external perspective. But it is important to stress the difference between Hume and other conservatives. Most certainly Hume was not a classical conservative who believed that the past patterning of institutions provides a rigid and permanent frame of reference. That is why Sheldon Wolin is incorrect in saying that "Hume cleared the way for political romanticism."[52] This might be true of Burke but not of Hume. Whereas Burke saw in political institutions objects of veneration, Hume saw those institutions as objects of loyalty and scepticism. For Hume, the function of social philosophy is to explicate the implicit norms of our past practice not as symbols of a supernatural order or of a teleological historical process but as guides to be adapted to new conditions. Unlike Blackstone and the common lawyers who tended to make the common law tradition into a metaphysical absolute, Hume could argue that the English Constitution evolved, that our cherished modern liberty sprang from the Puritans, that the Norman Conquest was modified by the inherent peculiarities in English feudalism.

Failure to perceive Hume's modern secular conservatism leads to the following kind of misunderstanding. In his *Life of Hume*, Greig asked:

How could the same man, and at the same time, be both, Edmund Burke and George III? How could he defend the colonists in North America for their resistance to the arbitrary power of king, ministers, and venal House of Commons and yet attack the old Whigs, and Patriots, and Wilkites, and democratic radicals of every sort for trying to resist the same agencies at home?....In metaphysics, theory of knowledge, economics, ethics and religion, and in politics as far as they concerned Americans, he deserved rather to be dubbed a Radical: he depended not upon authority, but upon his own reasonings;...he disintegrated and destroyed many settled notions by an acid logic of his own. Why therefore did he fail to bring the same acid logic to the politics of Charles I and Cromwell, George II and John Wilkes?[53]

The mistake is Greig's. Hume is consistently the conservative, the last appeal is always to custom and to common sense. What Hume's epistemology shows is that logic left to its own devices consumes itself. Rationality has nothing to do with that sort of logic. On the contrary, rationality has to do with explicating the implicit norms that inform our use of logic, and those norms are social and historical. The enemies of rationality are those who seek to read into our cultural norms a hypothesis about hidden structure, a doctrine of necessary and sufficient conditions, a magisterial archimedean point from which to legislate.

Just as there is no absolute atemporal frame of reference from which we can judge individuals, so there is none from which we can judge a particular society. Notice that we did not say there were no standards but only no absolute atemporal standards. Just as Hume refused to elevate some truth about human nature into a dogma, Hume consistently resisted the temptation to elevate any set of historical circumstances onto an abstract level where they freeze into dogmas. Hume could agree on the danger of state activism and the importance of private property and various freedoms within the historical context of the Anglo-Saxon moral consciousness, but he declined to recognize them as absolute values. Since traditions are historical products, and since there are no absolute frames of reference for understanding traditions, Hume denied that traditions can have a closure, i.e., a teleological endpoint beyond which they no longer evolve. Traditions are fertile sources of adaptation and reconstruction. One can explicate a tradition, but one cannot circumnavigate it. We cannot totally conceptualize a tradition or definitively state its hidden essential structure. There is no such structure. Understanding a tradition is a matter of practical, not theoretical, knowledge. Practical knowledge is not inferior to theoretical knowledge and is not to be rejected by appeal to theoretical criteria. On the contrary, as Hume was the first to show, such theoretical criteria are themselves meaningless and destructive unless grounded in practical knowledge. In order to gain theoretical knowledge we must follow certain procedures, i.e. engage in certain practices. One achieves this practical knowledge by internalizing its norms, not by seeing it as a distant object of contemplation, calculation, and manipulation. This notion of internalizing the norms, instead of seeing them as mere means, accounts for the stress on due process. Once achieved, this understanding must be protected not only from all human moral weakness but also from those who seek to turn that understanding into a timeless blueprint.

NOTES

CHAPTER ONE

1. Kant's concept of the categorical imperative can now be understood as an argument in favor of the existence of specifically moral motives not reducible to self-interest.

2. J.S. Mill, unlike Bentham, also argues for the existence of an internal sanction, and that is why Mill's utilitarianism is strikingly and problematically different from Bentham's.

3. All references are to the Selby-Bigge edition of *A Treatise of Human Nature* (Oxford: Clarendon Press, 1967).

4. This was brought to my attention by Tom Beauchamp.

5. *An Enquiry concerning Human Understanding*, 1748 edition, p. 15. Unless otherwise noted, all references to the *Enquiry concerning Human Understanding*, hereafter referred to as *EHU*, are from the Selby-Bigge 2nd. edition of the *Enquiries* (Oxford: Clarendon Press, 1951).

6. *Ibid.*, pp. 15-16.

7. This format for Hume's work was not unusual during the period. There is another famous letter, *A Letter from a Person of Quality to his Friend in the Country* (1675), which might very well have been written by Locke. This letter contains a statement of Shaftesbury's opposition program.

8. David Hume, *A Letter from a Gentleman to his friend in Edinburgh* (1745), ed. C.C. Mossner and John V. Price (Edinburgh: University Press, 1967), p. 30, hereafter referred to as *Letter*.

9. David Hume, *An Enquiry Concerning the Principles of Morals,* ed. Selby-Bigge, second edition (Oxford: The Clarendon Press, 1972). All references are to this edition unless otherwise noted and will be referred to hereafter as *EPM.*

10. Thomas Hobbes, *Leviathan,* chapter xi.

11. *Ibid.,* chapter vi.

12. Thomas Hobbes, *The Elements of Law,* 1.14.6.

13. *Sensus Communis:* An Essay on the Freedom of Wit and Humour in Shaftesbury, *Characteristics of Men, Manners, Opinions, Times,* ed. John M. Robertson (Indianapolis: Bobbs-Merrill, 1964), p. 79.

14. Adam Smith, *Theory of Moral Sentiments,* ed. A.L. Macfie and D.D. Raphael (Oxford: Clarendon Press, 1976), p. 13.

15. "Philosophers conceive of the passions which harass us as vices into which men fall by their own fault, and therefore, generally deride, bewail, or blame them, or execrate them...bestow manifold praise on such human nature, as is nowhere to be found...For they conceive of men, not as they are, but as they themselves would like them to be....no men are esteemed less fit to direct public affairs than theorists or philosophers." Benedict de Spinoza, *A Political Treatise,* ed. R.H.M. Elwes (New York: Dover,1951), p. 287. These remarks are in the first paragraph of the work. In the fifth paragraph (p. 289), Spinoza says: "For this is certain, and we have proved its truth in our Ethics, that men are of necessity liable to passions..."

16. There is indeed something novel about Hume's views on reason and passion. Hobbes is much more of a rationalist than Hume. Hutcheson followed Aristotle on practical reason, but Hume went further than anyone down to his own

age. Unlike these other thinkers Hume denied any version of natural law or any view of a fundamental human teleology which made it possible for reason to serve passion in a straightforward way.

As Peter Jones has pointed out in his book *Hume's Sentiments, Their Ciceronian and French Context* (Edinburgh: University Press, 1982), p. 5, Pierre Bayle's article on Ovid in Bayle's Dictionary describes Cicero as referring to "l'esclavage de la raison", later translated in 1739 in the English edition as "reason had become the slave of the passions."

17. See John Colman, *John Locke's Moral Philosophy* (Edinburgh: University Press, 1983). See also, John Dunn, *The Political Thought of John Locke* (Cambridge: University Press, 1982).

18. T.H. Green, *Hume and Locke* (New York: Crowell, 1968), pp. 301-02. This is also found in the original Green introduction to Hume's collected works edited by Green and Grose.

19. Richard Cumberland (1632-1718), in his work *De Legibus naturae disquisitio philosophica* (1672), argued that laws of nature could be inferred from the observation of physical and mental phenomena, all somehow ultimately produced by the will of God.

20. John Dunn has called attention to Locke's unfinished manuscript 'of Ethics in General' which Dunn suggests may have been intended as the final chapter of Locke's *Essay.* See John Dunn, *Locke* (Oxford: University Press, 1984), p. 84.

21. See Nicholas Capaldi, "Hume's Philosophy of Religion: God without Ethics", *International Journal for the Philosophy of Religion*, 21 (1970), pp. 233-40. See also J.C.A. Gaskin, *Hume's Philosophy of Religion* (London: Macmillan, 1978), pp. 149-58.

22. *Characteristics, op. cit.*, pp. 251-54, 258-66.

23. *EPM, op.cit.*, pp. 170-71.

24. *Characteristics, op. cit.*, pp. 281-82.

25. *Ibid.*, p. 264.

26. *The Fable of the Bees* (Oxford: Clarendon Press, 1924), p. 41.

27. See Chapter Eight.

28. *Sermons*, in Selby-Bigge, ed., *British Moralists* (Indianapolis: Bobbs-Merrill, 1964), I, p. 188.

29. It is also important to note that moral sentiments themselves are correctable by reference to perspective. This will become a crucial point in Chapter Six when we discuss difficulties in the account of sympathy.

30. David F. Norton, *David Hume: Common-Sense Moralist, Sceptical Metaphysician* (Princeton: University Press, 1982). In his discussion of Hutcheson (p. 61), Norton confuses two issues: (a) whether moral sentiments exist per se, and (b) whether these sentiments are "objective". A positive answer to (a) is not the same as a positive answer to (b). Hobbes denied both (a) and (b); Hutcheson and Hume had answered (a) positively but answered (b) negatively in the realist sense. This confusion on Norton's part is the result of using the expression 'moral scepticism' to cover a negative answer to both (a) and (b). I hasten to add that both Hutcheson and Hume had an intersubjective notion of objectivity. Finally, the point in Hutcheson and Hume is ontological, not simply epistemological. That is, the response of the perceiver is a constituent part of the moral sentiment. See note 38 below. As Alasdair MacIntyre has pointed out in his book *Whose Justice? Which Rationality?*

(Notre Dame: University Press, 1988), "...we discriminate the virtuous from the vicious by responding to causal stimuli with one kind of feeling rather than another" (p. 286). Please note, however, that we are discussing the moral sentiment and not the moral judgment.

31. This paragraph was omitted in the Selby-Bigge edition of *British Moralists*. The full text appears in F. Hutcheson, *Illustrations*, ed. B. Peach (Cambridge: Harvard University Press, 1971), p. 141.

32. *Ibid.*

33. *Illustrations*, Selby-Bigge, *British Moralists, op.cit.*, p. 460.

34. *Ibid.*, p. 455.

35. *Ibid.*, p. 447.

36. *Ibid.*, p. 449.

37. A. N. Prior, *Logic and the Basis of Ethics* (Oxford: University Press, 1949), p. 31.

38. N. Kemp Smith, *The Philosophy of David Hume* (London: Macmillan, 1949), p. 43.

    When Kemp Smith attempted to explain Hume's restatement of Hutcheson's moral theory, he did so in the form of a lengthy, insightful, but controversial thesis. Although recognizing the enormous influence of Newton upon Hume, Kemp Smith argued that the Newtonian and Hutchesonian strains were in conflict, a conflict allegedly exemplified in Hume's apparently contradictory remarks about the *self*. The conflict is explained by Kemp Smith on the hypothesis that Hume must have composed Books II and III of the *Treatise* prior to having composed Book I, despite the fact that Books I and II were published together before the publication of Book III. According to Kemp Smith the moral and psychological theories of Hutcheson were extended to matters epistemological and ontological. Kemp Smith concluded with the observation that "it is Hutchesonian, not Newtonian concepts (i.e. Biological not physical analogies) which prove to be more fundamental in Hume's thinking." (Kemp Smith, *op.cit.*, p. 76.)

Contrary to Kemp Smith, we note that in the advertisement to the *Treatise* the first two books (on the understanding and on the passions) are claimed by Hume to "make a complete chain of reasoning by themselves" and may thus be understood in Newtonian terms without reference to the theory of morals. Moreover, as we shall argue in chapter five, Hume's difficulties with the self can be explained without appeal to such an extraordinary thesis. Finally, I suggest that the fundamental conflict in Hume is between his Newtonian program and his Copernican Revolution, a point I shall pursue in Chapters Seven and Eight.

There are even more fundamental questions about Hume's philosophy which are raised by Kemp Smith's challenging thesis. Kemp Smith argued that what Hume took from Hutcheson is the view that sentiment is more fundamental than reason in morals, and that Hume then went on to make sentiment the basis of epistemology and metaphysics. Recently, David F. Norton has forcefully challenged Kemp Smith's views and has insisted (1) that both Hutcheson and Hume are moral realists and (2) that Hume remained a metaphysical sceptic. Norton is correct in insisting on the role of reason in the moral theories of Hutcheson and Hume, but I would urge that it is misleading to characterize Hutcheson and Hume as moral realists. Both believe in intersubjectivity to be sure, but this is far from and pointedly opposed to realists who define realism to mean the existence of a structure independent of mankind. What Hutcheson and Hume believe is that our moral insights are always relative to the frame of mind of human agents. This will never satisfy traditional realists.

Where Kemp Smith seems to me to be correct is in insisting upon the unity of Hume's moral philosophy, epistemology, and metaphysics, something Norton denies. As Hume put it in a letter to Hutcheson (1739): "I intend to make a new Tryal, if it be possible to make the Moralists & Metaphysicians agree a little better." *Letters of David Hume*, ed. J.Y.T. Greig (Oxford: Clarendon Press, 1932), #17. On the other hand, the intersubjectivity one finds in Hume's moral philosophy is certainly to be found in Hume's epistemology and metaphysics as well. Where Kemp Smith failed was in characterizing this intersubjectivity as a kind of sentiment, which makes it sound personal, subjective, and non-rational if not irrational. What Kemp Smith failed to see was the revolutionary character of Hume's philosophy as a whole, specifically the inherent social dimension of what I shall call the *We Do* perspective.

39. Francis Hutcheson, *Short Introduction to Moral Philosophy* (Glasgow: 1753), p. 68.

40. Duncan Forbes, *Hume's Philosophical Politics* (Cambridge: University Press, 1975), p. 59.

41. See Nicholas Capaldi, *David Hume: The Newtonian Philosopher* (Boston: Twayne, 1975). For a recent review of the influence of Newton on Hume see James E. Force, "Hume's Interest in Newton and Science", *Hume Studies* (1987), pp. 166-216.

42. This does not mean that there are no problems in Hume's Newtonian program both in specific areas like the understanding of the self and in his moral philosophy in general. At some point Hume will have to modify severely the New-

tonian program. Nevertheless, none of this indicates a fundamentally Hutchesonian framework.

43. The earliest recognition of something like a Copernican position in Hume was by Robert P. Wolff, "Hume's Theory of Mental Activity," *Philosophical Review, 69* (1960), pp. 289-310. The serious development of the thesis of Hume's Copernicanism is to be found in Nicholas Capaldi, "The Copernican Revolution in Hume and Kant," *Proceedings of the Third International Kant Congress,* ed. Lewis White Beck (Dordrecht: Reidel, 1972), pp. 234-40 and Lewis White Beck, "A Prussian Hume and a Scottish Kant," in *McGill Hume Studies,* eds. David F. Norton, Nicholas Capaldi, and Wade L. Robison (San Diego: Austin Hill Press, 1979), pp. 63-78. See also F. Dauer, "Towards a Copernican Reading of Hume," *Nous, 9* (1975), pp. 269-93.

44. See Nicholas Capaldi, "Copernican Metaphysics", in *New Essays in Metaphysics,* ed. Robert C. Neville (Albany: SUNY Press, 1987), pp. 45-60.

45. Gilbert Ryle, *The Concept of Mind* (London: Hutchinson, 1949), p. 31.

46. Nicholas Capaldi, *David Hume: The Newtonian Philosopher, op. cit.*

47. Donald W. Livingston, *Hume's Philosophy of Common Life* (Chicago: University Press, 1984).

48. *Treatise,* pp. 183-187.

49. Part of the problem in discussing the issue of scepticism in Hume's philosophy is the historical change in the use of the term. In ancient times, scepticism connoted a positive position and a form of wisdom to thinkers such as Sextus Empiricus. In addition, Sextus insisted upon a "practical

criterion" (natural instinct, inclination, tradition, and the instruction of the arts) unspotted by theoretical reflection about the ultimate. Sextus' practical criterion may very well have inspired Hume's pragmatic *We Do* orientation. On the other hand, there is an important difference between Hume's practical approach and that of the ancients. The latter still operated within the classical tradition which emphasized the extent to which the agent conforms his inner attitude to external structures. Hume, as a modern, thought in terms of the alteration and manipulation of the environment to reflect inner attitudes. Hence, despite some clear examples of his antecedents I would still emphasize the novelty inherent in Hume's use of his antecedents.

Starting with Descartes, however, scepticism began to connote a negative position. It is this switch in connotation that initially prompted my suggestion that we not speak of Hume as a sceptic. The switch in connotation is reinforced by the adoption of an *I Think* perspective since it encourages ignoring the perspective of an engaged agent.

50. I would make the same case about calling Hume a *naturalist*. To be a naturalist is to interpret mankind as a part of nature without appeal to supernatural explanation. Hobbes is a naturalist, but Hobbes does not begin with a *We Do* perspective. In subsequent philosophical history later versions of naturalism are often *I Do* perspectival accounts where human beings are interpreted as agents embedded in the world, but such accounts fail to see how social exchanges are constitutive of personal identity. Both Hume's appeal to the process of sympathy and his appeal to general social rules are ignored by this reading of him. To be sure, Hume sometimes wrote from an *I Think* perspective as in the first book of the *Treatise* and from an *I Do* perspective as in the second book of the *Treatise*. However, he adopted the first perspective in order to show its limitations, and he adopted the second perspective in order both

to overcome the first perspective and as a prelude to the *We Do* perspective of the third book of the *Treatise*. All of this is lost on those who never read beyond Book I. Note that the *We Do* perspective is incontrovertibly the only perspective one finds in *An Enquiry Concerning the Principles of Morals*.

51. Annette Baier has made a similar point about reading Hume in her book *Postures of the Mind: Essays on Mind and Morals* (Minneapolis: University of Minnesota Press, 1985). See especially chapter twelve.

52. The major difficulty for Hume, and it is one we shall see most clearly as we work through his moral philosophy, concerns his attempt to explain or to account for the *We Do* perspective. How are we to proceed in explaining the human nature which will eventually explain everything else? What methods and framework can serve to explain man himself? In the *Treatise* Hume proposed to answer methodological and ontological questions by taking as his paradigm the most extensive and coherent body of knowledge available in his time, namely Newtonian mechanics. This can be easily seen in the mechanical order of the principles of association, the transfer of vivacity, and the sympathy mechanism. As Hume subsequently discovered, there is no adequate way in which he can generate all of the elements of the *We Do* perspective using the Newtonian mechanical model. This will become most evident in his analyses of the self and the sympathy mechanism. In this very important respect Kemp Smith was correct to stress a conflict between the mechanical Newtonian model and the biological or organic metaphors Hume was forced to use. This has nothing to do, however, with the influence of Hutcheson. Instead, I would suggest that this represents a conflict between the Newtonian Program and the Copernican Revolution. Even more important, the me-

324

chanical account of the *We Do* perspective is not reflexive, i.e. we are still left with a conceptual dualism.

Hume's more considered response in *An Enquiry Concerning the Principles of Morals* was to drop the mechanical model as an explanation of the *We Do* perspective and to substitute a cultural account of the *We Do* perspective. James T. King has actively called attention to the differences between the *Treatise* and Hume's Second *Enquiry*. See "The Place of the Language of Morals in Hume's Second *Enquiry*" in *Hume: A Reevaluation*, eds. Donald Livingston and James T.King (New York: Fordham University Press, 1976), pp. 343-61. The cultural account, which is fundamentally social and historical, is the only one capable of being reflexive, i.e. the perspective and the ultimate form of order are mutually inclusive. This changes what the science of man meant for Hume into one in which we explicate the concepts of our ordinary understanding of what we do instead of looking for hidden structures. More will be said about this shift in the last two chapters of this book.

CHAPTER TWO

1. Hume's discussion of moral philosophy in Book III presupposes that the reader is already familiar with Hume's discussion of the passions and motivation in Book II. My reasons for beginning with Book III are: (1) we have distinguished three issues, namely, moral insight or apprehension, moral motivation, and the relationship between apprehension and motivation; the discussion of moral insight is logically prior to the other issues, and it is precisely in Book III part I that Hume initiates the discussion of that issue; (2) the complexities and subtleties of Hume's discussion of moral motivation will be more apparent after we have clarified his position on moral insight. Moral motiva-

tion is discussed in Chapter Five, to which the reader is referred.

2. For a similar argument against the distinction see Brand Blanshard, *Reason and Goodness* (London: Allen and Unwin, 1961), pp. 263-64.

3. Francis Hutcheson, *Illustrations Upon the Moral Sense*, ed. B. Peach (Cambridge: Harvard University Press, 1971), p. 146.

4. *Ibid.*, p. 123.

5. Wollaston has been defended by Stanley Tweyman in *Reason and Conduct in Hume and his Predecessors* (Hague: Nijhoff, 1974). Tweyman maintains that "the role of the observer is not at all as pivotal for Wollaston's view as Hume believes" (p. 110). What is immediately at issue here is not what Wollaston wants to believe but to what his position commits him. If the observer's presence is not important then the total objectivity of the action's message determines the morality as well as the truth of the action. The actions of animals give us a message. Hence, animals are morally liable. Tweyman fails to see Hume's arguments about animals and inanimate objects in this context. Any attempt to exclude animals on the grounds of qualifying factors within the agent and not just the act (or in the case of Locke factors in the observer and not just the object) is to compromise the alleged objectivity which is crucial to Wollaston and the rationalists. Once truths are only truths for certain agents or observers with special preconceptions then we are no longer dealing with objective truth but with intersubjective truth. Wollaston argued for objective truth.

6. Barry Stroud, in *Hume* (London: Routledge and Kegan Paul, 1978), claims that Hume failed to prove that "a feeling or passion must always be present for action to occur" (p.

167), and this failure is a result of Hume's propositional view of reason. To begin with, Stroud fails to note the historical context in which Hume is arguing and the fact that Wollaston is the object of Hume's rebuttal. More important, the dispute is not over a word, namely, 'reason', but the issues behind the word. The rationalists believed in the total objectivity of moral distinctions as well as the role of reason in apprehending them. Any change in the concept of reason which threatens total objectivity threatens the rationalists. Contrary to Stroud, Hume does have a rather broad conception of reason and does recognize as well as insist on practical knowledge in addition to theoretical knowledge. Extending the use of the word 'reason', an extension to which Hume would not object, does nothing to obviate the existence of different kinds of reason. It is theoretical reason to which the rationalists appealed, but it is precisely this kind of reason which is inert. Finally, the onus is on Hume's opponents to show that theoretical reason leads to action, not Hume. The whole tradition of philosophy from Plato to the present recognizes this as a serious challenge.

J.L. Mackie, in *Hume's Moral Theory* (London: Routledge & Kegan Paul, 1980), says: "Someone like Clarke, for example, might well concede that Hume's model of choice, will, and action is correct for all ordinary cases *where moral considerations do not play any significant part*, but say that where such considerations do come in, we have something radically different from what his model allows. A relation of fitness, Clarke might say, is out there in the objects....Yet this judgment, my awareness of this fitness, is also in itself a motive to action....the fitness of which it is a perception is something intrinsically and objectively prescriptive." (pp. 47-48). Mackie confuses two different things that Clarke, curiously, would not have confused. It is one thing to say that a judgment or an awareness actually motives us and quite another to say that a judgment or an awareness *ought* to motivate us. Hume, rightly in my opinion, is maintaining that such alleged judgments of fitness at best only account for what 'ought' to motivate us and not for what actually motivates us. Moreover, Hume is maintaining that no rationalist has ever clarified in a non-question-begging fashion what this 'ought' means. Finally, it is Hume who is insisting that this 'ought' is not any recognizable logical relation and that any explanation of 'ought' in legal or theological terms fails to capture what we mean and do in morals.

7. Hume's loose use of the term 'reason' is a source of endless confusion. One must also distinguish between 'reason' and 'reasoning' within his writings. In this chapter, I use the expression 'theoretical reason' to refer to philosophical relations as opposed to natural relations. Cause and effect reasoning can be of either type. Most of what Hume said about natural relations would be classifiable under the rubric of practical reason.

8. See Chapter Three for a detailed discussion of Hume's theory of the relations of ideas.

9. One of the few people who has made some attempt to determine the historical context of Hume's argument is Stanley Tweyman in his book *Reason and Conduct in Hume and His Predecessors, op.cit.* Tweyman notes that Hume has Clarke in mind. Tweyman also defends Clarke against Hume by arguing that "the relation of mathematical reasoning to moral reasoning is to be regarded as analogical" (p. 87). However, this really grants Hume his first point, namely, that moral approbation is not at all like mathematical reasoning. If Clarke is drawing an analogy, then it is important for Clarke to identify the analogous elements. The alleged analogy is between the compulsion of *a priori* reasoning and what Clarke refers to as the "fitness" of ac-

tions to circumstance. The Clarke notion of fitness, as critics have persistently pointed out, smuggles in a kind of
normativity which appears to be significantly different
from the compulsion of *a priori* reason. Again, it seems to
me that Hume's criticism is very much to the point. We
shall expand on this point below when we discuss Hume's
other argument against moral rationalism, its failure to account for the influence of morals on conduct. Finally,
Tweyman does not note that Hume's critique of relations
takes Locke into account as well as Clarke. The larger context of Hume's critique is that his adversaries have borrowed a word, 'relation', and have extended it to a context
where it ceases to have any clear meaning.

10. George Berkeley, *Works*, ed. Luce, I, 84.

11. D.D. Raphael, in *The Moral Sense* (London: Oxford University Press, 1947), tries to avoid Hume's objection that relations would apply to animals and inanimate objects.
Raphael proposes that the "relations imply such a knowledge or belief in their very nature, and cannot exist between terms where this element of cognition is lacking"
(p.59). This appears to be a restatement of Locke. To begin
with, the subjective element of cognition would make
moral relations different from the other relations and
thereby raises the question of whether we can still call it a
relation. Second, even if Raphael's proposal avoids one
horn of Hume's dilemma it falls prey to the other, namely,
that the total objectivity on which the moral rationalists insisted would be lost. Third, Raphael's view proposes a
subjectivism far more extreme than anything ever attributed to Hume. Any moral deviation could be defended
on the ground that the agent is unaware of any relation
and therefore the relation does not exist. If Raphael then
replies that the agent "ought" to be aware of the relation,
then we would have to explain this new moral relation of

"ought", which begs the question. Hume's own moral theory allows the moral agent to be mistaken and corrected because it appeals to intersubjectivty (*Treatise*, p. 416).

12. Francis Hutcheson, *Illustrations* in *Selby-Bigge, op.cit.*, p. 403.

13. Stanley Tweyman, *op.cit.*, tries to defend Clarke against Hume's objections on motivation by saying that for Clarke there is an identity of morality with our long range interests (pp. 114, 116). This is a correct assessment of Clarke, but what Tweyman fails to notice is that this makes the autonomous reasoned status of moral apprehension superfluous if not *ad hoc*. As Tweyman argues it, "the observations which...[Hume] makes are compatible both with his theory and theirs" (p. 174). But this works both ways. If Clarke's theory of motivation is practically indistinguishable from Hume's, what is the status of the assertion made by Hume's opponents that there is a fundamental conflict between reason and passion? We find that there is a crucial difference between Clarke and Hume on motivation in that Clarke requires a theological guarantee whereas Hume does not believe we can infer moral attributes in the deity. Recall that Clarke's Boyle lectures of 1705 are entitled "A Discourse Concerning the Unchangeable Obligations of Natural Religion, and the Truth and Certainty of the Christian Revelation."

For Hume, direct moral insight or perception is in the form of an impression. Moral impressions give rise to moral ideas. These moral ideas, in turn and under appropriate circumstances, *causally* give rise to the indirect passions. Moral motivation is thus no different from natural motivation. Therefore, the relationship of (a) to (b) in Hume is causal. For the rationalists like Clarke, this cannot really be possible; hence, the necessity for a concept of a special moral "ought" to bridge the gap. The fact that rationalists need this kind of "ought" while Hume does not shows the extent to which Hume's theory cannot possibly be compatible with that of the rationalists.

14. Francis Hutcheson, *Illustrations, op.cit.*, p. 163.

15. What these circumstances are will be discussed in greater detail in our Chapter Four. Keep in mind that pleasure and pain were traditionally categorized as tertiary qualities, thereby making them even more dependent upon the agent or observer. Keep in mind as well that the presence of external circumstances does not make the moral sentiment a referent of those circumstances, rather the sentiment is internally generated in the presence of those circumstances. Analogously, the color 'blue' only exists under certain circumstances but it is not merely a referent of those circumstances but of the agent's or observer's nervous system, etc.

16. A fuller discussion of the role of the passions in Hume's moral theory will be given in our Chapter Five.

17. It is important not to confuse moral sentiments with indirect passions. In his otherwise exemplary and ground breaking work on the passions in Hume, Ardal is guilty of this confusion. See Norton, *op.cit.*, p.115 for a criticism of Ardal. Tweyman, *op.cit.*, p. 180, is also guilty of this confusion.

18. See Nicholas Capaldi, *David Hume: The Newtonian Philosopher, op.cit.*, Chapter Nine.

19. This will be detailed in our Chapter Five.

CHAPTER THREE

1. W.D. Hudson, *The Is-Ought Question* (London: Macmillan, 1969), p. 11.

2. R.M. Hare, *The Language of Morals* (New York: Oxford University Press, 1952), pp. 29, 44.

3. A similar claim is made by D.D. Raphael, "Hume's Critique of Ethical Rationalism" in *Hume and the Enlightenment*, ed. W.B. Todd (Edinburgh: University Press, 1974), pp. 26-27.

4. *British Moralists*, ed. Selby-Bigge, *op.cit.*, p. 482.

5. *Ibid.*, p. 499.

6. *Ibid.*, p. 500.

7. *Ibid.*, p. 504.

8. *Ibid.*, p. 491.

9. *Ibid.*, p. 460.

10. Francis Hutcheson, *Illustrations Upon the Moral Sense*, ed. by B. Peach (Cambridge: Harvard University Press, 1971), p. 141.

11. The distinction between the vulgar and the philosophers is to be found in Berkeley as well. "My endeavours tend only to unite, and place in a clearer light, that truth which was before shared between the vulgar and the philosophers: – the former being of opinion, that those things they immediately perceive are the real things; and the latter, that the things immediately perceived are ideas, which exist only in the mind. Which two notions put together do, in effect, constitute the substance of what I advance." *Third Dialogue*

between Hylas and Philonous, ed. Jessop, II, 262; Fraser ed., I, 484.

12. "The vulgar, who take things according to their first appearance..." (*EHU,* p. 86).

13. A. MacIntyre, "Hume on 'is' and 'ought'", in *Philosophical Review, 48* (1959).

14. Thomas Reid, "Moral Approbation Implies a Real Judgment" in *Essays on the Active Powers,* in the *Works* of Thomas Reid, ed. Sir William Hamilton (London: Longmans, Green, 1895), 8th ed., II, p. 675. The essay is also included in the edition of the *Essays* ed. by B. Brody (Cambridge: MIT Press, 1969), p. 469.

15. *Ibid.*

16. *Ibid.*

17. *Ibid.,* p. 589.

18. *Ibid.*

19. *Ibid.*

20. *Ibid.*

21. *Ibid.*

22. T.H. Green, *Hume and Locke, op.cit.,* p. 354.

23. N. Kemp Smith, *The Philosophy of David Hume, op.cit.,* p. 201.

24. Bernard Wand, "Hume's Account of Obligation", *Philosophical Quarterly, 6* (1956), reprinted in V. Chappell, ed., *Hume* (New York: Doubleday, 1966), p. 325.

25. *Ibid.*, p. 328.

26. F. Hutcheson, *Illustrations upon the Moral Sense* in Selby-Bigge, *British Moralists, op.cit.*, paragraph 455.

27. What causes some confusion here is that Hume himself uses the term 'natural' equivocally. Hume believes in both natural and artificial virtues. Corresponding to each of these different virtues there may be moral obligations. Thus, there are moral obligations attending natural natures as well as moral obligations attending artificial virtues. At the same time there are 'natural' obligations of a totally different sort in non-moral contexts as when we say that you 'ought' to fly if you are in a hurry.

28. Most of the alternative interpretations I discuss and dismiss were suggested to me in conversation by colleagues and students over the past twenty years. Almost none of them appears in print, and hence the lack of direct references. To my knowledge, no one else has ever actually taken the is-ought paragraph apart and analyzed it. The objections to my interpretation would be much more formidable if they could be presented as a sustained argument about the text. I suggest that the attempt to present a sustained argument would underscore the totally *ad hoc* nature of most of these alternative interpretations.

    In this context I would like to mention that the only other author who has recognized that Hume is discussing the deduction of "ought" from philosophical relations is Stanley Tweyman, *op.cit.*, p. 143.

29. C.D. Broad, *Five Types of Ethical Theory* (Paterson, N.J.: Littlefield Adams, 1959), p. 112.

30. B.M. Laing, *David Hume* (London: E. Benn, 1932), p. 188.

31. J. Laird, *Hume's Philosophy of Human Nature* (London: Methuen, 1932), p. 215.

32. D. Daiches Raphael, *The Moral Sense* (New York: Oxford University Press, 1947), p. 65.

33. A.N. Prior, *Logic and the Basis of Ethics* (New York: Oxford University Press, 1949), p. 33.

34. W.K. Frankena, "The Naturalistic Fallacy", reprinted in W. Sellars and J. Hospers, eds., *Readings in Ethical Theory* (New York: Appleton-Century-Crofts, 1952), pp. 104-05.

35. MacIntyre, *op.cit.*, p. 465.

36. G. Hunter, "Hume on 'Is' and 'Ought'", *Philosophy, 37* (1962), p. 149.

37. D.C. Stove, "The Nature of Hume's Scepticism" in *McGill Hume Studies, op.cit.*, p. 221.

38. Jonathan Harrison, *Hume's Moral Epistemology* (Oxford: Clarendon Press, 1976), p. 69.

39. J.L. Mackie, *Hume's Moral Theory* (London: Routledge & Kegan Paul, 1980), p. 62.

40. See for example the following: R.F. Atkinson, "Hume on 'Is' and 'Ought': A Reply to Mr. MacIntyre", *Philosophical Review, 70* (1961), pp. 231-38; M.J. Scott-Taggart, "MacIntyre's Hume," *Ibid.*, pp. 239-44; A.H. Basson, *David Hume* (Baltimore: Penguin, 1958), pp. 94-95; A.C. Ewing, *Ethics* (New York: Free Press, 1962), p. 92; R.M. Hare, *The Language of Morals* (New York: Oxford, 1952), pp. 29, 44; P.H. Nowell-Smith, *Ethics* (New York: Philosophical Library, 1959), pp. 36-37; W. Salmon, *Logic* (Englewood Cliffs, N.J.: Prentice-Hall, 1959), p. 17.

41. T.H. Green, *op.cit.*, p. 354.

42. *Ibid.*

43. It is, of course, possible to construct a deductive argument involving matters of fact. However, such an argument or arguments would ultimately involve a non-deductive process for the apprehension of the initial matters of fact. Matters of fact are discovered through observation or they may be inferred causally. Neither observation nor causal inference is deductive or demonstrative. Insistence upon this point is a hall mark of Hume's epistemology.

    It should also be noted that what is being discussed in the is-ought paragraph and throughout this section of the *Treatise* is the apprehension of alleged moral relations. It was Hume's opponents, like Clarke, who alleged that moral relations were apprehended through an intellectual insight beginning with certain alleged facts. On epistemological grounds Hume denied this was possible.

    Hume himself permits the construction of deductive arguments from certain kinds of facts to values precisely because he believed that values were a special class of facts analogous to secondary qualities. This is possible for Hume because the original value-facts are apprehended through observation and not some kind of demonstrative process of thinking.

44. No claim is made in this context about the correctness or incorrectness of the views of Prichard, Moore, Cudworth, etc. Nor are we maintaining that Prichard had a theory of moral relations. What we are commenting upon are attempts to explicate Hume by analogy to these other positions.

45. R. David Broiles, *The Moral Philosophy of David Hume* (Hague: Nijhoff, 1964), pp. 89-93.

46. In his more recent treatment of Hume, Alasdair MacIntyre
    has argued that since there are two types of obligation in
    Hume, natural and moral, what Hume is denying is that
    we can infer moral obligation entirely from non-moral
    premises. MacIntyre, *Whose Justice? Which Rationality?*,
    op.cit., pp. 310-11. Aside from all of the textual arguments
    to show that this specific claim by MacIntyre is false as well
    as being irrelevant to the is-ought paragraph because the
    latter is not discussing inference from is to "ought", I would
    suggest that MacIntyre's error is partly the result of at-
    tributing to Hume an *I Think* perspective and thereby not
    seeing how Hume treats obligation from the perspective of
    an engaged agent. See Chapter Eight for my criticism of
    MacIntyre's general treatment of Hume.

47. MacIntyre, *op.cit.*

48. I have not mentioned J.R. Searle's *Speech Acts* (Cambridge:
    University Press, 1969) in the text because Searle did not
    present his views as an exegesis of Hume. Searle main-
    tained that ought statements could be deduced from
    "institutional" statements such as that some one had made
    a promise, etc. The is-ought paragraph aside, what Searle
    is discussing is what Hume would identify as the third
    great problem of moral theory, the relationship of insight
    to motivation. Distinguishing between "right" and "ought",
    we can always ask "Ought I to do x?" where x is dependent
    upon some social institution. Searle's answer is that we are
    obliged to do x, i.e. we "ought" to do x, where "ought" is
    understood as consistency with the social framework. The
    relationship of insight to motivation is explained legalistic-
    ally. This issue is quite distinct from the legitimacy of the
    social practice which is explained non-morally by Searle in
    terms of some kind of utilitarianism.

    I believe that Hume would have two objections to this
    approach (which is reminiscent of Hobbes). First, it fails to

capture the connection with motivation or actual human conduct. Consistency is a weak subterfuge for getting around this point. It amounts to confusing the issue of moral insight with the issue of how insight is related to motivation. Second, no social practice is intelligible without the concept of a promise being antecedently understood, and promising is only intelligible if morality already exists in some sense. Therefore, the promise as social practice cannot be the foundation of morality but presupposes it. We are still forced to rely on a more fundamental moral practice, and hence we are not going from simple facts to moral judgments as Searle thinks.

49. In the earlier edition of the Selby-Bigge collection on *British Moralists*, *op.cit.*, there was no selection from Reid. Moreover, in that collection the selections from Hutcheson had been excerpted so that one of the two key passages in which Hutcheson challenged "ought" had been left out.

50. Basson, *op.cit.*, p. 94; Broiles, *op.cit.*, pp. 86-87; V.C. Chappell, *The Philosophy of David Hume* (New York: Modern Library, 1963), p. 1; P.R. Foot, "Hume on Moral Judgment," in D.F. Pears, ed. *Hume, a Symposium* (New York: St. Martin's, 1963), p. 74; R.M. Kydd, *Reason and Conduct in Hume's Treatise* (London: Oxford, 1946), p. 53; Laing, *op.cit.*, pp. 188-89; Nowell-Smith, *op.cit.*, pp. 36-37; T.D. Weldon, *The Vocabulary of Politics* (Baltimore: Penguin Books, 1955), pp. 181-82.

CHAPTER FOUR

1. The distance between Hume and naive empiricist theories of language can be gauged by consulting Livingston, *Hume's Philosophy of Common Life, op.cit.*, pp. 60-111. Note as well that when Hume used his critical weapon in metaphysics and epistemology, more often than not what he discovered was that our ideas were complex not simple.

Since they were not simple there was no simple corresponding impression. Rather than declare all such ideas meaningless, Hume designated many of them as complex ideas. As complex ideas, he explicated them by reference to the association of ideas in the imagination, i.e. as natural relations. Here Hume could then bring to bear an elaborate theory of learning derived from an historical and social context of previous practices, i.e. the *We Do* perspective.

2. W.T. Stace, "Some Misinterpretations of Empiricism," *Mind, 67* (1958), pp. 465-84.

3. This was borrowed from Locke's *Essay.*

4. See also the *Abstract, op.cit.,* pp. 185-86.

5. See also the *Treatise,* pp. 189, 448-49.

6. *Abstract, op.cit.,* p. 185.

7. The confusion which leads to the mistaken assertion that vice and virtue are themselves passions is to be found in Ardal and Tweyman. We have already called attention to this.

8. R.M. Kydd, in her book *Reason and Conduct in Hume's Treatise* (New York: Oxford University Press, 1946), distinguishes between judgments of virtue and judgments of obligation (pp. 56-58, 72-73) on the grounds that the latter can move us to action but not the former. On the contrary, the distinction in Hume is based upon the kind of sentiment involved. Both are capable of moving us to action.

9. F. Hutcheson, *Illustrations,* ed. Selby-Bigge, *op.cit.,* p. 408 (#455).

10. What is meant here is that a moral judgment can sometimes be explicated in causal terms. We are not claiming that a moral judgment per se always involves an inference from cause to effect or effect to cause.

11. It is this sort of problem that appears in R.M. Kydd. See note 8 above.

12. Thomas Reid, "Moral Approbation Implies a Real Judgment," *Essays on the Active Powers*, in *Works, op.cit.*

13. *Ibid.*

14. *Ibid.*

15. *Ibid.*

16. *Ibid.*

17. See Chapter Three of this book for a further elaboration.

18. A. N. Prior, *Logic and the Basis of Ethics, op.cit.*, p. 33.

19. Reid, *op.cit.*

20. T.H. Green *Hume and Locke, op.cit.*, p. 354.

21. Selby-Bigge index to the *Enquiries, op.cit.*, p. 358.

22. In his earlier article in *Mind*, 46 (1937), Stevenson had accepted a view of Hume similar to Broad's, namely, that 'good' is defined as "what is approved by most people." By the time he wrote *Ethics and Language*, Stevenson had a more accurate view of Hume in which it was clear that the approval was determined by the sentiments of both the speaker and others, for Hume assumed the universality of sentiments under standard conditions.

23. J.N. Findlay, "Morality by Convention", *Mind* 53 (1944), pp. 142-169.

24. Paul Edwards, *The Logic of Moral Discourse* (Glencoe, IL.: Free Press, 1955), p. 47. Edwards cites both Prior and Raphael.

25. D.D. Raphael, *The Moral Sense, op.cit.*, chapter three.

26. *Ibid.*, p. 63. Ironically, Raphael explains why 'vice' is not like 'angry', but in doing so actually gives an example which restates the core of Hume's theory. "When we say that someone is angry, we can illustrate what we mean by putting the man to whom we are speaking in a position in which he will feel angry; or we can point to symptoms of the anger..." I submit that this is exactly what we do when, according to Hume, we say something is 'vicious'.

27. P.H. Nowell-Smith, *Ethics* (New York: Philosophical Library, 1959), p. 176. Nowell-Smith's book was first published in 1954. He cites Raphael.

28. M.J. Scott-Taggart, "MacIntyre's Hume," *Philosophical Review,* 70 (1961), pp. 239-44.

29. Alasdair MacIntyre, *Whose Justice? Which Rationality?, op.cit.,* p. 305. MacIntyre also claims that Hume differs from Hutcheson in adopting a noncognitivist account of the moral sense, *Ibid.*, p. 286. MacIntyre is correct about Hume but not about a gap between Hume and Hutcheson on this issue. What Hutcheson and Hume share is a non-realist account of the moral sense or moral sentiment. If MacIntyre had kept this account of Hume on the moral sense in mind as an account of moral sentiment and not treated it as an account of moral judgment, then he would have avoided the error of attributing a noncognitivist theory of moral judgment to Hume. How thought and action con-

nect in Hume is a crucial issue, but I believe that it can only be discerned by recognizing Hume's *We Do* perspective. See Chapter Eight.

30. W. Frankena, "The Naturalistic Fallacy," *Mind, 48* (1939), reprinted in Sellars and Hospers, *op.cit.*, pp. 104-05.

31. Prior, *Logic and the Basis of Ethics, op.cit., pp. x-xi.*

32. *Ibid.*, p. 61; see also p. 68.

33. *Ibid.*, p. 67.

34. *Ibid.*

Note that Raphael also objected to Hume because of the "absurd identification of obligation with causal necessity." Raphael, *Moral Sense, op.cit.*, p. 61.

35. Jonathan Harrison, *Hume's Moral Epistemology* (Oxford: Clarendon Press, 1976), p. 125.

36. *Ibid.*, pp. 25, 62, 85, 88-89, 103, etc.

37. *Ibid.*, p. 61.

38. *Ibid.*, back cover or dust jacket statement.

39. *Ibid.*, p. 105.

40. *Ibid.*, p. 107.

41. J.L. Mackie, *Hume's Moral Epistemology* (London: Routledge & Kegan Paul, 1980), p. 71.

42. *Ibid.*, p. 72.

43. David F. Norton, *David Hume: Common-Sense Moralist, Sceptical Metaphysician* (Princeton: Princeton University Press, 1982), especially the introduction and Chapters One through Three.

44. See Norton's criticism, for example, of Stroud (*Ibid.*, p. 151n).

45. See T.A. Miskell's review of Norton's book in *Hume Studies*, November 1984.

46. Norton, *op.cit.*, p. 140.

CHAPTER FIVE

1. V.C. Chapell's widely read and influential anthology, *Hume* (Garden City: Doubleday, 1966), contains not a single essay on the passions.

2. See Nicholas Capaldi, "Hume's Theory of the Passions," in *Hume: A Re-evaluation*, ed. Livingston and King, *op.cit.*, chapter eight.

3. My reason for reviewing the secondary literature chronologically both here and in other chapters is that the presence of a standard interpretation of a point or text in Hume frequently has no validity other than its repetition from one generation to the next of commentators. A misunderstanding by Reid, for example, becomes canonical by the twentieth century through repetition.

4. T. Reid, *Essay on the Active Powers, op.cit.*, III, iii,1.

5. T.H. Green, *Introduction to Hume's 'Treatise of Human Nature'* (New York: Crowell, 1968), pp. 332-33.

6. B.M. Laing, *David Hume* (London: Benn, 1932), p. 161.

7. John Laird, *Hume's Philosophy of Human Nature* (London: Methuen, 1932), p. 191.

8. *Ibid.*, p. 204.

9. *Ibid.*, p. 190.

10. *Ibid.*, pp. 191, 197.

11. *Ibid.*, p. 197.

12. Norman Kemp Smith, *The Philosophy of David Hume* (London: Macmillan, 1941), p. 11.

13. Laird, *op.cit.*, pp. 185-86.

14. A.B. Glathe, *Hume's Theory of the Passions and of Morals* (Berkeley: U. of California Press, 1950), chapter one; R. Popkin, "David Hume: His Pyrrhonism and His Critique of Pyrrhonism," reprinted in R. Popkin, *The High Road to Pyrrhonism* (San Diego: Austin Hill Press, 1980), pp. 103-132.

15. See note 38 of Chapter One.

16. Albert Glathe, *Hume's Theory of the Passions and of Morals*, *op.cit.*

17. J.A. Passmore, *Hume's Intentions* (Cambridge: University Press, 1980), p. 131.

18. P.L. Gardiner, "Hume's Theory of the Passions," in *David Hume: A Symposium*, ed. D.F. Pears (London: Macmillan, 1963), p. 38.

19. *Ibid.*, p. 39.

20. Alasdair MacIntyre, *Whose Justice? Which Rationality?*, *op.cit.*, p. 302. MacIntyre's claim is true only of the primary passions, about which Hume says very little. MacIntyre's claim reflects the mistake of attributing to Hume the *I Think* perspective.

21. Pall Ardal, *Passion and Value in Hume's Treatise* (Edinburgh: University Press, 1966).

22. *Treatise*, pp. 7, 13, 190, 212, 239, 242, 248, 340-41.

23. The myth of Hume's phenomenalism still haunts those who grapple with Hume's epistemology. That myth is largely the fabrication of positivism but has roots in Reid's critique of Hume. See Nicholas Capaldi, *David Hume: The Newtonian Philosopher*, *op.cit.*, chapter three. Robert Anderson in his *Hume's First Principles* (Lincoln: University of Nebraska Press, 1966) has argued brilliantly for the materialist foundations of Hume's philosophy.

24. *Treatise*, pp. 13, 275-76.

25. *EHU*, p. 10.

26. Laing, *op.cit.*, p.160.

27. Laird, *op.cit.*, p. 207.

28. *Ibid.*, p. 197.

29. See Nicholas Capaldi, "The Historical and Philosophical Significance of Hume's Theory of the Self," in A.J. Holland (ed.), *Philosophy, Its History and Historiography* (Dordrecht: Reidel, 1985), pp. 271-285.

30. Gardiner, *op.cit.*, p. 39.

31. Laird, *op.cit.*, p. 190.

32. Kemp Smith, *op.cit.*, pp. 112-13.

33. *Treatise*, p. 8.

34. *Treatise*, pp. 118-23. "The effect, then, of belief is to raise up a simple idea to an equality with our impressions, and bestow on it a like influence on the passions....This, then, may both serve as an additional argument for the present system, and may give us a notion after what manner our reasonings from causation are able to operate on the will and passions" (*Ibid.*, pp. 119-20).

35. It is important to note that the classification of the passions as given by Kemp Smith, *op. cit.*, p. 168, and followed by Ardal, is incorrect.

36. *Passions, David Hume: The Philosophical Works*, ed. T.H. Green and T.H. Grose (Aalen: Scientia Verlag, 1964) p. 148. Reprint of the new edition of London, 1886.

37. "What is the soul of man? A composition of various faculties, passions, sentiments, ideas; united, indeed, into one self or person, but still distinct from each other", Demea speaking to Cleanthes in *Dialogues Concerning Natural Religion*, Part IV, p. 159 of the Kemp Smith edition (Indianapolis: Bobbs-Merrill, 1947).

38. F. Copleston, *History of Philosophy* (Garden City: Doubleday, 1964), V,ii, pp. 172-73.

39. P. Butchvarov,"Hume on Personal Identity", *Philosophical Review, 68* (1959), p. 100.

40. The importance of pride and humility is not evidence of the priority of the first person, as MacIntyre, *op.cit.*, has suggested. The indirect passions of pride and humility are 'indirect', and what that means is that they are not original existences. On the contrary, it is requisite that there be preceding ideas that give rise to such passions. It is through others that we come to learn about ourselves. This underscores the importance of the *We Do* perspective. See Nicholas Capaldi, "The Historical and Philosophical Significance of Hume's Theory of the Self", in A.J. Holland (ed.), *Philosophy, Its History and Historiography* (Dordrecht: Reidel, 1985), pp. 271-285.

41. Hume's discussion of identity presupposes his theory of relations. He distinguished between natural relations and philosophical relations. Identity is a philosophical relations, that is, it is found, "only in philosophy" (*Treatise*, p. 13). Common sense, on the other hand, does not function in terms of philosophical identity but in terms of the natural relations of resemblance and causation. Those philosophers who employ identity as a strict philosophical relation are unable to account for personal identity. Therefore, the identity of the person is to be accounted for by means of resemblance and causation, which, as natural relations, are produced by association and the *transfer of vivacity*. It is precisely the distinction between strict philosophical identity and common sense resemblance upon which Hume insisted.

    Understanding is, for Hume, an organic, social, and historical activity. As such it itself cannot be understood analytically and incrementally. Organic activities, unlike mechanisms, grow and exist in a state of exchange with their environment. That is why it is only through action, not thought alone, that we discover who we are and add to what we are. "Understanding, when it acts alone, and according to its most general principles, entirely subverts itself" (*Treatise*, p. 267). In the course of such exchanges, organic activities or entities transform themselves. They do not exist just in space, but qualitatively transform themselves through time. Thus, even logical structures are intelligible only by reference to the history of structural transformations. The historical origin and development of any part is always a relevant and crucial condition of its meaning. Time, as Hume said, is the source of identity. (*Ibid.*, p. 200).

Once time is recognized as crucial then spatial relationships alone are never adequate for complete explanations. That is partly why Hume rejected monistic materialism and opted for a dualism in which he could say that some things exist without a place. This recognition also signals Hume's awareness that no mechanical explanation will be completely adequate. Hence, it is no surprise as we progress through Hume's thought that we begin to see qualifications of the Newtonian program and eventually its severe restriction.

42. Once more we remind the reader that Hume has two discussions of the self, that in his earlier discussion in Book I he warns us that there are two discussions, and that Hume himself stressed that the first discussion presupposes the second discussion in Book II. One could claim that in Hume we find the suggestion that there are two ideas of the self, one enriched and one impoverished.

43. Passmore, *op.cit.*, p. 126.

44. Kemp Smith, *op.cit.*, pp. 171-73.

45. Laird, *op.cit.*, pp. 160-61.

46. See Nicholas Capaldi, "The Historical and Philosophical Significance of Hume's Theory of the Self," *op.cit.*

Notes

Hume's dissatisfaction with his own theory is expressed in the Appendix:

> Philosophers begin to be reconcil'd to the principle, *that we have no idea of external substance, distinct from the ideas of particular qualities*. This must pave the way for a like principle with regard to the mind, *that we have no notion of it, distinct from the particular perceptions*.

> So far I seem to be attended with sufficient evidence. But having thus loosen'd all our particular perceptions, when I proceed to explain the principle of connexion, which binds them together, and makes us attribute to them a real simplicity and identity; I am sensible, that my account is very defective, and that nothing but the seeming evidence of the precedent reasonings cou'd have induc'd me to receive it. If perceptions are distinct existences, they form a whole only by being connected together. But no connexions among distinct existences are ever discoverable by human understanding. We only *feel* a connexion or determination of the thought, to pass from one object to another. It follows, therefore, that the thought alone finds personal identity, when reflecting on the train of past perceptions, that compose a mind, the ideas of them are felt to be connected together, and naturally introduce each other. However extraordinary this conclusion may seem, it need not surprize us. Most philosophers seem inclin'd to think, that personal identity *arises* from consciousness; and consciousness is nothing but a reflected thought or perception. The present philosophy, therefore, has so far a promising aspect. But all hopes vanish, when I come to explain the principles, that unite our successive perceptions in our thought or consciousness. I cannot discover any theory which gives me satisfaction on this head.

> In short, there are two principles, which I cannot render consistent; nor is it in my power to renounce either of them, viz. *that all our distinct perceptions are distinct existences*, and *that the mind never perceives any real connexion among distinct existences*. Did our perceptions either inhere in something simple and individual, or did the mind perceive some real connexion among them, there wou'd be no difficulty in the case. For my part, I must plead the privilege of a sceptic, and confess, that this difficulty is too hard for my understanding. I pretend not, however, to pronounce it absolutely insuperable. Others, perhaps, or myself, upon more mature reflexions, may discover some

hypothesis, that will reconcile those contradictions. (*Treatise*, pp. 635-36)

What Hume claims to be *defective* is his account of the *unity of consciousness*. Twice in his statement of the problem, Hume identified the unity of consciousness as the problem: (1) "...when I proceed to explain the principle of connexion, which binds them together...I am sensible, that my account is very defective" (*Ibid.*, p. 635); (2) "But all hopes vanish, when I come to explain the principles, that unite our successive perceptions in our thought or consciousness" (*Ibid.*, p. 636). For an excellent history of the discussion of the unity of consciousness prior to Hume, and by writers with whom Hume was familiar, see Ben Lazare Mijuskovic, *The Achilles of Rationalist Arguments* (The Hague: Nijhoff, 1974).

Precisely because he distinguished between the self and the idea of the self, Hume was able to perceive his problem. What Hume had explained was the idea of the self. But the idea of the self is not the same as the self, here understood as the unity of consciousness. What does Hume suggest would be a kind of account for the unity of consciousness? First, if there were a *real* connection among perceptions we would have such an account. Second, if perceptions inhered in a simple substance we would have such an account. Either inhesion or real connection could explain the unity of consciousness.

The difficulty for Hume is that he can accept neither. Hume denied real connections. He had also refused to consider seriously the possibility of inhesion in substances. Instead he had insisted upon the distinctness of every perception. So a conflict exists between the belief in the unity of consciousness and Hume's commitment to two principles. This explains the inconsistency Hume notes in his own theory. The two principles do not conflict with each other but with the belief in the unity of consciousness.

Hume drew a parallel between this conflict or inconsistency and "...those contradictions, and absurdities, which seem to attend every explication, that human reason can give of the material world" (*Treatise*, p. 633). The contradictions Hume had wished to avoid with regard to the material world were the difficulties of explaining the substance of external physical objects. Earlier, he thought that he had circumvented that issue by focusing on how the mind organized the data without committing himself to explaining the origin of the data.

> The intellectual world, tho' involv'd in infinite obscurities, is not perplex'd with any such contradictions, as those we have discover'd in the natural...concerning the material or immaterial substances, in which they [certain philosophers] suppose our perceptions to inhere. (*Treatise*, p. 232)

At one point Hume asserted that there were material foundations to the relations which unite (*Treatise*, p. 60). Subsequently, he realized that any attempt to account for the origin of such principles raised anew the issue of mind-body interaction or inhesion. Hume never despaired of identifying the principles that unite our successive perceptions. He had already identified those principles as resemblance and causation. His problem was to explain the origin of those principles.

By the time he wrote the first *Enquiry*, Hume was able to express his problem more clearly. "Is there not here, either in spiritual or material substance, or both, some secret mechanism or structure of parts, upon which the effect depends, and which, being entirely unknown to us, renders the power or energy of the will equally unknown and incomprehensible?" (*EHU*, pp. 68-69). Hume believed in the unity of consciousness but realized that he had failed to account for it.

This foregoing difficulty has no immediate effect on the doctrines Hume expounded in his moral theory. If anything, it could be argued that Hume came to realize that no conceptualization of the unity of consciousness was possible, rather that unity emerges as the pre-conceptual condition or context of conceptualization. Moreover, that unity could only be talked about from the point of view of common sense. Curiously the Copernican Revolution in philosophy with its emphasis on the *We Do* perspective leads precisely in this direction, and this may account for the revisions Hume makes in his treatment of moral issues in the second *Enquiry*. See Chapter Seven of this book.

Hume's last published statement on this issue may be in the *Dialogues*: "it is perfectly indifferent, whether we rest on the universe of matter or on that of thought; nor do we gain any thing by tracing the one into the other" (*op.cit.*, pp. 160-61).

47. Passmore, *op.cit.*, p.128.

48. Laird, *op.cit.*, p. 204.

49. Reid, *op.cit.*

50. Passmore, *op.cit.*, p. 129.

51. One must distinguish the question of how we originally come to identify our own internal states from the epistemological question of how subsequently we can be sure of our attribution of internal states to others. I would maintain that for Hume we come to know ourselves originally through others. Once this kind of knowledge is established, then we can have a basis for analogical reasoning on occasion about others. Passmore, I believe, is raising the epistemological question about causal inferences.

52. Rules as such can have no force whatsoever for Hume unless linked to the passions or to the imagination, in which case it is the passions or the imagination which is effica-

cious. This point will lead Hume to discover difficulties in his account of sympathy, difficulties we shall be discussing at the end of Chapter Six. General rules are also inherently social, but this is a point we shall stress later.

53. See John Boatwright, "Hume's Account of Moral Sentiment," *Revue internationale de philosophie, 30* (1976), pp. 79-90.

CHAPTER SIX

1. There is no single virtuous motive. Sometimes a natural motive is perfectly virtuous (parental love for a child), sometimes sympathy, sometimes long-range interest, sometimes concern for public interest, sometimes duty.

2. For some of those contexts, see *Treatise*, pp. 484-501, (a discussion of the origin of justice, which is an artificial virtue). Hume does not explain the origin of the natural virtues as due to self-interest. See also our discussion of this misrepresentation of Hume in Chapter Eight.

3. This point is often missed not only because many readers are unfamiliar with the historical context, but because Hume actually raised the question in Book II long before he dealt with the answer in Book III: "...*whether these moral distinctions be founded on natural and original principles, or arise from interest and education. The examination of this I reserve for the following book; and in the mean time shall endeavour to show, that my system maintains its ground upon either of these hypotheses; which will be a strong proof of its solidity*" (*Treatise*, p. 295).

4. Note that what I am calling the second variant account of sympathy occurs on pages 584-86 of the *Treatise* while the third variant account occurs on pages 580-84. I have re-

versed the order in order to emphasize an emerging difficulty in Hume's treatment of sympathy.

5. In order for Hume even to consider this objection he must already have distinguished judgment from sentiment. This confirms our contention in earlier chapters of the crucial importance of this distinction. Keep in mind that the sentiment is variable but not the moral judgment.

6. Hume said or implied that there is a moral sentiment in the following places in the *Treatise*: pp. 588-89, 591; in the following places he said or implied that there might be *no* sentiment: pp. 582, 583, 584, 585, 586, 589, 593, 603.

7. Raphael, in *The Moral Sense, op.cit.*, p.88, claims that the objection Hume is considering applies only to feeling theories. However, an examination of the context of the *Treatise*, especially pp, 581 and 618, makes clear that Hume has all theories in mind including moral theories which allege the existence of peculiarly moral relations. As I indicated in a note to Chapter Two, Raphael's own alternative theory is subject to an extreme kind of subjectivism.

8. Shaftesbury and Hutcheson had made much of this analogy. The importance of the analogy for Hume has been overestimated. First, Hume compared virtue to other secondary qualities as often as he compared it to the sense of beauty. This is an important corrective to the tendency to attribute to Hume a subjectivist account of value judgments in general. Second, Hume made it quite clear that an analogy is not an identity: "...if we compare moral beauty with natural, to which in many particulars it bears so near a resemblance" (*EPM*, p. 291). Third, and most important, moral sentiments are motives in a way that the sense of beauty is not. The point of Hume's analogies is to show that we correct our judgments. The following kind

of criticism by Raphael, The Moral Sense, op.cit., p. 89, misses the point: "...a landscape may be more beautiful when seen from a distance than from near at hand."

9. For a similar account of the difficulties in Hume's treatment of sympathy see Philip Mercer's very fine book *Sympathy and Ethics* (Oxford: Clarendon Press, 1972).

Mercer recognizes the importance of benevolence for ethics and the inability of the sympathy mechanism to serve as the general principle of morals. Mercer's account of the inability of the sympathy mechanism to serve as the general principle of morals is that sympathy is value-neutral. My merely being affected by what affects others doesn't make for approbation or disapprobation. What it makes for is replication. Sympathy thus plays a role secondary to that element in human nature which makes us approve and disapprove of affairs to which sympathy makes us sensible. Thus far, I would agree entirely with Mercer. Mercer, however, then attributes Hume's failure to the "inability to distinguish clearly between a psychological explanation and a logical one" (p. 21).

Our treatment of Hume's problem with the sympathy mechanism requires a distinction between (1) the issue of what constitutes the general principe of morals and (2) the requirements of Hume's theory of moral judgment. Hume's theory of moral judgment necessitates both the objectivity of such judgments in the intersubjective sense and the presence of a confirming moral sentiment. Although sympathy can achieve objectivity through the help of general rules and a change in perspective, sympathy cannot in key cases generate a moral sentiment. In order to be able to generate the requisite moral sentiment, Hume needed to appeal to benevolence or humanity. Hence, benevolence or humanity becomes the origin of morals or the general principle of morals. Sympathy still remains an important factor in the theory of moral judgment, but it no longer serves as the general principle of morals.

Mercer did not perceive this dimension of Hume's problem for the following reasons. First, Mercer does not relate the function of sympathy to moral judgment, and even admits his perplexity about Hume's views on moral judgment (p. 66). Second, Mercer does not discuss the analogy between sympathy and belief as inferential processes. Had he done so, Mercer would not have fallen back on the misleading charge that Hume confuses logic and psychology. Third, Mercer concentrated exclusively on the *Treatise*, and only mentioned in a footnote (p. 42) Hume's revision of sympathy in the *Enquiry*. This unfortunately gives the impression that Mercer is correcting Hume without making clear that Hume recognized and even remedied the difficulty in question. Finally, by failing to analyze the *Enquiry*, Mercer missed the opportunity of showing how Hume's revision throws light on the meaning and function of sympathy in the *Treatise*.

10. Terence Penelhum, *Hume* (New York: St. Martin's Press, 1975), makes the point that the willingness to be objective is not a purely epistemological matter but is "in itself a moral attitude" (p. 143).

CHAPTER SEVEN

1. Hereafter we shall refer to *An Enquiry Concerning the Principles of Morals*, Hume's so-called second *Enquiry*, as *Enquiry* for short; when we refer the so-called first *Enquiry* we shall give its full name.

2. My discussion of Hume's moral philosophy in the *Enquiry* is very close to that of James T. King's, to which it is indebted. See King's "The Place of the Language of Morals in Hume's Second *Enquiry*" in *Hume: A Reevaluation*, ed. Liv-

ingston and King, *op.cit.*, pp. 343-361. King suggests that switching from the idiom of ideas and impressions to that of language, where language is a shared, historical fact, underscores that for Hume "morality is not a private matter discovered through introspection or the analysis of perceptions, or something variable according to personal taste. Its positive, public reality vanquishes any suggestion of moral scepticism" (p. 344).

3. An interesting question which could be raised at this point is whether the sentiment of humanity is natural or artificial. Clearly it is both! More than anything this shows the extent to which Hume overcomes any atomistic conception of human nature.

4. Nicholas Capaldi and James King are the exceptions.

5. See his introduction to the Green and Grose edition of the *Treatise, op.cit.*

6. F.C. Sharp, *Ethics* (New York: Century Co., 1928), p. 348.

7. E. V. McGilvary, "Altruism in Hume's *Treatise*," *Philosophical Review* (1903), p. 272.

8. There are three possibilities here: (1) argue that individual interest is ontologically primary and that social interest is secondary or derivative, or (2) argue that social interest is ontologically primary and that individual interest is secondary or derivative, or (3) that the notion of any ontologically primary interest is misguided. The last is, I submit, Hume's more mature view.

9. "In the *Enquiry* the passages dealing with self-love, reason and passion, the equivalent of correction of judgment, and so on, do not dictate conclusions; rather, they are determined...by considerations involved in the common lan-

guage of morals. No theoretical assumptions stand in the way of Hume's arriving at factually well-grounded conclusions about human nature" King, *op. cit.*, p. 348.

10. Donald Livingston, *Hume's Philosophy of Common Life*, *op.cit.*, has made much of the dangers of false philosophizing in Hume's sense.

11. *A Dialogue*, p. 333, Selby-Bigge edition of the *Enquiries*, *op.cit.*

12. Two other revisions are worth noting. First, Hume himself expressed reservations about his own explanation of the self in the *Treatise*. For a further discussion of this see N. Capaldi, "Hume's Theory of the Self: Its Historical and Philosophical Significance", in *Philosophy, Its History and Historiography*, ed. A. Holland (Dordrecht, Holland: Reidel, 1985), pp. 271-85.

    Note as well that Hume's discussion of the continued and distinct existence of perceptions, that is, the belief in an external physical world, utilized the now suspect doctrine of the communication of vivacity. Hume did not include this item in his *Enquiry Concerning Human Understanding*.

13. "The other scientific method, where a general abstract principle is first established, and is afterwards branched out into a variety of inferences and conclusions, may be more perfect in itself, but suits less the imperfection of human nature, and is a common source of illusion and mistake in this as well as in other subjects" (*EPM*, p. 174).

14. "...the notion of morality to which Hume appealed in Part III [of the *Treatise*] is continuous with the view of morality which serves as the presupposition and starting point for the *Enquiry*." King, *op. cit.*, p. 354.

CHAPTER EIGHT

1. Given the *We Do* perspective and what we shall be saying shortly about explication, any sharp distinction between the moral and the nonmoral would not be in the spirit of Hume's philosophy. That is why Hume does not stress how we can move from nonmoral judgments to moral judgments. In this book we have highlighted the movement from the nonmoral to the moral as a response to readers who believe that there is an unbridgeable gap between the two.

   In the twentieth century, those philosophers, with whom I am familiar, who have come closest to exemplifying the *We Do* perspective include *Dewey, Heidegger, Ortega*, and the *later Wittgenstein*. Those moral and social philosophers with whom I am familiar and who most closely approximate Hume's conception of explication include *Oakeshott, Hayek*, and *Ortega y Gasset*.

2. Alasdair MacIntyre, *Whose Justice? Which Rationality?* (Notre Dame: University of Notre Dame Press, 1988), chapters xv and xvi, pp. 281-325.

3. *Ibid.*, p. 290.

4. *Ibid.* MacIntyre appeals to Norton, *op.cit.*, and Norton's thesis of a gap between metaphysical and epistemological scepticism on the one hand and the lack of scepticism concerning moral matters as further evidence of the transition necessary from Book I to Book III. I do not know if Norton would share this use of his thesis. In any case, I have already rejected the arguments for the existence of that alleged gap.

5. *Ibid.*, p. 306. Consider the following statement by MacIntyre about Hume: "...calculate where my long-run interest

and the long-run interest of those with whom I interact lie" (*Ibid.*, p. 309).

6. *Ibid.*, p. 293.

7. *Ibid.*, p. 295.

8. *Ibid.*, p. 298.

9. *Ibid.*, p. 292.

10. *Ibid.*, p. 317.

11. To his credit, MacIntyre (*Ibid.*, p.320) recognizes his disagreement with Livingston's position on this point in the latter's book *Hume's Philosophy of Common Life, op.cit.*

12. "...that to which in the longer run the majority assent" (MacIntyre, *Ibid.*, p. 318).

13. David Hume, "My Own Life," in *Letters of David Hume*, ed. J.Y.T. Greig (Oxford: Clarendon Press, 1932), p. 4.

14. Man has wants "precisely because he is social" (p. 108), D. Miller, *Philosophy and Ideology in Hume's Political Thought* (New York: Oxford University Press, 1981).

15. For an excellent discussion of this point see Duncan Forbes, *Hume's Philosophical Politics*, op. cit., chapter 4, "Social experience and the uniformity of human nature", pp. 102-121.

16. Hume specifically attacks natural law in the *Treatise, op.cit.*, on pp. 477, 483, 520, and 528.

17. David Hume, *Essays: Moral, Political, and Literary* (Oxford: University Press, 1963), p. 499.

18. *Ibid.*, p. 500.

19. *Ibid.*, p. 499.

20. David Hume, *Enquiry Concerning Human Understanding*, ed. Hendel (Indianapolis: Bobbs-Merrill, 1955), p. 34. This addition to Section 3 was added in 1748.

21. *The Letters of David Hume, op.cit.*, I: 33.

22. A strong case for the influence of Hume on Hegel as well as some of the differences between them can be found in Norbert Waszek's "Hume, Hegel, and History" in *CLIO* (1985), pp. 379-92.

23. David Hume, *The History of England* (London, 1841), Vol. 2, p. 497.

24. Hume, *Essays, op.cit.*, p. 372, "Of Some Remarkable Customs".

25. For Hume, the language of morals is more stable than the language of science. See *Essays, op.cit.*, p. 253, "Of the Standard of Taste".

26. See Nicholas Capaldi, "Hume as Social Scientist," in *Review of Metaphysics* (1978), pp. 99-123.

27. "Thought seems to have made little advance since David Hume and Immanuel Kant....It was they who came nearer than anybody has done since to a clear recognition of the status of values as independent and guiding conditions of all rational construction. what I am ultimately concerned with here...is the destruction of values by scientific error which has increasingly come to seem to me the great tragedy of our time – a tragedy, because the values which scientific error tends to dethrone are the indispensable

foundation of all our civilization, including the very scientific efforts which have turned against them. The tendency of constructivism to represent those values which it cannot explain as determined by arbitrary human decisions, or acts of will, or mere emotions, rather than as the necessary conditions of facts which are taken for granted by its expounders, has done much to shake the foundations of civilization, and of science itself, which also rests on a system of values which cannot be scientifically proved." F.A. Hayek, *Law, Legislation, and Liberty*, Vol. I, Rules and Order (London: Routledge & Kegan Paul, 1973), pp. 6-7.

28. In his landmark paper, "Some Implications of the Virtue of Reasonableness in Hume's *Treatise*", in *Hume: A Reevaluation, op.cit.*, pp. 91-106, Pall Ardal has argued that theoretical reason is judged as morally worthy, that the concept of virtue is fundamental to Hume's epistemology, and that Book I of the *Treatise* has to be understood in the light of Book III.

29. For a relevant and insightful comparison of Wittgenstein and Hume see Peter Jones, "Strains in Hume and Wittgenstein," in Livingston and King, eds., *Hume: A Reevaluation, op.cit.*, pp. 191-212.

30. The distinction between explication and exploration corresponds roughly to the distinction Livingston finds in Hume between true and false philosophy. See Livingston's *Hume's Philosophy of Common Life, op.cit.*

31. David Miller, *Philosophy and Ideology in Hume's Political Thought, op. cit.*

32. One is reminded here of Kant's subsequent discussion of the autonomy and heteronomy of the will.

33. Ralph Cudworth, *Treatise concerning Eternal and Immutable Morality*, in Selby-Bigge, *British Moralists, op.cit.*, pp. 813-16.

34. It is the dependence upon human beings and cultural evolution as well as the direct relation to practice or action that distinguishes Hume's account of moral knowledge from G.E. Moore's. Note that Hume would agree in general with Moore's critique of those who deny the existence of a moral dimension in human experience.

35. See David Lewis, *Convention: a philosophical study* (Cambridge: Harvard University Press, 1969).

    The conflict between those who think that we can explore the hidden structure of custom and those who claim that custom can only be explicated and never explored is a vital part of contemporary philosophical debate. In *Wittgenstein on Rules and Private Language* (Cambridge: Harvard University Press, 1982) Saul Kripke denies Wittgenstein's thesis that there is no underpinning to explain how we apply signs, not even by appeal to other people. Kripke suggests in a manner analogous to David Lewis that we can discover the underpinning in the user's relation to a community. Wittgenstein would deny that the user's relationship to a community has an underlying objectifiable structure. That is why for Wittgenstein we need explication instead of an independent exploration. Actions, including speech, for Wittgenstein, are not natural events but *symbolic events*. As symbolic events they involve tacit agreements which we may seek to explicate and they require the ability to follow rules. But symbolic action is not reducible to rule following. There cannot be a metalanguage relating acts to anything else. Acts can only be related to other acts as in Wittgenstein's example of the building site and the bricks.

    Kripke sees Wittgenstein's position as similar to Hume's and claims that both positions are *sceptical*. Kripke does not define what scepticism is, rather he distinguishes between a straightforward solution of the sceptic's challenge and the sceptical solution of the sceptic's challenge. The straight solution is to offer an argument which shows that scepticism is unwarranted. The sceptical solution, attributed to Hume and Wittgenstein, (a) concedes that the sceptic's negative assertions are unanswerable, and (b) claims that ordinary practice or belief is justified because such practices and beliefs do not require the justification the sceptic has shown to be untenable.

What Kripke fails to see is that for both Wittgenstein and Hume the sceptic's argument is incoherent. Hence there is no point in trying to answer it. Aside from trying to explain how we fall into the error of taking the sceptic seriously, Hume and Wittgenstein point out that the sceptic's position is parasitic upon the very beliefs he challenges and that the sceptic's own action reflects this. This is why it is important to point out that the action refutes the words.

In our endeavor to achieve intersubjectively shared understanding we do not go back to axioms or rules in order to achieve consistency, rather we go back to prior acts in order to achieve coherence. In trying to resolve disputes about what something means we return to the aims and activities which either originally gave rise to the disputed terms or from which the dispute evolved. This is why an historical accounting is so important.

36. David Gauthier has attempted to employ David Lewis' notion of convention in order to interpret Hume's theory of justice. Gauthier begins by distinguishing utilitarianism from contractarianism as follows: "The utilitarian considers overall well-being a sufficient condition for the conventions of property. The contractarian considers the well-being of each individual a necessary condition for such conventions" (p.10). Gauthier then interprets Hume as a

contractarian in the sense that Hume proceeds from the point of view of mutual advantage to each participant. David Gauthier, "David Hume: Contractarian," *Philosophical Review*, 88 (1979), pp. 3-38.

Part of the difficulty in evaluating the claim of how Hume differs from utilitarianism is what one understands by utilitarianism. From our point of view, Gauthier's argument makes a specious distinction between utilitarianism and contractarianism because utilitarianism usually assumes that there is a coincidence of individual and overall well-being. Hence, a contrast between overall well-being and individual well-being is a distinction without a difference. Second, Gauthier's argument presupposes that it is possible to conceptualize pre-conventional or extra-conventional self-interest. We have argued that Hume himself denies this very possibility. Working as he does from the *I Think* perspective, Gauthier cannot account for how a contractarian makes the transition from pre-conventional self-interest to post-conventional self-interest, i.e. Gauthier fails to capture the normative dimension of conventions.

37. This is what Lewis, *op.cit.*, does with his example of the telephone (pp. 36-40).

38. Hume, *Essays, op.cit.*, p. 469, "Of the Original Contract".

39. As usual in philosophy, any discussion about applying a label to a philosopher, a label such as 'utilitarian', is confounded by the equivocal use of the label. When I speak about utilitarianism, I have in mind the following family of characteristics. First, utilitarianism usually means beginning with an ontological conception of the individual as an ahistorical and acultural being (e.g. in a state of nature). Clearly, Hume would disagree with this. Second, utilitarianism usually means that all human motivation is construed as reducible to one fundamental principle (e.g. self-

preservation, self-love, maximizing pleasure, etc.) so that even where benevolent impulses are recognized such impulses are treated as epiphenomena. What is at issue is not whether benevolent impulses are recognized but whether it is being assumed at some level that self-interest always harmonizes with or is best served by taking the social interest seriously. The hidden structure is always construed as one of maximizing the self-interest of the atomic individual. One consequence of this notion of a hidden structure of maximizing self-interest construed as acultural is that utilitarians search for one supreme principle to which all of moral existence must submit. Clearly, Hume would disagree with this. Third, utilitarianism usually means the denial of the existence of an internal sanction or motive of duty in favor of the assertion that social order is to be maintained through a network of external sanctions and that agents will agree to the external sanctions in order to maximize self-interest. Clearly, Hume would disagree with this.

40. The importance and primacy of practical knowledge has been stressed by W.D. Falk in his paper "Hume on Practical Reason," *Philosophical Studies,* 27 (1975), pp. 1-18.

41. Areyh Botwinick in "A Case for Hume's Nonutilitarianism," *Journal of the History of Philosophy,* 15 (1977), pp. 423-35, argues against any utilitarian reading of Hume. Botwinick also emphasizes "Hume's repeatedly stated belief in the complete coincidence between the public good achieved by adherence of the rules of justice and our own individual goods" (p. 431). What has to be seen, however, is that the coincidence in Hume is not a metaphysical assumption or a rash empirical claim but the reflection of our basically social nature and the logical requirement of explication that there cannot be a discussion of pre-social interests or extra-social interests. The "coincidence" would be the product of an

historical development. The "coincidence" is to be distinguished from "consistency" where the latter is a logical requirement for the explication of morality.

42. There can, of course, be conflicts between self-love and
other interests. However, self-love is as much a malleable
social and historical entity as any other interest. Specifically, what cannot come up is the question whether I
should be such a being as is sensible of moral distinctions.
The question whether I should lay aside my interests when
they conflict with the requirements of morality, assuming
this question is not intended to question what is the relevant moral requirement, would be treated by Hume, I suggest, as a symptom of false consciousness (in our idiom).

43. "It follows that the recognition of the existence of the common language of morals is not like the recognition of plain
matters of fact; it is the recognition which belongs precisely
to the user of that language who, by participating in a set
of approvals and disapprovals, finds therein something to
which, by the constitution of his nature, according to
Hume, he subscribes. There is no contradiction in affirming that the language of morals is both normative and factual, so long as it is understood that the kind of facticity in
question is consequent upon the fact of common participation in the moral language as a normative system....Those
committed to upholding the viability of ethical naturalism
in its *strictest* form, therefore, ought perhaps to reconsider
whether the *Enquiry* may be appealed to as an instantia-
tion of that particular meta-ethical stance." King, *op. cit.*, p.
348.

44. Recent work by David Norton and Robert Fogelin has attempted to conceptualize our understanding of Hume in
terms of the scepticism vs. naturalism framework. I believe
this is the wrong way to grasp what Hume is doing, and

that is why I have suggested seeing Hume as a Copernican operating from the *We Do* perspective understood culturally.

Fogelin in *Hume's Skepticism in the Treatise of Human Nature* (London: Routledge & Kegan Paul, 1985) has insisted upon the sceptical element in Hume, an element which Fogelin thinks is neglected by those who see Hume as a naturalist. Fogelin attributes the 'naturalist' label to everyone who emphasizes the positive aspect in Hume. Herein lies Fogelin's error. Interpreting Hume as a Copernican who makes practical knowledge primary is not the same thing as making Hume a 'naturalist' in the Kemp Smith sense. Moreover, I do not know of any aspect of Hume's philosophy that is in any way illuminated by stressing what Fogelin calls the sceptical dimension. Finally, to frame the issue in sceptical vs. naturalism terms is itself to adopt a theoretical perspective. That is, Fogelin's conceptualization is itself an example of the *I Think* perspective and is therefore inherently incapable of grasping what Hume is doing.

Norton concedes the existence of scepticism in metaphysics but challenges it with regard to Hume's moral philosophy, which Norton sees as realist. We have argued that Hume is not a realist in the relevant sense but an intersubjectivist and that the intersubjectivism is best interpreted from the Copernican point of view. Norton makes a good case for the inappropriateness of Kemp Smith's designation of Hume as a naturalist who subordinates reason to instinct or feeling (*op.cit.*, p. 231). Despite all of Norton's careful qualifications of reason's role in Hume's theory, it still remains the case that (a) reason is the slave of the passions, and (b) that the qualified use of reason shows us nothing about the external structure of the world but only about the internal structure which we bring to the world. It is because Hume's structuring is internal that readers like Fogelin can insist upon the scepticism. In the end, scepticism means to Fogelin that we never grasp an external objective structure. As I have tried to argue, the search for objective structure is misguided as far as the Copernican position is concerned. It is not that Hume despairs but that he seeks to circumvent this way of thinking. *There is crucial difference between saying that Hume conceptualized his position as sceptical and saying that in spite of Hume we ought to conceptualize Hume's position as sceptical.*

When we turn our attention to Hume's insistence upon internal structuring principles we must raise the question are these principles personal or intersubjective? If it is the former then we would need God's guarantee in order to link up with the objective world and the social world, i.e. the position of the Scottish realists like Reid. This could not possibly be Hume's position. If the principles are already intersubjective (i.e., common sense) then we have all that we need for practical purposes. All of this is precisely what illuminates Hume's moral philosophy and is totally missed by trying to construe Hume as a kind of sceptical-naturalist. What Hume's philosophy presupposes is the interpersonal or intersubjective framework (*We Do*) understood culturally. This is precisely why Hume is most critical of religion and superstition. They both attempt to get outside the intersubjective framework and are, therefore, a threat to its stability.

45. Having mistakenly attributed to Hume the position that the motivation for justice is self-interest alone, Barry Stroud fails to see how Hume can explain our approval when an individual's self-interest is absent, for "there will be nothing to recommend justice to him at all" p. 210, *Hume* (London: Routledge & Kegan Paul, 1978).

46. Much has been made of this point by Livingston, in *Hume's Philosophy of Common Life, op.cit.,* and elsewhere. In another context I would argue that the evolution of classical liberalism into modern liberalism and the tendency of modern

liberalism to become totalitarian reflect the refusal to take the internal sanction seriously.

47. This argument is now known as King's Conundrum, after J. Charles King.

48. I am indebted to H. Tristram Engelhardt, Jr. for this insight.

In his otherwise admirable treatment of Hume's social philosophy, David Miller finds both liberal and conservative elements in Hume which Miller finds difficult to reconcile without appeal to Hume's social milieu. One such instance is Hume's refusal to embrace meritocracy without reservation and Hume's finding of a place for aristocracy. It could be argued that meritocracy presupposes that the value of efficiency is paramount, an indirect kind of utilitarian appeal. I suspect that Hume would find such an argument doctrinaire just as he would find abstract appeals to equality doctrinaire. See David Miller, *Philosophy and Ideology in Hume's Political Thought, op.cit.*

49. Duncan Forbes makes the following point. "Suppose a reader knowing Hume only from Book III of the *Treatise* and the *Enquiries* and certain of the essays, or parts of them, were to be told that Hume had written a *History of England*, and then asked to hazard a guess as to what sort of a history he would expect it to be. Might he not be justified in replying: 'I note what Hume has to say about sympathy, social experience, national character, the evolution of morality, social rules and institutions, and "moral" causes; so on the whole I expect to see a social history, with the emphasis on the gradual evolution of English society and social institutions, on national character (and possibly its development), on the Common Law and manners and customs, etc., neglecting "physical causes".' Would he not be surprised to learn that the narrative has often been criti-

cized for being too narrowly political?" *Hume's Philosophical Politics, op.cit.,* p. 121.

50. Adam Ferguson, *Essay on the History of Civil Society* (London, 1767), p. 187.

51. For a detailed examination of how Hume treated social philosophical issues and how this treatment reflects his cultural and historical approach as well as his uniquely secular conservative outlook see *Liberty in Hume's History of England,* eds. N. Capaldi and D. Livingston (forthcoming), a collection of essays by Peter Jones, Craig Walton, Eugene Miller, Donald Livingston, John Danford, and Nicholas Capaldi

52. Sheldon Wolin, "Hume's Conservatism", in Livingston and King, *op.cit.,* p. 243.

53. J.Y.T. Greig, *Hume* (London: J. Cape, 1931) pp. 375-76.

BIBLIOGRAPHY

Standard bibliographies of Hume's works can be found in (1) T.E. Jessop, *A Bibliography of David Hume and of Scottish Philosophy, from Francis Hutcheson to Lord Balfour* (London: Brown and Son, 1938); (2) W.B. Todd, "David Hume, A Preliminary Bibliography," *Hume and the Enlightenment: Essays Presented to Ernest Campbell Mossner*, ed. W.B. Todd (Edinburgh: University Press, 1974), pp. 189-205; (3) Roland Hall, *Fifty Years of Hume Scholarship: A Bibliographical Guide* (Edinburgh: University Press, 1978). Supplements to Hall's bibliography appear annually in Hume Studies.

Anderson, Robert F. *Hume's First Principles*. Lincoln: University of Nebraska Press, 1966.

Ardal, Pall S. "Another Look at Hume's Account of Moral Evaluation." *Journal of the History of Philosophy* 15 (1977).

_____. *Passion and Value in Hume's Treatise*. Edinburgh: University Press, 1966.

Atkinson, R.F. "Hume on 'Is' and 'Ought': A Reply to Mr. MacIntyre." *Philosophical Review* 70 (1961).

Baier, Annette. *Postures of the Mind: Essays on Mind and Morals*. Minneapolis: University of Minnesota Press, 1985.

Basson, A.H. *David Hume*. Baltimore: Penguin, 1958.

Bayle, Pierre. *The Dictionary Historical and Critical*. 5 vols. 2d English ed. London, 1734-1738.

Beattie, James. *An Essay on the Nature and Immutability of Truth, in Opposition to Sophistry and Scepticism.* 4th ed. London, 1773.

Beck, Lewis White. "A Prussian Hume and a Scottish Kant." *McGill Hume Studies,* eds. David F. Norton, Nicholas Capaldi, and Wade L. Robison. San Diego: Austin Hill Press, 1979.

Berkeley, George. *The Works of George Berkeley, Bishop of Cloyne,* 9 vols. A.A. Luce, and T.E. Jessop, eds. New York: Macmillan, 1948-1957.

_____. *The Works of George Berkeley,* 4 vols. ed. A.C. Fraser. London, 1871.

Blanshard, Brand. *Reason and Goodness.* London: Allen and Unwin, 1961.

Boatwright, John. "Hume's Account of Moral Sentiment." *Revue internationale de philosophie* 30 (1976).

Botwinick, Areyh. "A Case for Hume's Nonutilitarianism." *Journal of the History of Philosophy* 15 (1977).

Broad, C.D. *Five Types of Ethical Theory.* London: Routledge & Kegan Paul, 1930. Reprint ed., Littlefield Adams, 1959.

Broiles. R. David. *The Moral Philosophy of David Hume.* Hague: Nijhoff, 1964.

Butler, Joseph. *Sermons.* London, 1726.

Capaldi, Nicholas. *David Hume: The Newtonian Philosopher.* Boston: Twayne, 1975.

_____. "Hume as Social Scientist". *The Review of Metaphysics* 32 (1978).

Bibliography

_____. "Hume's Philosophy of Religion: God Without Ethics." *International Journal for the Philosophy of Religion* 21 (1970).

_____. "The Copernican Revolution in Hume and Kant." *Proceedings of the Third International Kant Congress.* ed. Lewis White Beck. Dordrecht: Reidel, 1972.

_____. "Copernican Metaphysics." *New Essays in Metaphysics.* ed. Robert C Neville. Albany: SUNY Press, 1987.

_____. "The Historical and Philosophical Significance of Hume's Theory of the Self." A.J. Holland, ed. *Philosophy, Its History and Historiography.* Dordrecht: Reidel, 1985.

Chappell, V. ed. *Hume.* New York: Doubleday, 1966.

Clarke, Samuel. *A Demonstration of the Being and Attributes of God.* 1705 and *A Discourse concerning the Unchangeable Obligations of Natural Religion.* 1706. Faksimile-Neudruck der Londoner Ausgaben. Stuttgart-Bad Cannstatt: Fredrich Fronmann Verlag (Gunther Holzboog), 1964.

Colman, John. *John Locke's Moral Philosophy.* Edinburgh: University Press, 1983.

Copleston, F. *History of Philosophy.* V, ii. Garden City: Doubleday, 1964.

Cudworth, Ralph. *The True Intellectual System of the Universe: wherein all the Reason and Philosophy of Atheism is Confuted, and its Impossibility Demonstrated, with a Treatise concerning Eternal and Immutable Morality.* Translated by J. Harrison and edited by J.L. Mosheim. 3 vols. London, 1845.

Cumberland, Richard. *De Legibus naturae disquisitio philosophica.* Translated by John Tower. Dublin, 1750.

Dauer, F. "Towards a Copernican Reading of Hume." *Nous* 9 (1975).

Edwards, Paul. *The Logic of Moral Discourse*. Glencoe: Free Press, 1955.

Falk, W.D. "Hume on Practical Reason." *Philosophical Studies* 27 (1975).

Ferguson, Adam. *Essays on the History of Civil Society*. London, 1767.

Findlay, J.N. "Morality by Convention." *Mind* 53 (1944).

Fogelin, Robert. *Hume's Skepticism in the Treatise of Human Nature*. London: Routledge & Kegan Paul, 1985.

Forbes, Duncan. *Hume's Philosophical Politics*. Cambridge: University Press, 1975.

Force, James E. "Hume's Interest in Newton and Science." *Hume Studies* (1987).

Frankena, W. "The Naturalistic Fallacy." *Mind* 48 (1939).

Gaskin, J.C.A. *Hume's Philosophy of Religion*. London: Macmillan, 1978.

Gauthier, David. "David Hume: Contractarian." *Philosophical Review* 88 (1979).

Glathe, A.B. *Hume's Theory of the Passions and of Morals*. Berkeley: University of California Press, 1950.

Green, Thomas Hill. *Hume and Locke*. New York: Crowell, 1968.

Greig, J.Y.T. *Hume*. London: J. Cape, 1931.

Hare, R.M. *The Language of Morals*. New York: Oxford University Press, 1952.

Harrison, Jonathan. *Hume's Moral Epistemology*. Oxford: Clarendon Press, 1976.

Bibliography

Hayek, F.A. *Law, Legislation, and Liberty.* Vol. I, Rules and Order. London: Routledge & Kegan Paul, 1973.

Hearn, Thomas K. "General Rules and Moral Sentiments in Hume's *Treatise.*" *Review of Metaphysics* 30 (1976).

Hedenius, I. *Studies in Hume's Ethics.* Stockholm, 1937.

Hobbes, Thomas. *English Works of Thomas Hobbes,* 11 vols., and *Opera Philosophica* (Latin Works), 5 vols., Sir William Molesworth, ed. London, 1839-1845; reprinted, Oxford: University Press, 1961.

Hudson, W.D. *The Is-Ought Question.* London: Macmillan, 1969.

Hunter, Geoffrey. "Hume on Is and Ought." *Philosophy* 37 (1962).

Hutcheson, Francis. *Essay on the Nature and Conduct of the Passions and Affections. With Illustrations on the Moral Sense.* 3d ed. London, 1742; reprinted, Gainesville: Scholars' Facsimiles and Reprints, 1969.

_____. *Illustrations on the Moral Sense.* ed. B. Peach. Cambridge: Harvard University Press, 1971.

_____. *An Inquiry into the Original of our Ideas of Beauty and Virtue; In Two Treatises. I. Concerning Beauty, Order, Harmony, Design. II. Concerning Moral Good and Evil.* London, 1738; reprinted, Farnborough: Gregg International Publishers, 1969.

_____. *Short Introduction to Moral Philosophy.* Glasgow, 1753.

_____. *System of Moral Philosophy.* 2 vols. Glasgow, 1755.

Jones, Peter. *Hume's Sentiments, Their Ciceronian and French Context.* Edinburgh: University Press, 1982.

King, James. "The Place of the Language of Morals in Hume's Second *Enquiry.*" in *Hume: A Reevaluation,* ed. Livingston and King. New York: Fordham University Press, 1976.

Kripke, Saul. *Wittgenstein on Rules and Private Language.* Cambridge: Harvard University Press, 1982.

Kydd, Rachel. *Reason and Conduct in Hume's Treatise.* London: Oxford University Press, 1946.

Laing, B.M. *David Hume.* London: E. Benn, 1932.

Laird, John. *Hume's Philosophy of Human Nature.* New York: Dutton, 1931.

Lewis, David. *Convention: a philosophical study.* Cambridge: Harvard University Press, 1969.

Livingston, Donald W. *Hume's Philosophy of Common Life.* Chicago: University Press, 1984.

Livingston, Donald W. and King, James. eds., *Hume: A Re-Evaluation.* New York: Fordham University Press, 1976.

MacIntyre, Alasdair. *Whose Justice? Which Rationality?* Notre Dame: University Press, 1988.

_____. "Hume on 'is' and 'ought'." *Philosophical Review* 48 (1959).

Mackie, J.L. *Hume's Moral Theory.* London: Routledge & Kegan Paul, 1980.

Mandeville, Bernard. *The Fable of the Bees: or, Private vices, Publick Benefits.* Edited by F.B. Kaye. 2 vols. Oxford: Clarendon Press, 1957.

Mercer, Philip. *Sympathy and Ethics.* Oxford: Clarendon Press, 1972.

Bibliography

Mijuskovic, Ben Lazare. *The Achilles of Rationalist Arguments.* Hague: Nijhoff, 1974.

Miller, David. *Philosophy and Ideology in Hume's Political Thought.* Oxford: University Press, 1982.

Morice, G.P., ed. *David Hume: Bicentenary Papers.* Edinburgh: University Press, 1977.

Mossner, E.C. *The Life of David Hume.* Edinburgh: Thomas Nelson and Sons, 1954.

Norton, David Fate. *David Hume: Common-Sense Moralist, Sceptical Metaphysician.* Princeton: University Press, 1982.

Norton, David Fate, Capaldi, Nicholas, and Robison, Wade L., eds. *McGill Hume Studies.* San Diego: Austin Hill Press, 1979.

Nowell-Smith, P.H. *Ethics.* New York: Philosophical Library, 1959.

Passmore, John. *Hume's Intentions.* Cambridge: University Press, 1952. Reprinted in 1980.

Penelhum, Terence. *Hume.* New York: St. Martin's Press, 1975.

Popkin, Richard H. *The High Road to Pyrrhonism.* San Diego: Austin Hill Press, 1980.

Price, Richard. *A Review of the Principal Questions in Morals.* Edited by D.D. Raphael. Oxford: Clarendon Press, 1948.

Prior, A.N. *Logic and the Basis of Ethics.* Oxford: University Press, 1949.

Raphael, D.D., ed. *British Moralists, 1650-1800.* 2 vols. Oxford: University Press, 1969.

_____. *The Moral Sense.* London: Oxford University Press, 1947.

Reid, Thomas. *Works of Thomas Reid.* 2 vols. ed. Sir William Hamilton. London: Longmans, Green, 1895.

Ryle, Gilbert. *The Concept of Mind.* London: Hutchinson, 1949.

Searle, J.R. *Speech Acts.* Cambridge: University Press, 1969.

Scott-Taggart, M.J. "MacIntyre's Hume." *Philosophical Review* 70 (1961).

Selby-Bigge, L.A., ed. *British Moralists.* 2 vols. Oxford: Clarendon Press, 1897; reprinted, New York: Bobbs-Merrill, 1964.

Shaftesbury, Third Earl of (Anthony Ashley Cooper). *Characteristics of Men, Manners, Opinions, Times.* Edited by J.M. Robertson. Introduction by Stanley Grean. 2 vols. New York: Bobbs-Merrill, 1964.

Sharp, F.C. "Hume's Ethical Theory and Its Critics." *Mind* 30 (1921).

Smith, Adam. *Theory of Moral Sentiments.* ed. A.L. Macfie and D.D. Raphael. Oxford: Clarendon Press, 1976.

Smith, Norman Kemp. *The Philosophy of David Hume: A Critical Study of its Origins and Central Doctrines.* London and New York: Macmillan, 1941; reprinted 1964.

Spinoza, Benedict de. *A Political Treatise.* ed. R.H. M. Elwes. New York: Dover, 1951.

Stevenson, C.L. *Ethics and Language.* New Haven: Yale University Press, 1944.

Stroud, Barry. *Hume.* London: Routledge & Kegan Paul, 1978.

Tweyman, Stanley. *Reason and Conduct in Hume and his Predecessors.* Hague: Nijhoff, 1974.

Wolff, Robert P. "Hume's Theory of Mental Activity." *Philosophical Review* 69 (1960).

STUDIES IN MORAL PHILOSOPHY is a book series publishing original works devoted primarily to the problematic or historical examination of the nature of good lives, character and its development, and virtues and vices. The consideration of these and related topics in the light of literary works is particularly welcome. Books in the series are intended to be readily accessible to nonspecialists, and thus they are written in plain English. The editor is:

Professor John Kekes
Department of Philosophy
State University of New York at Albany
Albany, New York 12222

Paul Allen III

PROOF OF MORAL OBLIGATION IN TWENTIETH-CENTURY PHILOSOPHY

American University Studies: Series V (Philosophy). Vol. 45

ISBN 0-8204-0568-X   199 pages   hardback US $ 31.65

Recommended price – alterations reserved

Since Plato's time, philosophers have concentrated on developing moral theories to guide our actions. They have said we ought to act to maximize happiness; we ought to act to fulfill human potential; etc. But all of them have largely ignored a key question: Regardless of *which* acts are morally obligatory, *can moral obligation as such be proven?*

Early in his book, Allen clarifies what sort of demonstration or justification can suffice as a proof that we are subject to moral obligation. He analyzes some twentieth-century ethical theories which initially appear to serve as such a demonstration. Next, he examines at length the theory of contemporary English philosopher R. M. Hare. And finally, he reworks Hare's ideas into a complete proof that we are bound by moral obligation.

Philosophers should value this book because it brings to light and defines a neglected but critical problem, and develops an innovative, thought-provoking solution. Serious students, too, will find it helpful because it provides a clearly written historical study of a central theme in twentieth-century ethics.

 PETER LANG PUBLISHING, INC.
62 West 45th Street
USA – New York, NY 10036

Gregory Mellema

INDIVIDUALS, GROUPS, AND SHARED MORAL RESPONSIBILITY

New York, Bern, Frankfurt/M., Paris, 1988
American University Studies: Series 5, Philosophy. Vol. 3
ISBN 0-8204-0855-7   224 pages   hardback US $ 33.50/sFr. 47.10

Recommended prices – alterations reserved

This volume is a conceptual analysis of issues in group responsibility. An attempt is made to identify factors which affect the degree to which individuals sharing responsibility for what happens bear responsibility for it, as well as factors which are erroneously judged to have such an effect. An examination of these issues leads to extended discussions of acting or failing to act in the company of others, the sequence in which the agents in a group perform acts, and group risk taking. It is argued that the failure to understand such issues has contributed to a widespread uncertainty in contemporary society as to the moral implications of participating in group actions.

Contents: Discussions of moral responsibility have traditionally been limited to the responsibility of individuals. Although some contemporary treatments have begun focusing on the responsibility of groups and collectives, this volume attempts to unravel in depth some of the complexities of sharing responsibility.

«The book makes a strong, worthwile, and much-needed contribution to our meagre understanding of the topic of shared moral responsibility.»
(Michael J. Zimmerman, Brown University)

«A lucidly written and carefully argued book . . . The fact that this is the first sustained discussion of this issue, and that the conclusions arrived at often affront the received informal wisdom, make Mellema's book a pathbreaker.»
(Nicholas Wolterstorff, Calvin College & The Free University of Amsterdam)

PETER LANG PUBLISHING, INC.
62 West 45th Street
USA – New York, NY 10036

Barry R. Arnold

THE PURSUIT OF VIRTUE
The Union of Moral Psychology and Ethics

New York, Bern, Frankfurt/M., Paris, 1988.
American University Studies: Series 5, Philosophy. Vol. 68
ISBN 0-8204-0819-0   XIV, 252 pages,   hardback US $ 37.75/sFr. 52.85

Recommended prices – alterations reserved

This book offers an antidote to the modern demise of virtue. While greatly admiring the contributions of Alasdair MacIntyre's *After Virtue,* Professor Arnold moves beyond his critique to the construction of a positive psychology of virtue. Rapprochement among moral philosophy, moral psychology, and theological ethics is Arnold's most innovative contribution toward the amelioration of the demise. Students and scholars of philosophy, theology, psychology, psychiatry, and the humanities will find this book particularly helpful and hopeful.

Contents: Arnold uniquely intertwines moral philosophy, moral psychology, theological ethics. A creative antidote to the modern demise of virtue.
«Rejecting the nay-sayers, Barry Arnold brings his own ethical analysis to ‹the human jigsaw puzzle›. He advocates a new ‹pursuit of virtue› that takes account of psychological, spiritual, and communitarian factors too often slighted.»
(Dr. James Sellers, Rice University)
«Barry Arnold addresses this in a discerning and fresh manner, thereby helping to redefine the purview of ethical thought.»
(James I. Laney, President, Emory University)

PETER LANG PUBLISHING, INC.
62 West 45th Street
USA – New York, NY 10036